CHRYSANTHEMUMS AND THORNS

Also by Edwin Reingold

Made In Japan (with Akio Morita
and Mitsuko Shimomura)

CHRYSANTHEMUMS and THORNS

The Untold Story of Modern Japan

EDWIN M. REINGOLD

ST. MARTIN'S PRESS
New York

Design by Paul Chevannes
Production Editor: Suzanne Magida
Production Manager: Marni Siskind

Library of Congress Cataloging-in-Publication Data

Reingold, Edwin M.
    Chrysanthemums and thorns : the untold story of modern
Japan / Edwin Reingold.
        p.   cm.
    ISBN 0-312-08160-X
    1. Japan—Civilization—1945–   2. National characteristics,
Japanese.   I. Title.
DS822.5.R45   1992
952.94—dc20   92-25053
                                                      CIP

First Edition: November 1992
10 9 8 7 6 5 4 3 2 1

Japanese names are presented here in the western style, given name before family name.

For Ellen

CONTENTS

ACKNOWLEDGMENTS

Many Japanese have helped me to know something about Japan and the Japanese. Two late colleagues and friends, Frank Iwama and Shoichi Imai, helped to open up the world of Japanese business, politics, and social life. The redoubtable S. Chang, critic, connoisseur, and confidante, exercised much patience in leading me through the journalistic minefield in a land where things are seldom what they seem to be. Keiko Nagasaka helped to organize my quest and with unfailingly good humor kept me in touch with Japan, no matter whether I was in Seoul, Beijing, Manila, Hong Kong, Los Angeles, or any point in between. Eiko Reed provided calm and efficient support.

The contacts and sources that have been generous with their knowledge and wisdom in the past two decades are innumerable: farmers, mayors, bureaucrats, fishermen, shop owners, cooks, ladies of the "water trade," and others. Many foreign businessmen and scholars based in Japan offered insights and friendship, though they may disagree with my conclusions. Japanese journalists and Japanese, European, and American diplomats provided valuable reflections. Many of the keen gleanings from the Japanese press by the Asia Foundation's Al Seligman and Jerry Inman can be found throughout the text, and thanks are due them for that, as well as for past assistance as the insightful diplomats they proved to be. Thanks are also due Tom Ginsburg of the foundation's Translation Service Center. The staff of the Foreign Press Center, Tokyo, has been supportive since its founding and the facilities and archives of the Foreign Correspondents Club of Japan and its obliging staff were invaluable.

Despite all the help from so many quarters, any errors in fact or judgment are my own. A warm note of appreciation is due Richard M. Clurman, who, as Chief of Correspondents of the Time-Life News Service, sent me on a dizzying series of assignments that became an education and a reward for myself and my family. Finally, my thanks go to Julian Bach, for insisting that I write the book, and to Robert Weil, whose advice and shrewd editing made it happen.

INTRODUCTION

Who are these people, the Japanese, suddenly so visible in the world, buying property and high-tech companies, selling more and more, dominating markets? Are they economic saviors or moneyed ogres? Are they teachers or takers? Must we take them seriously?

More and more Westerners find themselves asking these questions, but answers are hard to come by. In the last half of the twentieth century, Westerners have invested a lot of hope and wishful thinking in their postwar relationship with Japan. Allies vowed to crush Japan's dream of an Asia totally dominated by and obedient to the Tokyo emperor. They set out to mold Japan into a representative democracy with values and practices very much like those of the United States.

Japan, however, has turned out rather differently from what was planned. It has become a permanent force in the economic well-being of the world's peoples and their politics. How this nation of once reclusive Asians has thrust itself, as the United States did in its time and in a decidedly different way, into the forefront of world affairs in less than a century and a half is one of the most complex tales of modern twentieth-century history.

Few Japanese, not to say foreigners, could have foreseen Japan's emergence as the dominant economic powerhouse it has become in these fifty years since Pearl Harbor. Until 1945, Japan had never suffered such calamitous military or economic defeat. The future was cheerless and uncertain, but the clues to the resilience of the Japanese were there to be seen. Even in peacetime the Japanese had lived under the world's heaviest tax burden and were forced to learn sacrifice and discipline. After the war everyone understood what was needed: the reconstruction of the country. Hated in Asia and around the world, postwar Japanese had only themselves and the generosity of the West, particularly the Americans, to rely on.

But starting afresh, Japan had advantages the victors did not have. Freed of the burden of rearming itself, Japan could devote virtually all its available resources to mercantile development. In a classic economic move, Japan chose to close the nation's ports to all but essential imports and channel this development into manufactured exports. At the time, senior American political figures and economic experts were not encouraging. They advised Japan to seek third-world trading markets, seeing no American market for anything Japan could make. Even in Japan, government and finance officials were skeptical of Japanese industrialists. These builders wanted to bring raw materials to Japan from halfway around the globe and create steel, ships, and automobiles for export to the West. Powerful bureaucrats scoffed at dreamy tinkerers who wanted to make and export motorcycles and consumer electronics.

Defying what seemed like logical skepticism, the people built a massive industrial machine on the volcanic mountaintops that comprise Japan. In America's view, the idea that a constitution—largely written by the Occupation forces, translated into Japanese, and approved by the parliament of the then impotent and impoverished nation— could create a like-thinking partner was idealistic, if not

naive. No nation has been able to ram democracy down the
throats of any conquered people. Besides, Japan's worldview
was different from America's. But the Japanese are among
the world's best adapters, and they created their own version
of government and capitalism from available models. The
war was quickly regarded as an aberration, and when it
was over, the new "democratized" government looked, not
surprisingly, like the prewar one. Although the Japanese
have established a form of quasi-representative government,
the system falls well short of the ideal glimpsed by the
conquerors.

In the late 1940s, the balance of power was changing rapidly. Japan eagerly embraced the strategic partnership with
the United States in the Cold War against the Soviet Union.
Nurturing and maintaining cooperative defense rather than
trade congruence and teamwork has been the centerpiece of
American policy toward Japan. So long as the Japanese stood
firmly with the United States in the United Nations, continued to allow U.S. troops in Japan, and promised trade concessions, successive American governments felt satisfied with
the relationship. But now the Cold War is over, and despite
promises Japan has not created the full economic partnership the United States hoped for. The balance of power in
the 1990s has changed yet again, and Japan is evolving, not
necessarily in synchronization, with the United States and
other European powers.

It was a chilly, snowy night in Tokyo when I arrived with
my family at Haneda Airport in February 1969. I had spent
nine years covering developing nations of the Caribbean and
Africa, and I was eager to leave the developing world for
what appeared to be an overdeveloped one. Japan was flexing
its new industrial muscle, and it was a striking sight. I had
seen nothing like it in Latin America, in Africa, or even in
the United States. The signs of rising self-confidence were
everywhere as Japan prepared to host the world for its first
world's fair in Osaka.

The industrial growth of the new Japan was astonishing. New machinery was scrapped for even newer machinery. The concept of industrial robots, avoided in America, was being embraced. Ideas about quality control, taken from the United States, and foreign technology were being emphasized, along with the people involved. Bureaucrats, industrialists, politicians seemed dedicated to development. The people were the most surprising; they never seemed to stop working. There was building everywhere, though very little of it for the comfort and safety of the builders, for parks, libraries, or playgrounds. Those who remembered the war now sacrificed for the future. Even so, life was different from the experience of wartime. Despite their cramped housing, the people were soothed by the blandishments of room air conditioners, automobiles, and color television. And they found the money to pay for cram schools for the children.

Foreigners like us, new to Japan, found life full of wonder and challenge. With four young children to place in school and a baby about to make an entrance, our family had to learn a lot in a hurry. With a barely rudimentary grasp of the language, what's a housewife to do when the collector from the gas company arrives at the door with his clipboard to collect the bill that she hasn't even seen and can't read? How fast will the children figure out the subway system? Where will they find friends?

Practicing journalism was a particular challenge, but one alleviated by a remarkably efficient bilingual staff, which helped me avoid mistakes. A journalist spends much time waiting for heads of state and bureaucrats to make up their minds. It is not a good way to learn patience. Without a course in Zen meditation or the benefit of indulgent editors with flexible deadlines, I had to practice Western-style journalism despite the elliptical practices of the Japanese.

In Japan the media is part of the establishment. No Japanese government functionary tells a foreign reporter anything for attribution that he has not already told the Japanese press—that is, if he can help it, because the Japanese press assigned to his ministry, competitive in a collegial way, will call him to account.

Such pressure had its results. At a high tension point during one trade dispute, Kiichi Aichi, the late foreign minister, agreed to steal away to a secluded tea house for a quiet dinner with a small group of frustrated foreign journalists. We began to hold these secret but valuable dinner meetings monthly, and Aichi was often surprisingly frank. I am sure, however, that what he disclosed to us was no secret to the Japanese press.

And as I learned early on, no enterprising reporting by outsiders can escape scrutiny. On my first interview with the prime minister, I learned to my chagrin that the folding screen at the far end of the room was more than a decoration. During the interview a Japanese newspaperman assigned to the prime minister's office sat behind it, taking notes. His report on my interview was in his paper before it reached the pages of *Time*.

Barred from official press conferences except under very special circumstances, the foreigners banded together, petitioning the ministries to open them. Some progress seems to have been made; more and more Japanese officials on their own are making themselves available for interviews. But I myself have seen the situation change little in over twenty years. As in any society, personal contact and travel away from the capital (and its bureaucracy) remain the best ways to gather news and keep a sense of people's concerns.

American journalism relies heavily on what is said, and editors have difficulty dealing with what is meant. In Japan, what is *not* said is usually more important. It was therefore refreshing in 1991 to see novelist/politician Shintaro Ishihara speak out on the unhappy state of relations between Japan and America. Ishihara's slender volume, *The Japan That Can Say No*, said things long left unsaid, or only whispered. Among his assertions: United States policy toward Japan is dictated by conscious and unconscious racism; Japan has the technological power to cripple the United States and perhaps should use that power for political ends. Ishihara wants Japan to play a leading political role to match its economic prowess. Such a part is what successive American administrations have said they wanted. But Ishihara sees Japan going its own way and not necessarily following United States foreign policy initiatives. Moreover, his criticisms of the United States, its shortcomings in education and in disposing of industrial waste, as well as his assertion that the country is shortsighted, were tinged with scorn. The rudeness of the presentation shocked many Japanese who are in agreement with his premise.

The study of Japan can be as frustrating as it is challenging and fascinating. For every insightful haiku there is a ton of trash. That doesn't make the haiku any less valuable, only more so. The contradictions of Japan and the Japanese render them and their nation more, not less, human. For more than a century we have seen the Japanese people as they see themselves—as unique and separate, in many ways significantly different from everyone else. Looking at the Japanese close up, one cannot but marvel at the way they have put together the ancient and modern, letting nothing stand in the way. The common sense of wasting nothing, saving a lot, making things right, and fixing what is wrong is irrefutable. But all is not well, and thoughtful Japanese worry a lot about the future. No nation can achieve the economic sophistication of Japan—the world's major financier and most efficient industrial producer—and expect the world's indulgence. If the role Japan must play seems clear to outsiders, it is far from clear to the Japanese.

Playing a part in the world is a major political dilemma for Japan, one not being solved. Japan still has severe problems at home. Having offered up their own well-being on the altar of progress and national pride, the Japanese today find themselves still working as hard as ever to adjust their lives to new realities.

All nations have trouble adjusting to new realities. Europe is in the midst of once unthinkable change. The disbanding of the Soviet Union has changed the military and political circumstances of Eastern Europe, Africa, and the Far East. Japan emerges from the turmoil, despite its internal difficulties, with what may turn out to be the most manageable set of problems. Its industry is strong, its economy has withstood the deflation that follows heady growth, and its social problems, although serious, are far from explosive. Dealing with the rest of the world is Japan's major challenge.

Not long ago I had a conversation with Kiichi Miyazawa, now prime minister, on the subject of understanding and cooperation between Japan and West. Must nations have a deep understanding of each other to become partners?, I asked. Miyazawa is a thoughtful man, and he was silent for a long moment. "My wife is fond of cats," he began, with a smile. "I told her I don't like them very much because I don't understand them. My wife said, 'Well, do we know each other so well, you and I, after almost fifty years of marriage?' "

"It's a kind of joke," he said, but then he made a point: "Although we can't understand each other fully, perhaps we should be prepared to find some area beyond my understanding and beyond your understanding and leave it as it is." It does not mean that the marriage must end by the lack of complete understanding.

Japan and her partners around the world may not understand each other fully, but they must cooperate. It discomforts many to see an economically powerful Japan that has yet to recognize the kind of leadership it can and should provide. But at the same time it is not clear whether Japanese leadership is even desired by the West. When Miyazawa toasted President Bush in January 1992, he said, "The days are gone when the question of world peace and stability could be left in the hands of the superpowers." To some observers this gnomic statement meant that Japan is eschewing the title of superpower, at least in the traditional sense of a militarily and economically powerful nation. But what other nation than Japan most effectively fits the new idea of an *unarmed* superpower? A related question looms: Can Japan and the U.S. find common ground beyond understanding? Knowing more about the Japanese may help us understand the answer if, or when, we see it.

Japan is a nation still hidden by the image of rich, camera-toting tourists, exported cars, chrysanthemums, and expensive golf courses. This book is written in the hope that it will help its readers see the Japanese and their institutions as they appear from close up. Or as close up as this outsider could get.

Looking at the Japanese close up, one cannot but marvel at the way they have put together the ancient and modern, letting nothing stand in the way. The common sense of wasting nothing, saving a lot, making things right, and fixing what is wrong is irrefutable. But all is not well, and thoughtful Japanese worry a lot about the future.

PROLOGUE

The emperor lay on his sickbed. He was arthritic and myopic, of quiet mien, studious, detached, and often frustrated. For three and a half months, he received around-the-clock medical attention, but the doctors fighting to save his life—doctors who in an earlier time were allowed to touch the man's body only with silk gloves—were dealing with a man suffering from a terminal case of duodenal cancer. Even in good health, the emperor seldom weighed more than 125 pounds, and at the age of eighty-seven, he had little strength left to fight the cancer.

His many blood transfusions were supervised by a medical team that included some of the nation's most practiced physicians. His passage toward death was chronicled prominently in the nation's press and broadcast to all reaches of the volcanic archipelago over which he reigned. Along with him, a nation waited (and some citizens not too patiently) for an era to pass.

Hirohito was the one-hundred and twenty-fourth sovereign to be entrusted with the mystical symbols of his inherited rank: the Mirror, the Sword, and the Jewel. Hirohito saw his nation through a tumultuous cycle of aggression, domination, and devastation, followed by political and economic redemption. And all this occurred during the era of *Showa*, or "Enlightened Peace."

Once Hirohito's mythical divinity had been removed by the victors of the war, the studious monarch remained a political figurehead and revered national grandfather. To many he remained a living god—after all, faithful adherents to Japan's pantheistic Shinto religion become gods after death, and the imperial family line, unbroken "for ages eternal," had never withstood historical scrutiny. So in important ways, historic verisimilitude did not matter. As he was dying, Hirohito, whom General Douglas MacArthur described in his memoirs, *Reminisces*, "the first gentleman of Japan in his own right," commanded respect from those who continued to believe in the institution. Hirohito's son, Emperor Akihito, falls heir to this sense of respect, with or without the godly overtones.

But dissident voices called out as well. They said that Hirohito's passing was the passing of an era. It seems unlikely that today a Japanese soldier would die with the emperor's name on his lips or that any Japanese businessman would conclude a deal by blessing the emperor. The new emperor eschews the obscure courtly language of his predecessors. As crown prince, he even danced in public with his wife, Michiko, the daughter of a wealthy miller and not of aristocracy. His children, reared at home and educated abroad, show signs of willfulness unheard of in Japanese royal families.

To Westerners who share the experience of World War II and its Pacific battles, Emperor Showa will most likely be remembered as Hirohito; the enigma of the man will persist. The person who ended the war despite the pleading of his remaining generals was the same man who signed the declaration of war in bold calligraphy. From 1931, when Japanese military forces manufactured an incident in Manchuria to justify their annexation of the territory, until the end of war in 1945, Hirohito was seen in public only in full military uniform, often sitting stiffly on his horse White

Snow. When Singapore fell in February 1942, Hirohito appeared on horseback at the *Nijubashi*, the double bridge that leads to the entrance of the Imperial Palace in the center of Tokyo. As the crowd gathered below, he sat stiffly motionless for a long time, peering down sternly at the throngs who came to hail the victory over mighty Great Britain's colonial forces.

And yet for all the saber rattling, the studies of Hirohito depict a different kind of man. He spent many years studying marine life, authoring or coauthoring a dozen scientific books. During the war he was almost always on palace grounds, conferring frequently with his military mentors, his aides, and advisers in the air raid shelter deep below the library. The shelter contained a kitchen and bedrooms as well as his conference room. Toward the end of the war, when the devastating B-29 incendiary bombings became incessant, he seldom ventured out, even to go to his laboratory. Was the image of a quiet, studious, introspective, and peaceful man a carefully constructed sham?

Enigmatic Monarch

The conundrum of Hirohito, whose signature in effect doomed more than 2 million Japanese soldiers and close to 1 million Japanese civilians, symbolizes the problem that faces any outsider attempting to understand Japan and the Japanese. Hirohito symbolizes the blend of myth and reality, fiction and fact, tradition and innovation that are the paradoxes of modern Japan itself.

On Hirohito's death, the reaction was mixed. British tabloids did not treat him kindly. "Hell's waiting for this truly evil emperor," *The Sun* declared. Left-wing groups protested the "self-restraint" the government asked of people as the elderly man lay on his deathbed. Businessmen cut short their trips abroad and hurried home to be in the country when he died. Public celebrations were canceled, weddings postponed as inauspicious, and the gaudy neon lights of the Ginza, Shin-

juku, and Shibuya dimmed. Economic analysts speculated
that such self-restraint might cost as much as $600 million,
the equivalent of two-tenths of 1 percent of the nation's all-
important gross national product. Nevertheless, tens of thousands journeyed to the palace to sign books wishing the emperor a speedy recovery, even as people demonstrated in
Tokyo and elsewhere against plans for the government to
finance a Shinto funeral. Some Japanese, particularly members of the Japan Socialist Party, worried in print and
through bull horns about a revival of prewar authoritarian
politics supported by forced emperor veneration; they called
for an end to the imperial system.

A few days before Hirohito's death, Hitoshi Motoshima,
the mayor of Nagasaki, was asked his views of Hirohito's war
responsibility during a city assembly meeting. The sixty-six-
year-old official, at the time a member of the nation's ruling
party, pondered the question for a moment. He replied, "If
I look at the descriptions of Japanese and foreign histories
and reflect on my experience in the military in the educational training of soldiers, in that regard, I think the emperor
has war responsibility." Explaining his wartime activities to
reporters after the meeting, Motoshima said, "I taught recruits to die for the emperor. I, too, share a heavy responsibility."

Motoshima's comments brought about threats. Right-
wing fanatics, self-styled defenders of the imperial system,
made hundreds of ominous telephone calls to Motoshima's
family. On police advice, the mayor abandoned his customary walks. One man was apprehended trying to break into
the mayor's office carrying a can of gasoline. Another sus-
picious person was found carrying a knife. Even as nearly
300,000 people signed a petition backing the mayor's statement, right-wing groups sent convoys of sound trucks around
the city blaring, "Death to Motoshima!"

Mayor Motoshima is a Roman Catholic who was persecuted in the army during the war for following his own religion—rather than Shinto, the official state religion. "I guess
the real mistake was that I waited to say it until now," Mo-

toshima told local reporters. The harassment seemed to
abate after several weeks. But the incident was not forgotten.
A year later, as Motoshima was leaving city hall, a right-
wing activist from Tokyo shot him in the back and later
appeared on television to boast about it. After Motoshima
was released from the hospital, his own political party (the
Liberal Democratic Party) disciplined him for violating an
unwritten taboo against speaking about the emperor disres-
pectfully. Not all the reaction was bad: Motoshima received
generous press coverage abroad and many letters from
strangers wishing him well, even an offer to dedicate to him
the Japanese language edition of Salman Rushdie's *Satanic
Verses*, the book that put Rushdie under sentence of death
by outraged Muslims. Throughout, Motoshima took the situation philosophically. "When it comes to the Imperial family," he told some magazine writers many weeks later,
"people get very emotional."

An End and A Beginning

Emperor Hirohito's funeral drew mourners from around
the world. There were 10,000 invited guests, including representatives of 163 governments. Some claimed it was the
largest and most distinguished funeral guest list ever assembled. United States President George Bush and French President François Mitterand headed the list of notables, which
also included princes, princesses, and prime ministers, all of
whom braved the chilling March drizzle to see Hirohito's
body carried in state on a gold-draped bier, shouldered by
fifty-one Imperial Guard members dressed in gray and black
robes and headdresses in the style of the eighth-century
Heian court. Some said the visitors came out of curiosity or
a sense of history, to acknowledge the passing of the last
great figure of World War II. The funeral procession, broadcast on all channels, wound through virtually deserted
streets of an unusually quiet Tokyo. Many businesses and
offices were closed for this official day of mourning—the

video rental stores, however, reported brisk business with customers who wanted more to watch than the funeral events and endless documentaries.

Left-wing radical threats to disrupt the funeral did not materialize, nor did the expected clashes with right-wing loyalists. Perhaps it was because of the 30,000-odd police, who for weeks had sifted through the city looking for old-time troublemakers and potential new ones. To the dismay of the small number of civil liberties advocates in Tokyo, the police made surprise searches, spot-checked all vans at impromptu roadblocks, and passed out leaflets encouraging citizens to report abnormal behavior in the neighborhoods near the funeral site. Local air freight shipments were put on hold five days before the event. Several dozen suspected troublemakers were arrested on a variety of convenient charges to keep them out of circulation. There was only one incident, a minor explosion along the funeral route before the procession arrived.

Behind a curtain at the rain-drenched site of the ceremony, Shinto priests and the new emperor to be, Akihito, could be glimpsed presenting offerings to the gods. The curtain was the Imperial Household Agency's bow to those who insisted no public religious ceremony should be held, but opponents of the Shinto ritual complained that the curtain was only a half-hearted attempt to make the religious service private (from time to time, wind gusts revealed the ceremonial affairs taking place). The thousands of foreigners, little concerned about the niceties of that dispute, were impressed with the pageantry. As each head of state arrived and approached the bier, his or her name was announced and broadcast nationwide over television and radio. But because of the angle of the cameras, the faces of the leaders did not often match up with the names being announced. It didn't seem to matter. "People finally noticed how important we are," exclaimed a Japanese businessman watching the broadcast. "They can see the world coming to pay homage."

Hirohito's moundlike tomb, similar to that of his father, was completed in 1990, at a cost of $18 million. Fears that many aged and loyal devotees would voluntarily join their emperor in death were unfounded, though two such deaths were recorded. The relentless security may have been responsible for preventing serious incidents that might have marred the day's simple ceremony or discomfited any of the distinguished visitors who came to see the passing of Hirohito and his era.

CHAPTER ONE

THE SMALLEST GIANT

The Japanese invariably describe their country as small. But modesty and understatement is ingrained in the Japanese character. The description of Japan as a small country is accurate only in a relative sense. Japan is bigger in land area than Great Britain or Italy and not too far behind France and Spain in size. Its landmass—about the size of the state of Montana—may be meager by some standards, but its agricultural productivity is better than that of many countries. This largesse is produced with effort: of the twenty-five largest nations in the world, only Egypt has less usable area for growing crops. Yet with a mere 14.4 percent of its land dedicated to agriculture, and much of that agriculture accomplished by part-time farmers, Japan considers itself virtually self-sufficient in the production of rice, vegetables, fruit, meat, eggs, fats and oils, fish, and shellfish.

Japanese society is often characterized as antlike, its millions crammed together in sprawling cities—human form-icaries—overgrown conglomerations of neighborhoods, and villages. The numbers are stunning. Japan's concentration of people—332 per square kilometer—exceeds that of the United Kingdom, 233 persons. It takes a backseat in numbers only to Bangladesh (740 per square kilometer) and Korea (428 per square kilometer). The land-rich United States is low on the list, with a density of twenty-seven persons per square kilometer. But that is only part of the picture, and in Japan's case, an understated one. The number of persons crammed into the *habitable* area of Japan is a remarkable 1523 per square kilometer. The figures from other countries are nowhere near as high. In the United States, it is 54 persons per kilometer; in the United Kingdom, 365 persons; and in France, 165 persons. Japan's population of 123 million makes it the seventh most populous in the world, and few people live as closely together as do the Japanese.

Despite the heavy population concentration, the overcrowding, and the frenetic pace, the Japanese live longer than anybody. The average Japanese female baby can be expected to live to nearly eight-two years, the Japanese male newborn to seventy-six years. Nobody knows why the Japanese live so long. They have one of the highest rates of smoking in the world. The men drink prodigiously. The traditional diet is heavy in salty, brine-soaked foods.

Newly developed appetites for the fatty foods of the West is creating a younger generation with a growing number of overweight and physically unfit people. Stomach cancer for many years was a leading cause of death, and now lung cancer is chasing it. Even so, this crowded nation of disciplined, hard-working, and hard-drinking achievers has become the world's second largest industrial power and the major creditor nation. Contrary to all the conventional wisdom that has seen Japan as a tiny, resource-poor land, it is gigantic in many ways that count in modern world society. The people are its most abundant, important, and valuable resource. And yet the Japanese today are not even sure of who they are or where they came from.

Mountain Tops for Immigrants

The land itself stretches like a cat sprawled across the doorway to northern Asia. Guarding the rim of the Asian continent, its claimed Kurile Island extremities in the north—seized by the Soviet Union—are frigid and subarctic. Its far-flung Ryukyu outposts to the south are tropical. These points span a distance of more than 1700 miles. The arc of Japan's islands shields the Yellow Sea and the Sea of Japan from the Soviet Kamchatka Peninsula and the American Aleutian islands to Taiwan.

Japan's land surface, the Far East's version of South America's Andes mountains, is a chain of mountain tops shoved above the Pacific Ocean by tectonic plate movement. Geologists say they did not appear until sometime between the Paleozoic period and the age of dinosaurs, 500 million to 160 million years ago. Japan sits on—is part of—the most unstable part of the earth's crust. One of its active volcanoes, Mt. Aso, has the world's largest caldera. Dozens of active volcanoes and hot springs not only delight vacationing Japanese bathers, but sometimes also overflow and destroy valuable farmland because of the water's acidity. Mt. Sakurajima, an active volcano a stone's throw across the bay from Kagoshima, sends plumes of smoky-gray ash skyward every day, and the hearty inhabitants of the island go about their business among the solidified remnants and eerie reminders of earlier eruptions. Children often are required to wear hard hats to and from school to protect themselves from falling volcanic debris.

The spine of Japan's main islands comprises a sparsely populated but breathtaking mountainscape with remote wooded areas and hidden valleys seldom visited except by the most intrepid trekkers. But this soaring mountain cordillera, covered with cedar, cypress, camphor, and pine, stands as a hurdle that tempers the wintry Siberian winds. Spring winds bringing converging weather systems from northwest and southeast collide over Japan and douse most of the country, especially the western regions, in midyear.

Typhoons, spawned in the south, tend to strike southern Japan and exempt the capital from all but rain, light snow and moderately strong winds. In summer most of the nation is bathed in moist warm air. Winter's brisk winds tend to sweep the pollution offshore and winter days can be crystal clear under brilliant cerulean skies. Early woodblock prints show a snow-capped Mount Fuji visible from foreground scenes hundreds of kilometers away. On clear days in winter, the scenes come to life again. On some cold and crisp winter weekends, one could wander through the outer gardens of the Imperial Palace in Tokyo and sometimes glimpse Mount Fuji through a gate or under an eave.

The northernmost main island, Hokkaido, once known as Ezo, is subject to long, frigid, snowy winters. Its northern and western extremities jut into the edge of the Siberian air mass; but the southernmost main island, Kyushu, where Portuguese and Dutch traders landed in the fifteenth century, is spared winter almost entirely.

To this land came the people who became the Japanese. Steep mountainsides, sharply cut precipices, and deep valleys served as natural protection for the early dwellers. On the main shore of Honshu facing the Asian continent they found long stretches of sand beach and dune; the coastline of Kyushu was punctuated with craggy bays and harbors. The Inland Sea, between what is now Honshu, Shikoku, and Kyushu, was usually as calm as a lake, studded with islands covered with trees, shrubbery, and wildflowers. It was also fat with fish. Japan's early peoples found it shallow enough and placid enough to serve as a convenient water highway for travel between coastal villages.

Anthropologists conclude that the inhabitants came in waves, from the Asian continent and the islands to the south, and from the north, the snowy reaches of what is now Kamchatka, Sakhalin, and the far-eastern extremity of the continent. Adventurers from fishing cultures of the coastal waters of Asia, hunters from the Arctic and island-hopping fishermen, and hunters and gatherers from the south converged on what we now call Japan. Neolithic artifacts, stone tools and implements, pottery vessels, masks, and axes unearthed in widely separated parts of the island nation indicate a disparate assortment of visitors. It is even thought that among the late Neolithic settlers from northeast Asia were members of a linguistic group that includes Mongols, Huns, and Finns.

Melanesians brought taro root with them, together with stone axes and pots. Archeological finds and certain linguistic clues give rise to the possibility that some of Japan's earliest settlers sailed from what is now called Indonesia and New Guinea. Ceramic artifacts in eastern Japan prove similar to Alaskan and Eurasian finds. The Ainu, a race of hirsute, bearded wanderers from the north, inhabited what is now Hokkaido, and for many years the people from the south traded with them at arm's—or weapon's—length. Eventually the settlers of Kyushu and Honshu conquered and colonized the Ainu, who are now considered the closest thing to an indigenous population of the islands. Over the years since 1799, when laws designed to protect Ainu culture and property were laid down, the Ainu have dwindled in number. Many have assimilated, leaving only scant numbers today, less than 15,000. Their few remaining villages are tourist attractions.

Rice-growing migrants from the Yangtse region of China are thought to have brought a matrilineal social system with them when they arrived about 300 B.C. The major Chinese influence is thought to have come through the Korean peninsula, and communications with China and with China-influenced Koreans have been constant since the first century B.C. These people are believed to have originated the myth of the sun goddess, and with it the beginnings of the idea of nationhood. It took many centuries for the settlers in diverse parts of Japan to make contact, fight, make peace, mingle, and assimilate, and Japanese ethnographers today are still trying to solve the riddle of the origins of the Japanese people. Expeditions are occasionally dispatched to Southeast Asia and elsewhere to seek more clues.

The dominant physical characteristics of a Mongoloid

people have come to identify the Japanese. Almost all Japanese babies are born with the Mongolian spot, a bluish coloration at the base of the spine which disappears, usually by the tenth year. They have soft brown or dark brown hair; an epitheal, or Mongolian, fold at the inner edge of the upper eyelid; a low and straight but small nose; and widespread eyes that give the appearance of a flat face. They tend to have little body hair. Northern Japanese dispose toward light brown or yellowish-brown skin. Those from more southern regions often have darker skin tones. They are not so homogeneous as to look alike.

City Slickers, Country Roots

The energetic people of Japan today recognize and celebrate their regional differences. Pride in local and regional traditions, mostly rooted in the nation's agricultural past, and a long history of warring clans have led many to consider the Japanese a tribe, or a congeries of tribes. The nation's sophisticated city dwellers have always felt superior toward their country cousins. Even among these sophisticates from Japan's major cities there are cultural clashes. The Tokyoite, who hails from the seat of power in the nation, speaks what has become standard Japanese. To most other Japanese, the Tokyoite is brash, talks too fast, acts too haughty. Japanese from the hinterlands have their own dialects, idioms, and idiosyncrasies, which the Tokyoites often imitate mockingly. The dialect of the Tohoku region of north central Japan served as the Japanese Eliza Doolittle's equivalent of Cockney when *My Fair Lady* was performed in Tokyo. Regional differences persist. In Osaka, the historic commercial center where most of Japan's major industrial enterprises began, it is still common to hear people greet each other with, "How's business?" or, "Did you make any money today?" rather than a standard, "Good morning."

Although it is still possible to find remote and virtually inaccessible regions of Japan, for the most part the nation has been opened up to modernization. The island of Kyushu, once a sleepy and slow-moving outpost of seaports, fishing villages, small farms, and ceramic kilns, is now becoming home to some of the nation's highest technology in steel-making and chemical and electronics industries. It is now described as the "silicon island" of Japan. In the suburbs of Kagoshima, ancestral home of the powerful Satsuma clan, I drove an experimental automobile with an engine made almost entirely of ceramics. It seemed fitting that a new "Stone Age" should be dawning on the island where the famous kilns of Imari produced some of the world's finest ceramics. And it is intriguing that the ancient ceramic techniques practiced in Kyushu were learned from Chinese and Korean teachers, many of whom were kidnapped expressly for the purpose. The broad and vacant plains of the northern reaches of Hokkaido have not escaped the developers' bulldozers and trenchers. An undersea tunnel now connects the main island of Honshu with Hokkaido, 780 feet under the Tsugaru strait, and one of the world's largest suspension bridges now provides easy access to Shikoku, the smallest of the four main islands. Good highways and an abundance of cars—77 percent of Japanese households own at least one—plus efficient rail and air transit, have brought the countryside to the city, or the city to the countryside. The lure of the metropolis, of high paying jobs and a life-style glamorized by television, which reaches the most remote corners of the land, have taken their toll: they have helped to produce a countryside of more or less wealthy elderly. Agriculture produces less than 2 percent of Japan's gross national product, but the profits are going to a smaller number of farmers.

A slow drive through the countryside of Hokkaido, from Chitose to Wakkanai, for example, reveals town after town resembling town after town. Everywhere there are Japanese and foreign chains of fast food stores, along with the ubiquitous neon signs and blinding lights of the *pachinko* parlors. The megalopolis from Tokyo to Osaka reveals short flashes of countryside, and soaring images of the 12,390-foot symbol of Japan, Mount Fuji, cone shaped and snowcapped. Small farms are hemmed in by industrial buildings, and a halo of air pollution all too often hovers over them. Through the snow country the lack of usable land and the Japanese mania for skiing have persuaded builders to bring ski runs and lifts right down into the new villages, almost to the right-of-way of the bullet train.

Seeking recreation, citified Japanese return to the countryside. They are prepared to suffer for their pleasures, jamming trains to double capacity on their way to the cemeteries of their ancestors, or to beaches and the mountains. The railroad and subway pushers, hired to shove passengers into already tightly packed cars, do so with the acquiescence of the pushed. Because the system has forced the rudeness on them, there is no need for those pushed to apologize for intruding on another's privacy.

There is still peace and beauty to be found off the beaten path. Even in the center of Japan's noisiest, smoggiest cities one can find in almost every neighborhood a temple or shrine, a garden or small cemetery, where the noise and disruptions of city life are surprisingly remote. (One is best advised, however, to find a place not on a popular tour bus itinerary.) In the gardens of Japan, horticultural artists have created new realities of nature. One of the triumphs of the Japanese aesthetic is the courtyard garden, in which the illusion of natural space is created where there is none. The ancient capitals of Kyoto and Nara, with their myriad religious and historical sites and imperial palaces and gardens, are a surprise and delight in that regard. Attempts by developers to build giant commercial projects in these cities have been rejected, although Kyoto's elegant, brooding wooden shrines and temples suffer the indignity of a soaring concrete showcase tower downtown.

The jarring juxtaposition of ancient and modern doesn't seem to bother the adaptable Japanese. My family, vacationing at a lakeside not far from the Sea of Japan, decided one morning to drive to the coast and look toward Korea, perhaps even to dip our toes in the sea. It was not a long drive, and as the crowded vacation land hurly-burly of tour groups and neon yielded to verdant farmland and eventually to the blue and white coast, a sense of spaciousness struck us all. The beach's wide, white sand in this part of Japan seemed so different from the rugged cliffs and precipitous coastline of most of the Pacific side of the nation. I parked the car on the wind-swept street of a small village facing the sea. As we crossed the road toward the ocean and the hissing surf, another sound intruded in the still morning. It was a crunching sound, almost like someone walking lightly on gravel. We all heard it and stopped to listen. The sound was coming from the houses where we had just parked the car. Filled with curiosity, we walked back, listening keenly, and as we did, the sound grew louder. Peeking cautiously under the eaves and into one of the houses, we could see the source: stacked in racks were flats filled with finger-size silkworms busily munching on mulberry leaves. The ancient practice of sericulture was still alive, and the worms were well in modern rural Japan. So were the silk farmers: beside the house was parked the owner's car, a large, new Mercedes Benz.

Indeed, with the rising land values of the 1980s and the continued protection of the nation's agriculture, the farmers of Japan, the mainstay force of conservatism, have profited handsomely. The bank with the largest deposits in the nation for many years has been Norin Chukin, the farmer's cooperative bank. As one of the bank's officials explained it to me, "Japanese farmers are very rich these days. You see, the outlook for farming is not so bright, so very little investment is being made in new equipment. They are just watching. So their savings and deposits are very big." So big—the bank has three times more money in deposits than it has made in loans—that the bank has been lending money abroad for agricultural development projects, such as grain-storage facilities in the United States.

But the social cost of rural prosperity has been hard. For most Japanese who farm, tilling the soil of the small family plot is only a part-time job. Ninety percent of these farmers work at jobs other than farming, and in more and more cases, farming is the sideline, not the town job. Taking care of the rice paddies has become, for many, a weekend occupation. When the cultivating has to be done, others are hired to do it.

The government's plan to encourage farmers with small plots to sell their land and rely on other jobs has failed. The larger and more economical farm units that the planners were encouraging did not materialize. Yet fertilizers and modern agricultural science, together with the government's financial encouragement, have resulted in ever bigger rice crops. By keeping their small plots, farmers are guaranteed a subsidy—the government still buys the rice at a specific price, regardless of supply and demand. Because of the high price of usable land, few wish to sell, preferring to see their holdings appreciate. For many years Japanese farmers have grown more rice than the nation can consume, and rice consumption continues to decline. Moreover, the Japanese favor a glutinous variety not popular abroad, so export markets are virtually nonexistent. The government larders are full: at one point there was so much old and dessicated rice in storage that it was being sold as a sandblasting material to clean industrial machinery.

For those farm households still intact in Japan's countryside, life has lost much, but not all, of its hardship and tedium. The children often choose to leave their farm homes for the city, and husbands and wives commute to the nearest town for a job at the electronics factory, the boutique, or the restaurant. But the standard of living for many rural families now rivals and in some areas surpasses that of the envied city dwellers. The countryside has cleaner air, more living space, a healthier environment, increased entertainment. Still, the excitement is missing, and so the children leave. There are even some remote villages that have been abandoned after the children moved away and the elderly died. There are shrunken villages in Japan where nobody will run for local office, and where joint community effort to build public facilities has come to a standstill. Japan today is essentially an urban country whose people, paradoxically, see themselves, almost nostalgically, as being rooted in the volcanic soil of the countryside.

The Other Part of Japan

At the nation's southern extremity lies an anomaly. Okinawa is a prefecture of Japan, but Okinawans are considered by the Japanese to be remote and different from, and somehow inferior to, main islanders. Their past seems more rooted in the foreign cultures of the south Pacific and less influenced by mainland Asian cultures. Okinawa's several local dialects are all but undecipherable to most Japanese, and the local festivals carry overtones derived from cultures removed from those of main island Japan's. Shinto and Buddhism are practied, but shamanism is common. To many Japanese, Okinawa and the forty-odd small islands that make up the Ryukyu chain are thought of as little more than a vacation spot.

From the Okinawan side, feelings of being Japanese compete with memories of World War II, when a third of the island's civilian population, at least 150,000 people, was slaughtered. Japanese soldiers forced some into service or ordered them into the path of the invading Americans. Many committed suicide, and there are heart-rending stories still told today of Japanese soldiers who killed Okinawan children to keep them from crying and giving away a hidden military position.

Oppression and occupation were not novelties to the people of Okinawa when American forces took over after the war. Okinawans did complain, however, when the United States continued to rule the islands and use it as a military base for two decades after the occupation of Japan had ended. (Okinawa was not returned to Japanese sovereignty until 1972.) During those years the medium of exchange was the dollar, and everybody drove on the right side of the road—contrary to Japanese custom, which matches the British. The American flag was a common sight, and Americans were the final authorities at law. When the United States returned sovereignty, the Okinawans had some initial difficulties adjusting to Japanese control. Some Okinawans wanted independence after the war, and they say American military officers helped to foster the idea of remaining separate from Japan. At the signing of the World War II peace treaty, it was envisioned that the United States would propose a United Nations trusteeship arrangement for the islands. But then the United States maintained jurisdiction. Anti-American demonstrations by students and political activists were common throughout the Vietnam War era, even after reversion to Japan, because the United States still maintained many of its military bases. Giant B-52 bombers carried their bomb loads from the Kadena Air Force Base as antiwar protesters chronicled their coming and going and demonstrated against the missions to Vietnam.

Most galling to many older Okinawans today is the widespread belief that Emperor Hirohito gave his tacit consent for the United States to remain in control of Okinawa for twenty-five to fifty years after the peace treaty. Okinawans saw themselves as sacrificial lambs. It was at a time when the road to recovery in Japan proper looked long and difficult: Okinawa seemed to the Japanese a burden that the Americans could afford and they could not. Once most of the American military presence withdrew from the main islands, 75 percent of what was left was based in Okinawa. Along with American changes came the increased presence of Japanese Self Defense Forces to replace the Americans. Okinawans saw themselves as paying the price for main island Japan's security and prosperity.

When Hirohito made a postwar nation-healing tour of ravaged Japan he did not visit Okinawa, and he did not visit in 1972, when Okinawa was returned to Japanese sovereignty. Aware of anti-Japanese sentiment along the left in Okinawa, the government thought they would test local sentiment by sending the crown prince and princess. Nobody on Okinawa was surprised by the violent protests the visit caused, including an attempt to firebomb the couple. A dozen years later, in 1987, a royal visit was scheduled to inaugurate the National Athletic Meet, but the emperor canceled because of illness. Again the crown prince and princess went in his place. Protest demonstrations were fewer this time, but one was particularly significant.

During the battle for Okinawa, the Japanese built an airstrip near the village of Yomitan. When American invasion forces zeroed in on the field, 139 villagers fled and 82 killed themselves to avoid capture. After the war the Americans used the site as an air base, and when they finally withdrew, it was turned into an athletic field. When the government in Tokyo began requiring the display of the flag and the singing of the national anthem at the playing field, some members of the village assembly opposed what they considered an act of enforced nationalism.

Yomitan's mayor challenged the government, saying, "a brute force is now attacking the citizens of this prefecture." Its demands, he said, represent "the second coming of the ideology of loyalty and patriotism which should have been negated under the new postwar constitution. This is a return to prewar [times]." At the emotional opening ceremony of a championship softball game, a member of the assembly, Shoichi Chibana, hauled down the Japanese flag and burned it.

Dealing with outsiders has been a problem for the island since 1372, when the people of Okinawa sent their first mission to China bearing tribute. They have been paying tribute one way or another ever since. Their position at the apex of a triangle 600 miles from Kyushu, 600 miles from Taiwan, and 600 miles from China has been a blessing and a curse.

At the beginning of the seventeenth century, samurai from Kagoshima swarmed over the island and assumed control. But because the Japanese were interested in maintaining trade and diplomatic relations with China, the samurai played an elaborate trick. To convince the Chinese inspector general that Okinawa was nothing more than a Chinese tributary, the samurai hid in the mountains until the Okinawans had performed the ncessary rites of obeisance. Then the warriors would reestablish their suzerainty. When Japanese generalissimos visited, the samurai also forced Okinawan officials to dress in Chinese costume to give the impression that Japanese rule ranged far and wide.

The West intruded on the Okinawans as well. Commodore Matthew C. Perry landed a small force from the U.S.S. Mississippi in 1853, marched his men to the royal castle on Shuri Hill, and asked for Okinawan cooperation in exchange for American friendship. What he really wanted, and soon demanded, was permission to set up a military base in the capital city of Naha while he awaited the outcome of his ultimatum to the Japanese emperor and shogun to sign a treaty. Perry had euphemistically proposed to President Franklin Pierce that the United States take Okinawa "under surveillance." Pierce's reply, in the light of history, shows him to have been prescient: "If, in the future," he wrote, "resistance should be offered and threatened, it would be rather mortifying to surrender the island if once seized, and rather inconvenient and expensive to maintain a force there to retain it."

Perry's appearance in Japan set off turmoil within the shogun's government, but in 1854 the shogun reluctantly agreed to open trading ports to American ships. The same year, Perry's ships visited again and left with only a "compact of friendship" to show for the effort. Then the British, the French, and the Dutch all rapidly showed up, demanding trade treaties with the Japanese and the bewildered Okinawans. Such interest in the Ryukyu Islands alarmed Japan, and with the abolition of the shogunate and the restoration of the Mikado to political power in 1868, the Japanese declared all the islands an integral part of Japan. Okinawa became part of the Kagoshima prefecture.

The Okinawans grew prickly over the turn of events. When an Imperial military force landed at Naha, the Okinawans protested, saying that a garrison might attract Japan's enemies and embroil them in a fight they had no interest in. For some years the Okinawans bickered with the Japanese over this issue. Then the Japanese deposed the king in 1879, abolished the royal government, and made Okinawa a full prefecture of Japan (it was also the poorest). The king was banished to Tokyo, where he received a modest pension. Since then the Japanese have tried to win the loyalty of the Okinawans in an effort to assimilate them. The attempt has not been a success.

As Okinawans made their way to the main islands seeking a better life, they experienced discrimination. It continues.

Time has helped to ameliorate many of the hard feelings of Okinawans. (Pointedly, the Okinawan administration failed to invite Emperor Akihito and Empress Michiko to the 1992 ceremonies commemorating the twentieth anniversary of the return of Okinawa to Japanese sovereignty.) As the Japanese economy prospers, some of the wealth trickles down to Okinawa, together with inflation. Okinawan incomes are still only about three-quarters of the national average, and Japan's promises to develop the economy have not been successful. Many American servicemen remain stationed at eight U.S. bases in Okinawa, and in the face of the high cost of living, not a few have augmented their military pay with part-time jobs.

A writer for the *Asahi Shimbun* found a vengeful Okinawan who confided his dream: to hire an American officer's wife as a maid. The bitterness lingers, a prickly thorn in the lovely chrysanthemum of the nation's cherished image.

Today's Japan still has many other social thorns to deal with, despite its vaunted homogeneity. Contrary to a common view of itself as a vulnerable, land-poor nation, it is seen abroad increasingly as a predatory economic superpower. By almost any measure, Japan is a big and powerful country. The Japanese have yet fully to come to grips with this reality.

CHAPTER TWO

THE HIROHITO RIDDLE

In Tokyo's Shibuya district during Hirohito's last days, at one of hundreds of rallies around the country, demonstrators against the imperial institution carried a large banner reading, "Even if the emperor passes away, the memory of what he did in the war will remain in history."

Hirohito's responsibility for the war is not fully understood now, nor is it likely to be anytime soon. Mariko Terasaki Miller, whose father Hidenari Terasaki was one of Hirohito's interpreters in the immediate postwar era, found papers that seemed to shed light on the question. Notes by Terasaki, made on one hundred sheets of memo paper, quoted Emperor Hirohito as saying he didn't oppose the beginning of the war with the U.S. because he feared a coup would take place if he opposed it. The war hysteria had been built to such a pitch, he was quoted as saying, that if he alone had resisted it the public opinion would have questioned why Japan's strong military had to bow to the United States. He believed his resistance would have brought about the coup. And the war would take place, anyway.

As for the high level meetings at which grave national

issues were decided, the Terasaki papers quote the emperor as saying, "All the members except the president of the Privy Council come to the meeting after they have discussed issues and reached a consensus. The president of the Privy Council is the only one who can speak. It is just a formality, and the emperor has no authority to make decisions ruling the meeting."

The subject is not one pursued by the Japanese press, who fear the disfavor not only of right-wing fanatics but also of the political establishment, including the Imperial Household Agency, which operates as a quasi-independent power. The diaries of the emperor's wartime attendants and political operatives have failed to disclose evidence that makes Hirohito the author of Japan's bloody expansionism.

Some analysts insist that the details of Hirohito's direct involvement were suppressed not only by the zealous guardians of the Imperial image but by General Douglas MacArthur himself. The general used the emperor and the Imperial institution to help him create the environment for what was undoubtedly to be the most benign and constructive occupation in history.

Hirohito was "a captive of forces beyond his control. He never possessed the absolute powers often ascribed to him," says Naohiro Amaya, a prominent former postwar government bureaucrat. "Hirohito faithfully observed the principle that a sovereign should reign, not rule. The militarists took advantage of this using his name shamelessly for their own ends." The records show that Hirohito participated in military strategy sessions with Prime Minister Hideki Tojo, who led the militarists that held power, and with others. Sometimes the answers he got to his questions at these sessions worried him. At the outset of the war, he asked Admiral Osamu Nagano, "Will you win great battles like the Battle of Tsushima?" (Hirohito was referring to the conflict that resulted in the defeat of the Russian Baltic Fleet just after the turn of the century.) Nagano was frank: "I'm sorry," he said, "but that will not be possible." To which the emperor is said to have responded, "Then the war will be a desperate one."

Major figures in the war crimes trial in Tokyo testified that Hirohito reluctantly consented to the war. Tojo, the general and politician, was found guilty of war crimes and hanged, but Hirohito was never charged with any offense. James Flood Webb, the chief justice at the trials, considered the Allies' decision twenty-five years later, in the introduction to *Japan's Imperial Conspiracy*, by David Bergamini:

> It may seem rather quaint for an alliance of democratic governments to wage war upon an autocratic government at great expense in life and material, and then leave the chief autocrat of that government in a position of leadership. But Hirohito was not only an individual; he was a symbol. However culpable he was individually, he was also the spiritual embodiment of his entire nation. In 1945 a majority of Japanese believed, as a matter of religious faith, that Japan and the Emperor were indivisible and must live or die together.

Caged Phoenix

Chamberlains have told of hearing Hirohito shout behind closed doors as early as 1940. They thought it was the only outlet he had available to express his opinions about many decisions made in his name. Historian Robert J. C. Butow writes in *Japan's Decision to Surrender*, "It was recognized that theoretically possessing the right to do many things, the emperor was actually allowed, for the good of the state and for the sake of the imperial institution, to do very little. He was permitted only a limited discretionary power, nothing approaching the power of veto." The late Edwin O. Reischauer, historian and former United States ambassador to Japan, pointed out in his book, *The Japanese*, that up to the end of the war, "the Japanese leadership was able to combine an extreme reverence for the emperor with a complete willingness to force decisions on him regardless of his own wishes. . . . None of the three modern emperors made any real effort to assert his own will against the decisions of his ministers." Except, of course, for Hirohito's tie-breaking decision to end the war.

Hirohito did try to change the course of his nation's history at least three times. The first was during Japan's drive into Manchuria to establish the puppet state of Manchukuo, when the expansionist General Giichi Tanaka, then prime minister, came to him with what would have been a *carte blanche* for further military actions against the Chinese mainland. Hirohito's simple response was a stunning rebuke: "We cannot trust your words." Tanaka resigned and his government fell. Others who advocated Japan's continued thrust onto the Asian continent took up where Tanaka left off, however, and the course of history was not changed.

The second time was in 1936, during a coup attempt by young military officers. Two of the emperor's most trusted men, the finance minister and the keeper of the privy seal, were assassinated by the rebels. Prime Minister Keisuke Okada escaped death by hiding in a closet in the servants' quarters when troops stormed the residence and mistakenly gunned down his brother. As usual, the bloody uprising of some 1200 soldiers, including some from the palace guard, was staged by purist officers who felt Hirohito was being wrongly advised. Hirohito was furious when he learned of the killings. His top military aide, Shigeru Honjo, wrote about the Emperor's rage in his diary. Hirohito is quoted as saying, "How can we not condemn even the spirit of these criminally brutal officers who killed my aged subjects who were my hands and feet?" Later he said of the act, "To kill the old subjects whom I trusted the most is akin to gently strangling me with floss-silk." Hirohito had had enough. "Subjugate those mobsters immediately," he ordered.

Honjo said he demurred from the emperor's use of the term "mobsters." The word he used, *boto*, can also mean rioters or mutineers, but the angry emperor obviously meant the term to carry its strongest connotation. "Such a term, Your Majesty, might just antagonize these fellows," cautioned

Honjo. Hirohito replied, "Those troops mobilized without Our command cannot be called Ours at all."

The military officers, reluctant to fire on their own men and partially in sympathy with them, fast-talked the soldiers into dispersing. The soldiers' request to have a royal witness at their ritual suicide, whereby they would atone for their actions, was denied. The military prosecuted 140 of the mutineers. Thirteen officers and two civilians were executed.

During World War II Hirohito wasn't known to have taken decisive action against his military advisers until its last days, after the United States bombed Hiroshima and Nagasaki and after the Soviet Union entered the war against Japan. In 1945 the invasion of Japan's home islands was considered imminent, yet Hirohito's cabinet ministers were unable to decide whether to end the war by accepting the Allied terms of unconditional surrender or to continue fighting. In a momentous meeting in the underground bunker, Prime Minister Kantaro Suzuki rose and stood before the emperor. He bowed deeply and begged for an Imperial ruling to break the deadlock. There is no official transcript of the meeting, but participants later said the atmosphere was heavy with anguish and that Hirohito was in tears. In a voice cracking with emotion, he said, "We have to bear the unbearable. . . . It is Our desire that you accede to Our wishes and accept the Allied reply. . . . In order to make the people know our decision we should broadcast it by radio."

In contrast, there had been a kind of melancholy but no tears on September 6, 1941, three months before Pearl Harbor, when the agreement was reached that Japan had no choice but to go to war against the United States and Britain. Hirohito surprised everyone by reciting a poem, cryptic in this setting, written by his grandfather, the Emperor Meiji:

> On the seas surrounding all quarters of the globe
> All peoples are kin to each other
> Why, then, do winds and waves of conflict
> Disturb peace among us?

A week before the attack, Tojo said he would put the emperor's mind at rest by quickly accomplishing the military and political objectives. The diarists do not record a response by the emperor, but on the day of the attack, Marquis Koishi Kido, Lord Keeper of the Privy Seal, noted that Hirohito looked "calm and collected."

Defeat, Demythification

Hirohito gradually became aware of Japan's changing fortunes during the course of the war, although much of the bad news was kept from him. He was said to be powerless to do anything about the situation; the nation was committed, and the generals and admirals in charge continued to promise victories. But there is evidence that the emperor knew long before surrender that defeat was inevitable. Why didn't the emperor end the war sooner, before Hiroshima and Nagasaki? In 1986 a former Imperial chamberlain provided Kyodo, the Japanese wire service, with copies of two letters the emperor is said to have written to his son near the end of the war. In one, dated September 9, 1945, six days before the actual surrender, Hirohito apologized for not speaking frankly: "Accept my apology for having refrained from telling you the truth because I had to tell you something completely different from what your teachers were saying." He explained Japan's defeat to his son: "Our people believed in the Imperial state too much and despised Britain and the United States. Our military men placed too much significance on spirit and were oblivious to science."

The wisdom and the professionalism of the victorious army and navy commanders of the Meiji era were no longer available to the nation. The modern commanders "did not take a wide view of the situation, just as in Germany at the time of World War I. They could only advance but had no knowledge of withdrawal." As to his own role, the emperor is quoted as saying, "[I] made efforts to swallow tears and protect the species of the Japanese nation."

Advising the emperor were military men who originally questioned the wisdom of going to war with the United States. Predominant among them was the highly popular Admiral Isoroku Yamamoto, a sophisticated and widely traveled man. While assigned to the Japanese diplomatic mission in the United States, he studied English at Harvard and enjoyed the drinking companionship of other naval officers on the diplomatic circuit. Yamamoto was an inveterate gambler, and although he thought the attack on the United States was foolhardy, he did not formally oppose the declaration of war. Years before he had visited the River Rouge plant of the Ford Motor Company in Dearborn, Michigan, and had seen modern industry and mass production at work. He had also seen the oil fields of Texas. A long war, he reasoned, was the road to disaster for Japan, which had long supply lines and comparatively little steel-making capacity.

Yamamoto intended, instead, to deliver a short and crippling blow to demoralize the enemy into negotiating peace. Three months before Pearl Harbor, according to Yamamoto's biographer, Hiroyuki Agawa, he told Prime Minister Fumimaro Konoe, "I can promise to give them hell for a year and a half, but I can guarantee nothing as to what will happen after that." Given the order to proceed, he set to work planning the successful surprise attack. But he was unable to make good on his promise of eighteen months of victories. The attack on Pearl Harbor, devastating as it was, had failed to destroy the crucial oil reserves at the submarine base. The aircraft carriers of the Pacific Fleet were not in the harbor at the time of the attack. Despite its losses—eight battleships damaged, three destroyed, and a fourth capsized—only six months after Pearl Harbor the U.S. Navy crippled the Japanese fleet irreparably in the Battle of Midway. The losses to Japan were serious—four aircraft carriers, 2500 casualties, and 332 aircraft. The United States was no longer on the defensive. Yamamoto gamely pursued naval strategy until April 1943, when a flight of American P-38 Lightning fighters intercepted his Betty bomber over Bougainville, and two young pilots shot it down. The Japanese Navy reported Yamamoto was found still strapped to his seat, sword in hand.

A God No More

To this day it is not clear whose idea it was for Hirohito to renounce his supposed divinity or "de-god himself" as some Occupation hands crudely put it. MacArthur wrote later that it was not his idea, although some Japanese who remember the era insist that the request that the emperor do so came from the Supreme Commander of the Allied Powers. Others say that it came directly from the palace and that it was a move calculated to appease the conquerors. Hirohito later commented that he never considered himself a sacred being or a god in the Western sense. In his notes, Hirohito's aide, Hidenari Terasaki quotes him as saying, "I do not remember who it was, but they called me god, so I told them I am not a god, for the structure of my body is no different than that of a normal human being. I continued to tell them that it is a nuisance to be called such."

But to his nation and to the inner circle of some 8000 employees of the Imperial Household Ministry, most of whom were thrown out of work by the Occupation authorities, the idea of his symbolic divinity could not have been more ingrained. And until his death countless Japanese considered him more than a mere symbol. During the last twenty years of his life, Hirohito was a thin, bent, sometimes impatient old man who walked with a shuffling gait. His hunched shoulders and downcast gaze gave him a decidedly unregal and uncommanding presence.

During the war his words were memorized and recited like holy writ. Every child's school day began by reciting the Meiji rescript, on education. Written by Hirohito's grandfather, this edict commanded the Japanese to sacrifice for the nation's good: "Offer yourselves courageously to the state, and thus guard and maintain the prosperity of the

Imperial throne coeval with heaven and earth." Spurred on by such injunctions, entire high school classes interrupted their studies to enlist en masse in the Army or Navy. By the end of the war, the enthusiasm was not so great. Military recruits took many blows from Japanese army noncommissioned officers, notorious for their sadism. Offenses might be real, or they might be imagined: failing to show the proper respect for the food or the battle equipment or the spirit of the emperor was considered a major transgression.

It is clear from the diaries of those close to him that the war pained him, especially the war on Britain, whose royalty had been kind to him during his only trip abroad as crown prince. He complained about the overseas freebooting of his generals, who did what they pleased despite Hirohito's reservations. Mothers who privately wept for their sons' death smiled in public because dying for the emperor was a glorious fulfillment of duty. A 1934 guidebook for foreign tourists illustrates the concept of *bushido*, the Japanese ideal of warrior knighthood, with the story of a patriotic wife of a young soldier:

> This woman . . . just before he left for the Manchurian front, committed suicide in the traditional manner for women (a dagger slashing the throat) so that in the risks and dangers to which her husband would be exposed he would have no consideration for her to hamper him, and so that he would be untrammeled in his devotion to the Emperor and to his country, and so that he would gladly sacrifice his life, if necessary, without the slightest thought of her.

At Tokyo's Yasukuni Shrine, where the souls of Japan's war dead are enshrined—including those of war criminals such as Hideki Tojo—stands a bronze relief depicting three soldiers known as the human bombs. These men carried a live torpedo into enemy lines to clear an obstacle to the Japanese approach to Singapore in 1932. Soldiers who went into battle against heavy odds often called to each other, "See you at Yasukuni!" In the past ten years covert support for Yasukuni and its glorification of emperor-inspired martyrdom has become a matter of public knowledge and some protest. The first prime ministers who made formal visits to the shrine three decades after the war took pains to answer criticism by saying they came as private citizens. But by the late 1980s the pretense was dropped, and government ministers made routine visits to pay homage to the war dead. Hirohito was not one of those visitors.

Until the end of the war it was considered an act of *lèse-majesté* for the ordinary citizenry to gaze at the emperor except on special occasions; as passersby approached the gates of the Imperial palace grounds in Tokyo, they were required to avert their gaze. On the streetcars that passed the palace, conductors warned passengers of their approach. Sometimes a particularly patriotic streetcar operator would stop, get out and genuflect, urging his passengers to join him, before moving on. Hirohito traveled in automobiles with drawn shades, and during the war the police saw to it that no one would be able to look down on him as his car passed. For some, gazing at his picture was considered a violation.

If Hirohito was not divine, it was a secret closely guarded by those who wanted to control the nation during the war. "MacArthur may have said he wasn't divine, the emperor may have said it," remarked a Japanese journalist just after Hirohito's death, "but many people in Japan never believed in his recantation." Besides, the journalist went on, foreigners do not grasp what Japanese mean by the word "god," and they misconstrue its use. In Japan there are gods for everyone—family gods, gods of rocks and trees, gods of the sun, moon, and rainstorm, gods of fertility and good business. Generals became gods, and so did "successful" kamikaze pilots. Hirohito was certainly seen as a very special person at least, the living embodiment of the nation's spiritual and temporal history. His existence lent continuity and meaning to the traditions of the state.

Politics and Court in a Newer Japan

Japanese emperors lived out their lives in aristocratic detachment, sometimes in elegant and sumptuous surroundings and sometimes in penury. For a thousand years in Nara and Kyoto, the royal courts busied themselves perfecting and patronizing the arts of painting and poetry. As Lady Murasaki tells us in her tenth-century work, *The Tale of Genji*, they were also adept at womanizing.

Hirohito's grandfather was chosen in the mid-nineteenth century by dissatisfied samurai from western Japan. They had deposed the last and ineffectual shogun and supplanted him with Emperor Mutsuhito (known as Emperor Meiji after his death), in the magnificent 284-acre palace in the center of Edo, now Tokyo. In 1868 Mutsuhito and the Meiji Restoration, as it was called, created modern Japan. The modernizing samurai and the progressive merchants did the work to build a strong nation, forging in less than a generation a formidable industrial empire and a military that would defeat the mighty army and navy of Imperial Russia.

Although Meiji's grandson Hirohito saw Japan march to its glory and its shame, he would also live to see his nation redeemed. The military men behind Hirohito created for a short time the world they wanted—an Asia dominated by Japan that was the military of the West. They believed that driving the British from Hong Kong and Singapore, the Dutch from Indonesia, and the Americans from the Philippines would make way for Japan's more logical Asian colonialism. In the words of one group justifying overseas expansion, "We have sought the spread of humanity and righteousness throughout the world by having the Imperial purpose extend to neighboring nations."

But the Imperial purpose failed. By the first day of 1946, most of the nation was in ruins. The emperor issued a new and striking Imperial decree divesting his personage of divinity:

We stand by the people and We wish always to share with them their moments of joy and sorrow. The ties between Us and Our people have always stood upon mutual trust and affection. They do not originate in mere legends and myths. They do not have their basis in the fictitious idea that the

Emperor is manifest God and that the Japanese people are superior to other races and fated to rule the world.

It is said that after he made the statement he turned to his wife, Empress Nagako, and using his pet name for her, remarked, "Do I look any different to you, Naga?"

As the first gentleman of Japan, Hirohito's previous divine status did not preclude him from being the wealthiest former god in the nation. When the tax authorities assessed his fortune during the Occupation, they put his net worth at $245,708,000. Like ordinary Japanese, Hirohito and members of the royal family who had holdings in banks and companies then saw the value of those assets disintegrate. (The royal family's remaining holdings were in land, then as now a rare and valuable commodity.) After taxes were exacted, the emperor was left with a modest net worth for a monarch, of $24,863,000. But the new constitution returned all property of the Imperial household to the state, and so the family was rendered impoverished. A generous annual stipend appropriated by the nation's parliament solved the crisis for the direct family. The allowance runs well over $60 million a year for upkeep of the palaces and villas and the palace bureaucracy, and another $20 million or so maintains the royal family.

Japan's postwar constitution, the original document written in English by the occupying forces, clearly outlined the emperor's new role. The first article in the Meiji constitution had decreed that: "the Empire of Japan shall be ruled over by Emperors of the dynasty which has reigned in unbroken line of descent for ages past. . . . The person of the Emperor is sacred and inviolable." The Occupation constitution, which took effect in 1946, rejected that idea totally. It decrees only that: "The Emperor shall be symbol of the state and of the unity of the people." And hoping to bring about democratization of Japan, the Allies specified that the emperor derives his position: "from the will of the people with whom resides the sovereign power."

Sobering Travels

In shabby, unpressed suits, scuffed shoes, and a battered fedora, Hirohito toured the nation in 1946. He traveled some 33,000 kilometers to bring hope to his defeated people. His sympathetic demeanor was in sharp contrast to the rigid, aloof, and forbidding wartime image. Once a personage not to be gazed on by his common subjects, the now human emperor peered at his subjects through thick-lensed glasses and tried in vain to master the art of small talk. It was his presence, say those who remember the visits, that helped many starving and dejected people to hold out hope for the future. His active presence in the countryside also kept at bay the fierce nationalism of the right-wing, defenders of Imperial rule who might have caused considerable trouble for Occupation forces and their plans for democratization. Having seen Japan through the heady heights of early victory and the depths of defeat, Hirohito, in Justice Webb's opinion, "was better qualified to profit by the lessons of defeat and to lead his people in new directions than any other Japanese." Webb's assertion paraphrased Ieyasu, the first Tokugawa Shogun of Japan, who said, "If you know only what it is to conquer and not what it is to be defeated, woe unto you, for it will fare ill with you."

Hirohito began acting and talking more like a mortal man. But the obscure courtly language in which he addressed the nation when he broke the news of his surrender was understood by few citizens. He did not even have in common with the people the words for father and mother. The Japanese industrialist Akio Morita, who founded Sony Corporation with a fellow scientist, was a Navy lieutenant in August 1945. He had just arrived at his parents' home at Nagoya when he was told the emperor would address the nation the next morning. Morita recalled the event in his book, *Made in Japan:* "I put on my full uniform, including my sword, and I stood at attention while we listened to the broadcast. There was a lot of static on the radio and a lot of background noise, but the high, thin voice of His Majesty came through. Although the people of Japan had never before heard his voice we knew it was the emperor. He spoke in the highly mannered old-fashioned language of the court, and even though we couldn't follow the words exactly, we knew what the message was. The war was over."

Hirohito tramped through countless bombed-out factories and residential neighborhoods. As he attended exhibitions and festivals and national sports meets, he was seeing firsthand the harm his people had suffered. But even though he visited all the major cities of the four main islands in the war's aftermath, Hirohito did not visit Okinawa, and many Okinawans—recalling the last great battle of the war, in which 150,000 civilians died together with 110,000 Japanese soldiers—have ever since been resentful.

In Japan's bombed cities, people were still living in makeshift shelters thrown together with scraps of metal and wood. Subway and train stations had become home to tens of thousands. Those who still had anything of value, such as a kimono or fine art or furniture, traveled to the countryside to barter their possessions piece by piece, until they had nothing.

"I saw him for the first time in 1945," recalled a Japanese journalist, Toshio Iwama. "It was his first appearance after the surrender, the first time he had ever appeared in public. He didn't know how to act. The chamberlain whispered to him to take his hat in his right hand and hold it up in greeting to the crowd. He did it and stood there holding the hat out stiffly, waiting for more instructions. He didn't know what to do next. The chamberlain had to tell him to put it back on his head." On a visit the emperor made to a factory near Osaka, the company president introduced the leader of the company's union, who shocked everyone by striding forward with an outstretched hand. "In the name of all the laborers in Japan," he said boldly, "I would like to shake your hand." Hirohito was clearly taken aback. "Let us do it the Japanese way," he said, bowing and eliciting a bow from the union leaders. After a long moment Hirohito urged, "Please work hard for the sake of your union." He then moved on.

A taciturn man not schooled in the making of small talk, Hirohito usually made stilted remarks or said little on his visits outside the palace. Some folks even began to joke about his response to almost any situation, *"Ah, so-desu-ka?"* (literally, Is that so?) The visits with his subjects are said to have opened his eyes to reality and to have made him a more sympathetic person. He was by no means unaware of the outside world, having visited Europe as a young man and having moved about Japan (if only between royal villas). But the bombed-out ruins outside the palace in 1945 were a different world than the one he had known.

The people had to get accustomed to the emperor as he to them. Generally unknown to those along the routes of his travels was Hirohito's dislike of hot tea and scalding baths. His doctors revealed that Hirohito soaked in a very hot bath only about once a week. It was not widely known that he also had what the Japanese call a "cat's tongue," which meant he was unable to tolerate very hot food or drink. Hot green tea is ubiquitous in Japan, a part of normal hospitality at home or business. A host or hostess does not ask whether the guest would like tea; it is served automatically. Even during the postwar period, when shortages existed, a cup of steaming hot tea was placed before the emperor everywhere. To let it cool, he did not touch it for a long time. Invariably, a well-meaning and worried host would have it replaced with a fresh, hot cup. And when it was learned that he liked broiled eel, everywhere he went the bill of fare featured broiled eel.

In 1921 the Crown Prince Hirohito traveled to Europe on the battleship *Katori*, a trip he was to recall fondly and remark upon frequently until his death. In Paris he spent money for the first time in his life. He bought a bust of Napoleon and a ticket on the Metro, which he refused to surrender at the end of his ride. (Sixty years later he acknowledged that he kept the ticket as a souvenir in his desk drawer, where he could see it often.) In London he was the house guest of King George V at Buckingham Palace, an experience that made him a lifelong Anglophile and admirer of the British royal family. The King took a friendly and

familiar approach to the awkward young prince, striding
into Hirohito's bedroom early one morning in trousers,
braces, shirt sleeves, and carpet slippers. He is said to have
sat down on Hirohito's bed and joked, "Well, no geishas in
London. Her Majesty would never allow it." He then discussed military strategy with the young man and suggested
some European battlefields to visit.

On his return to Japan, Hirohito emulated some of the
ways he had observed on his trip. He enjoyed a Western-style
breakfast, slept in a bed rather than on futon quilts. To the
day he died he eschewed traditional Japanese clothing, preferring Western dress to the kimono. (He did, however, wear
Shinto ceremonial robes and the lacquered hat of a Shinto
priest to attend private rites on the palace grounds.) He
didn't own a wallet, and he may have been the only gentleman of Japan who did not have calling cards.

When the emperor was asked during a rare press conference what had left the deepest impression during his long
life, he said it was his trip to Europe. Not wishing to dwell
on the war and postwar years of hardship, he said, "What is
most deeply impressed on my mind today is that visit overseas. That is because my life until then was like that of a
bird kept in a cage. I experienced freedom for the first time."
And perhaps never since. The lingering memory of Hirohito
in later life is of a frail figure being herded to and fro by
court chamberlains, the most notable of whom towered over
him by more than a foot.

Although Hirohito was fond of Japanese arts and of watching the seventeenth-century sport of sumo wrestling, he was
most happy among his marine specimens, his microscope,
and his books in the private laboratory where he worked
three days a week. A student of the flora of Japan, he had an
encyclopedic knowledge of the subject. As he was dying Hirohito asked to see a small branch of a maple tree from the
spacious grounds of the Canadian Embassy in Tokyo, not far
from the palace. When it was brought to him, he examined
it closely and remarked that it was a different species from
the tree he remembered, which he had not seen since the

1960s. (The comment set off a research project to classify types of maples on the embassy grounds.)

When his health permitted, the emperor made it a practice to visit the sumo matches at least once during the three yearly tournaments in Tokyo; he often sat on the edge of his seat urging the giant wrestlers on. He spent many of his days dealing with formal documents that required his approval, receiving the credentials of foreign ambassadors, and greeting foreign dignitaries visiting Japan. But most of Hirohito's time was spent in pursuits unseen by outsiders, his privacy jealously guarded against intrusions except for special occasions. Each year he appeared with the immediate family to greet as many as 80,000 Japanese on his birthday, waving to them from the palace veranda, behind thick glass. Requests for him to pose for photographs were always refused by the chamberlains. Even a request to photograph the palace gardens would be routinely refused by the Imperial Household Agency. In 1963, however, after long consideration, the agency suggested in response to a request from *Life* that a photographer might wait at a certain point along the road at the beach near Hayama, where the emperor and the empress maintained a detached villa.

Sure enough, at the appointed hour the emperor's specially built Nissan, bearing the royal chrysanthemum insignia, pulled up on the beach side. The emperor, in shorts, tennis shoes, and a floppy Panama hat, waded into the water in search of marine specimens while the late photographer Larry Burroughs snapped his shutter from a distance. A chamberlain saw to it that Burroughs didn't get too close to the imperial personage. The emperor examined some sea urchins, took some specimens, and in due course drove away. No words were spoken; there was no eye contact. The incident was not mentioned, but the picture appeared on a full page in a *Life* issue devoted to coverage of Japan's recovery from the war. The emperor seemed quite human.

CHAPTER THREE

BEYOND THE PAST

Since the end of the Occupation in 1952, there has been a gradual return of interest in the war years among Japanese veterans. One can often hear the old war songs reverberating through the paper partitions of teahouses during reunions and conventions. This was once frowned on by a public sick of war, propaganda, and warrior bravado. Such gatherings have become prevalent and more public, more or less indulged by older people and viewed as curiosities by younger. However, public attitudes toward the military are generally still so negative that military uniforms are almost never seen on the streets of the capital. To fill the gap, private paramilitary right-wing organizations increasingly tour the city in trucks with banners bearing nationalist slogans and with loudspeakers blaring the old war songs. For decades one diehard nationalist, Bin Akao, daily delivered patriotic, anticommunist diatribes from the top of his flag-draped van at one of the busiest pedestrian crossings in downtown Tokyo. Such blatant belligerency, while ignored by many, is tolerated by most. The right-wing groups are regarded as fringe political elements, but they often express popular sentiments—such as the return of the four northern islands seized by the Soviet Union in 1945. These groups are well financed with money donated by prominent figures from the right and sometimes with funds extorted from large companies.

In Tokyo, an occasional hapless military man in uniform may be reviled by an uninhibited drunken commuter late at night. Many officers who must report to Self Defense Force headquarters in Tokyo either travel in civilian clothes or change when they get to the city. Some officers who must visit headquarters often maintain rooms in the vicinity, where they change into their uniforms just before reporting and then slip into mufti for the trip back to base. Even today, the armed forces stage their annual review for the prime minister before a carefully selected audience of local civilians, military families, foreign military attachés, and diplomats. Held on an army base north of Tokyo, the review is secure and far from either left-wing or right-wing extremists.

One reason youth are encouraged to get close to the men and their equipment is that Japan has never been able to recruit enough volunteers to bring its military forces up to authorized strength. As the population ages and the number of eighteen-year-olds decreases, there is deep concern in the defense agency. The idea was even floated that eventually Japan may have to recruit mercenaries from other countries to fill out the ranks. And during the war against Iraq, some critics saw Japan's refusal to send troops as evidence of exactly such a notion. Each year between 10 and 17 percent of the graduating class of the National Defense Academy decides against a military career and resigns; after getting a four-year education at the expense of the taxpayers, these young men are free to go without obligation. For years, the University of Tokyo was reluctant to accept graduates of the academy in postgraduate programs, so many candidates were sent abroad to study.

Nevertheless, the meetings of survivors of World War II military units and the singing of old war songs in the *karaoke* bars are quite common. It took a couple of decades after the end of the Occupation for models of Japanese warplanes and replicas of weapons to become popular. Now a surge of revisionism about the war and its causes is washing over the Japanese, fostered by an assortment of right-wing politicians, social critics, historians, intellectuals, and journalists.

Newly publicized revisionist views of modern Japanese history have confronted not a few old-timers who for many years struggled under the conventional postwar perception that they were losers, inferior to the victorious West. Now that Japan has recreated itself as the second largest economic system in the world, the views and revisions and so-called clarifications of history fall on newly proud, some say conceited, ears. To many Japanese the nation's history has been distorted by a victor's justice, the imposition of a set of beliefs on the defeated, defenseless, and morally distressed citizens of a ruined Japan.

In defeat the Japanese impressed the Allied powers with their eagerness to learn from those who have defeated them. They seemed surprisingly amenable to the idea of taking on the changes the Occupation forces wished to impose. Many Japanese welcomed the New Deal reformers who came to remake Japan in a new image. They were thankful the United States prevented the Soviets from occupying a portion of the main islands, having witnessed the unnerving sight of the division of Germany. The changes included a new constitution as well as an evangelical document forswearing the rights of belligerency and of maintaining "war potential."

The constitution also contained concepts out of tune with customs and practices then common, which for the most part have since been honored mostly in the breach: an equal rights amendment and guarantees against self-incrimination, double jeopardy, and retroactive justice. It also mandated compulsory education, the separation of church and state, protected the rights of marriage and divorce. One lofty passage of Article 97, said to have been written by General Douglas MacArthur himself, declares: "The fundamental human rights by this Constitution guaranteed to the people of Japan are fruits of the age-old struggle of man to be free; they have survived the many exacting tests for durability and are con-

ferred upon this and future generations in trust, to be held
for all time inviolate."

In 1957, a Japanese Commission on the Constitution
sought the views of some eminent international constitutional scholars with an eye to possible changes that would
make it more consonant with Japanese reality. It was considered then that perhaps the constitution should be revised
or rewritten as a truly Japanese document rather than an
imposed war artifact that had been written in English and
then translated into Japanese. Some aspects of the constitution were long ago out of date—particularly Article 9,
which prohibited the maintenance of "land, sea, and air
forces, as well as other war potential." (The article's violation
was legally sanitized by the Nation's Supreme Court when
the National Police Reserve, later called Japan's Self Defense
Forces, was formed at the Occupation's insistence at the out-
break of the Korean War. America's Occupation troops were
needed elsewhere).

In the commission's report of 1964, the scholars found
much to comment on. The scholars found MacArthur's por-
tentous Article 97 rhetorical, redundant, even meaningless.
Distinguished historian Richard Storry, then at St. Antony's
College, Oxford, wrote the commission:

> When the new Constitution came into force I confess that I
> was rather doubtful as to whether it really would survive for
> many years unaltered . . . nevertheless I have come to the firm
> conclusion that this present constitution has indeed taken
> root—just as the potted plant that we bring into our own
> garden from outside can take root and prosper. The reason is
> this, I think. The basic concepts embodied in this constitution,
> though to some extent inspired by American influence, are
> surely of universal validity. Therefore, they make an appeal
> to the majority of the Japanese people.

Nothing came of the commission's investigations but a
lengthy report and some scholarly studies. The constitution,
as it stands, seems inviolate.

Periodically, nationalist politicians have attempted to develop a popular consensus for revision of the constitution. They have had no success contending against the disapproval of opposition parties, whose leaders say the move signifies a return to fascism. In actuality the guarantees of the constitution are often only selectively enforced. For example, despite the guarantees of equal rights for women, an insignificant number of cases of discrimination have been brought and adjudicated, and even in the face of Supreme Court rulings that electoral districts are unfairly drawn, movement to redraw the districts has been slow and ineffective.

Article 9 still rankles many Japanese, not because the Japanese want to go to war, but because the decision to have such a policy, they feel, should be written by Japanese for Japanese. The conservative former prime minister, Yasuhiro Nakasone, has campaigned for revision of the constitution in general and Article 9 in particular, explaining that Japan cannot fulfill its destiny as a world power without its own constitution. One American historian, Donald C. Hellmann of the University of Washington, argues that even though Occupation authorities were willing to discuss the wording of Article 9, the Japanese insisted on keeping it as written so that it would remain in accord with the charter of the United Nations. Why? So that they could one day be accepted as full members. In fact, older politicians have suggested that their predecessors got much of what they wanted by convincing occupiers that the latter had forced their decisions on a weakened Japanese political structure. For example, conventional wisdom in the West asserts that the massive and liberating postwar land reform ending feudalism in Japan was the brilliant planning of Wolf Ladejinsky of the U.S. Department of Agriculture. Many Japanese now claim land reform was on their minds at the time, that a land reform plan was in preparation before the Americans even broached the subject, and that it would have been implemented without the Americans.

The New Look Westward

Since the mid-1970s, Japanese politicians have enjoyed noting in speeches that the postwar era has ended, but that era did not truly draw to a close until Emperor Hirohito died in 1989. In the final years of the postwar period, a great deal changed in Japanese attitudes toward individual and nation. What many Japanese had felt for many years could now be said unguardedly. America, Great Britain, and Western Europe were no longer to be emulated. In fact, even some people in America, long patronizing toward Japan, were saying that the United States could learn from its Far East contemporary ally. Japan was not always gracious about its new prowess. "You are over the hill," an audacious economic official told me one day, referring to the decline of American economic performance.

This kind of talk used to shock. Even today Japanese find it difficult to speak their thoughts except in close company. *Tatemae*, or the official line—what outsiders want to hear and can accept—is still often the only way Japanese can talk with foreigners, at least while sober. Young people have less trouble talking directly. Indeed, the more adventurous of them have been making candid and insulting remarks to and about foreigners on trains and busy sidewalks for twenty years, commenting on their odd looks, their smell, even their gait. *Honne*, true feeling, need not be different from *tatemae* but usually is.

For Japanese growing up during postwar deprivation, Westerners, particularly Americans, were seen as guides and role models. Complaints about the way the occupiers acted, or how the flood of foreign businessmen operated, were made under one's breath, or at least in Japanese, which few outsiders could understand. Learning from the West became popular again. Foreigners were still *gaijin* (outside persons), but they presented virtually limitless opportunities for clever Japanese.

When Carl Mydans, the *Life* magazine photojournalist, and his wife Shelley, also a journalist, returned to Japan in 1970 after a hiatus of more than twenty years, they were greeted by Yasuo Kitaoka, soon to be the general manager of the American company's extensive Japanese operations. After passing some pleasantries, the dapper Kitaoka regarded Mydans impishly and asked in impeccable English, "Carl, don't you remember me?" Mydans confessed he did not. With a delighted smile, Kitaoka said, "Don't you remember the day your Jeep got stuck in the mud and the houseboy from next door came to help push you out?" Mydans remembered. The houseboy had grown up in adversity to represent one of America's giant publishing companies.

For a generation of Japanese, one appealing route to success in business was with foreigners. Fluency in English or another European language was required. Today there is a long and distinguished list of Japanese who have made successful careers in foreign enterprises in Japan. Their numbers are growing, and the stigma of being employed by foreigners has declined. Today, Japanese executives are running many subsidiaries and joint ventures of such multinational companies as IBM and Xerox in Japan. A few progressive Japanese companies have admitted foreigners to their boards, but the lure of the pure Japanese enterprise is still strong, and college recruiters for the giant Japanese companies have their pick of the new college graduates. Some observers suggest that as Japanese have more options than ever, their ideal choices narrow to the Japanese megacorporations.

Japan's economic success has engendered a sense of pride. Jobs at world class wages are plentiful, and in fact, Japan looks toward a labor shortage as the population ages. Housewives are increasingly joining the work force as part-timers. Thousands of illegal aliens are discovered each year working the menial construction and service jobs that Japanese increasingly eschew. It is hard to ignore a sense of smugness among many of the young; foreigners, once catered to in shops and deferred to on the street and on crowded subways, may now be treated as rudely as a Japanese might treat another Japanese unknown to him.

Critics complain that the intellectual curiosity of contemporary Japanese is more often than not self-serving and self-centered rather than wide ranging. When United States President George Bush visited Japan in January, 1992, Prime Minister Kiichi Miyazawa rose to toast his guest during a banquet. Miyazawa told of his visit to California in 1939 as a college freshman to attend a student conference at the University of Southern California. "It was a fresh surprise for us Japanese students," Miyazawa recalled, "that some of the American students freely voiced their criticism of their government's Asia policy at a time when our bilateral relations were turning bitter." In the opinion of many, there is not enough criticism in Japan today, even though, unlike 1939, everyone is free to speak out. Criticism of Japan by the Japanese is becoming more acceptable, but criticism of Japan by outsiders is tolerated less passively than before. A foreign critic of Japan is often scolded, ostracized, and branded a Japan basher or even an enemy for saying things that a few years ago might have been taken, albeit grudgingly, as constructive criticism.

Professor Shuichi Kato, a prominent social critic, complains of the lack of focus in his fellow countrymen's recent nationalism:

> Today every Japanese is in a way nationalistic, but that neonationalist feeling has not yet crystallized into any political philosophy, let alone into a party or a political program. After the war everything about Japan was wrong. The Japanese [then] were very self-critical, but today the Japanese don't like to be criticized.

An American university professor of Japanese studies, looking back on his forty-five-year association with Japan, echoes Professor Kato's sentiments. He points out that the growing sense of nationalism does not make all Japanese enthusiastic about the pace at which Japan is being reorganized into multinational and multiregional organizations. "I've had a lot of discussion with one Japanese professor who has fought the good fight in his university on behalf of developing a more international outlook among the faculty, and that is not easy, apparently," he says. "If there is ever an issue which divides the nativists and the internationalists, the nativists are going to win out every time. This is likely to continue. The Japanese see themselves besieged by foreign criticism and they cannot respond to that very effectively, and they tend to withdraw into their shells. The feeling emerges that 'Maybe we are superior to everybody else. But on the other hand, if everybody is kicking us in the shins, maybe we are inferior.' "

Tensions seem to be building among older Japanese because of the push of new ideas about Japan's role in the world. Younger people, unencumbered by either defeat by or gratitude toward foreigners, find the notion of Japan as a world power easier to cope with. Some of today's Japanese are trying to speak out, and when they do it is often to say things Westerners are unaccustomed to hearing. When American trade negotiators said there were 240 Japanese "structural" impediments to free and fair trade between the two countries, the Japanese produced a list of 80 practices that inhibit America's ability to perform and compete with the Japanese. The negotiators called for more United States government frugality, higher gasoline taxes, longer-term business thinking, and even the limited use of credit cards. Many Americans were surprised. The *New York Times* commented, "In a stroke, the Japanese have shown how preposterous it is to think that national norms can be reordered by negotiation." By and large, the *New York Times* said in an editorial, the items on the Japanese list make sense, and "they don't stand a chance of being adopted." The items on the list were no more implausible than a United States suggestion that Japan's giant business conglomerates make public the minutes of their monthly meetings. Such public disclosure is not practiced anywhere, not even in the United States.

What is new and important about the exchange of ideas on structural impediments is that it happened at all. At the end of the twentieth century, Japanese have begun to speak their mind more freely. It is equally clear that this new candor is as new for Westerners as it is for the Japanese. It is likely to cause considerable friction.

In 1991 Shintaro Ishihara wrote boldly that the United States defense umbrella for Japan was "an illusion," that racism is at the base of America's policy toward Japan, and that Japanese technology is so far ahead of the United States that defense planners are "beside themselves with fear" that Japan will withdraw it. Despite the kernel of truth about Japanese high technology, especially American dependence on Japanese microchips, American defense officials and industrialists say they are more annoyed at Ishihara's oversimplifications than they are fearful. What is there to fear? Economic subservience? Political domination? Another war? Japan's top politicians will not declare what it is: they cringe at the idea of their nation as world leader, of introducing a Pax Japonica. Perhaps the people of Japan don't know where they are going because they haven't fully examined where they have been.

Looking Inward and Backward

The political events of the last decade of the twentieth century stunned the world. Debate about Eastern Europe and its relationship to Russia and the outside world is popular even in Japan. Looking at themselves and the world through eyes unclouded by, some say without the benefit of, a close public examination of the first half of the twentieth century, Japanese head toward the twenty-first with a new sense of pride.

But on the world's political map, the area named Japan remains largely undefined. Much of the lack of definition originated with the Japanese. The Japanese government was paralyzed for a time in response to the United Nations' reaction to the Iraqi invasion of Kuwait. Physical noninvolvement is a preoccupation, virtually a political philosophy. Underneath the view of the Japanese that negotiation and sanctions against Iraq were a wiser course than force lay the common perception that what the West saw as broader issues were not all that important to Japan. It was even said publicly that no matter who controlled the oil of Kuwait, Japan would be able to buy it. Even though the nation gets 71.5 percent of its oil from the Middle East, many voices insisted that the United Nations effort to expel Iraq from Kuwait was not Japan's affair. The idea of contributing medical personnel and other noncombatants (the constitution forbids the sending of soldiers) was debated and initially rejected. Money, vehicles, and other goods were pledged and finally sent. And several minesweepers helped the navies of the United States and other countries clear Iraqi mines after the war. The contribution, while substantial, took so long that the largesse seemed a grudging thing in the world's eyes. Furthermore, the contribution of Japanese goods, rather than people or cash, made their aid look like an advertisement for the vehicles and office equipment they brought to the Saudi Arabian desert.

The criticism stung. In 1992, the Japanese government succeeded in passing an ambiguous bill that will allow Japanese troops to participate in United Nation's peace-keeping operations, subject to certain conditions. Japan's view, that there are options other than those proposed by the United States, is seldom expressed forcefully. Although Japan's impact on the world's economy and technology is immense, its voice in world councils is muted. One reason is that much of what takes place in Japan ends up inconclusively in compromise.

"We talk but we don't debate," explains Professor Kato. "In Japan the people try to avoid individual responsibility, saying that the best way to go is to do nothing, take no initiative, avoid argument. We have sentiments and personal disagreements, and some are extremely combative, yet we rarely have arguments."

Charting a course for the future is made difficult by the war memories of all involved—Asians, Europeans, and Americans. Memories—and the histories taught in school—

differ from those of Japan. What happened in Japan during the 1930s is dismissed by Japanese textbooks as an aberration, in which the military merely seized power, used the name of the emperor to enforce its will, and embarked on a voyage to national disaster. This historical rendering does not provide a satisfactory explanation for those who have studied the acts of wartime Japan. People who remember the old Japan now face a new generation, accomplished and often cocky, who see the first fifty years of this century quite differently.

Japanese now view the events of the war rather defensively. The course toward war, the invasion of the Asian mainland and Southeast Asia, Pearl Harbor, Manila, Bataan, Iwo Jima, Okinawa, Hiroshima, the Occupation, the war crimes trial, the imposition of the postwar constitution, the dissolution of the *zaibatsu* industrial combines, the land reform, the patronizing and condescending claims of the Occupiers that they were responsible for Japan's resurgence— all the incidents are now seen from a different perspective. Yasuaki Onuma, of Tokyo University, author of a book on war responsibility, characterized what he feels is the prevalent thinking in Japan. "With regard to the United States," he wrote in *Mainichi Shimbun*, "we have a vague notion that with Pearl Harbor on the one hand and Hiroshima and Nagasaki on the other, the wartime account between Japan and the United States more or less balances out." The argument goes this way: "Admittedly we acted meanly in launching a surprise attack. But you killed 200,000 innocent civilians with your brutal atomic bomb. So we're even."

For most Japanese the crucial acts of the war remain the firebombing and the atomic bombing, which created a strong sense of victimization. The decade and a half of Japanese aggression, beginning on the Asian mainland, tend to be compressed into the three and a half years of the war between Japan and the United States, culminating with the atomic bombing.

At the museum of the Peace Park at Hiroshima, the artifacts of the atomic holocaust are displayed with matter-offactness: shadows of human figures etched on stone, descriptions of the victims and survivors, clothing, melted metal objects, and a chillingly detailed model of the destroyed city. In Japan the event seems to live in all its ghastliness as an incident isolated in history, as though it had no prelude. The conflagration does not appear as the culminating horror of a long series of mutual horrors, but as a kind of wanton, vengeful, and undeserved assault on a city in an innocent nation. Aside from the question of whether the bombs should ever have been dropped, it should be noted that Hiroshima and Nagasaki were, after all, important strategic military ports and staging areas, not neutral, international cities. Nor, of course, were Tokyo and Nagoya, where much of the firebombing took place. It is worth noting that Kyoto and Nara, Japan's ancient capitals, were deliberately spared during the bombing campaign.

Some Tokyoites begrudge Hiroshima's claim to the world's compassion. They complain that the nation's capital suffered as many direct casualties in conventional firebombing by American B-29 Superfortresses, specifically during the gigantic March 9–10, 1945, raid (the attack leveled most of the central city and made the water of the canals and rivers boil). Tokyoites who survived feel they have never received the outpouring of sympathy and compensation and medical aid that victims of the Hiroshima and Nagasaki bombings have received. The strange jealousy of Tokyo survivors finds expression in their complaints that the *hibakusha*, victims of the atomic bombing, and their families are overcompensated. In actuality, descendants of the *hibakusha* continue to suffer; they are pariah people, shunned by those who fear some kind of contamination, and by prospective spouses, who have a lingering fear of genetic damage.

In 1945 it was commonly thought that nothing would grow in Hiroshima for a hundred years. But Hiroshima thrives, and the Peace Park, with its understated monuments and stark outlines, no longer dominates the landscape as it did when I first visited the site. Now new high-rise buildings dwarf the site, the epicenter of the first atom bomb. Most

citizens do not dwell on the history anymore, but the city is
unable to escape its fate: it is a mecca for foreign antiwar
and antinuclear crusaders.

Today the Japanese feel that the International Military
Tribunal for the Far East, the war crimes trial, was grossly
unfair and involved no more than a victor's justice. But Professor Onuma has pointed out how inaccurate and mistaken
a view the Japanese have of the period from 1931 to 1945.
He, like some others, has insisted that the Japanese should
not allow pride to rewrite the history of the time. Pride in
the nation should not be gained "by stubbornly insisting that
one's country's past errors were not errors," noted Onuma.

History textbooks approved for use throughout the nation
by the Ministry of Education persist in whitewashing Japanese colonial depredations in China and Korea, Singapore,
and elsewhere. They gloss over the undeclared attack on
Pearl Harbor. The invasion of China is routinely referred to
as an "advance" into China. The scores of young Koreans
hanged for rebellion during Japan's annexation of Korea are
described in offhanded terms. At one point during the textbook controversy, I asked a Korean editor about the future
of relations between Korea and Japan. His reply was suc-
cinct: "Let's face it," he said. "They hate us and we hate
them." Although changes have been made, Japan's textbooks
still fall far short of the candid view of history that Japanese,
as well as foreign critics, wish to be taught the nation's students."

Japan has begun to acknowledge exploitation of the Koreans. At a state dinner in Japan, on the occasion of the
Korean prime minister Chun Doo Hwan's visit to Japan (the
first ever), the emperor obliquely apologized for Japan's annexation and occupation of Korea. Koreans and others read
into his remarks an acknowledgment of Korean blood in the
Japanese royal lineage. Akihito has also alluded with regret
to the inglorious history of Japan in Korea.

In the revisionist view, the war with the United States,
Britain, and the Allies was an Asian crusade against white
imperialism. This view was echoed by Axis powers during

the war. After Japan had swept through Indochina in 1942, the German propagandist Furst Urach declared in a radio broadcast: "Asia, with her old and highly cultured peoples, will no more be exploited by pillaging foreign powers, but will be a co-prosperity sphere for its millions of inhabitants. . . . The peoples of East Asia are acknowledging Japan's leadership because they know it is in accordance with the spiritual laws of Asia." Some people in the colonized nations of Asia welcomed the Japanese overthrow of European power. Invading Japanese forces in the Philippines, Malaysia, and elsewhere found willing support from some citizens. It is no surprise that those in India fighting British colonialism encouraged the victorious Japanese to help end the hated colonialism of Great Britain. Many Japanese, then and now, characterize the war as a struggle for liberation. This view is, of course, a simplification. Collaborators such as Jose Laurel in the Philippines and Ba Maw in Burma did exist, as did supporters such as Subhas Chandra Bose of India, although Bose's emphasis was anti-British, not pro-Japanese. No nation welcomed the invaders. The oppression of conquered peoples by the Japanese is still vivid in many countries, and the animosity has not yet completely died.

Colonialism was in trouble at the time of World War II. The winds of change that blew through Africa and Asia after the war were already gathering force; colonies were becoming anachronisms, as their own internal liberation movements dramatically demonstrated. There is little beyond rhetoric that the Japanese dream of an Asia made noble by the spirit of the Showa Emperor had anything to do with a genuine desire to liberate peoples. Evidence indicates that the dream was one of exploitation of the peoples and resources of Asia. The British novelist George Orwell, in one of his weekly British Broadcasting Corporation commentaries on the war in 1941 (before the fall of Singapore) commented to his listeners, "What it would be like to be free under the heel of Japan the Chinese can tell us, and the Koreans."

In his surrender speech, Emperor Hirohito told his subjects in what must have been a bit of an understatement that "the war situation has developed not necessarily to Japan's advantage." He insisted, even while accepting Allied terms, that the war was fought "to ensure Japan's self-preservation and the stabilization of East Asia, *it being far from Our thought either to infringe upon the sovereignty of other nations or to embark on territorial aggrandizement.*" This remarkable statement, which flew in the face of simple fact, was little commented on. The war was now ending because the enemy, he said, had begun to use "a new and most cruel bomb." To fight on would lead not only to the obliteration of the Japanese nation but also to the "total extinction of human civilization." Some skeptical Japanese journalists say the bomb provided everyone with excuses: Japan was now a symbol of victimization because of the suffering at Hiroshima and Nagasaki; the bombing also gave the world a warning and a prophesy, therefore serving a lofty purpose.

Japanese writers have suggested that the generation born at the end of the war are children of a void, growing up uncomprehending in a devastated land. Children in Germany experienced a similar emptiness; however, German authorities have been much less reluctant to reveal the truth of the past. Japanese war atrocities were committed abroad, whereas Germany's death camps existed inside the country and in occupied territory nearby.

"We were taught that for inexplicable reasons the entire country had gone mad, thinking it could achieve the impossible and convinced that wrong was right," Professor Michiko Hasegawa writes. Hasegawa has noted that after the war, adults talked to children of soldiers who "died in the war" or "died when the atomic bomb fell." At the time, it appeared to young students "as if God, by some slip of the hand, had let the bombs drop from heaven." This is not a question of phrasing. In reviewing the events of the war, the Japanese intentionally omit the word 'enemy.' Like others, Professor Hasegawa suggests that once the Japanese decided that the war was caused by militarists, who kidnapped the country and took it on an insane excursion, "we . . . closed our eyes to the true dangers of war."

Other historians and analysts suggest that the war really began nearly a century ago, when Europe and America began to impose themselves on an unwilling, naive, and cruelly exploited Asia. They suggest that Japan rose up against decades upon decades of onslaughts, the final insult coming when the U.S. embargoed Japan's vital oil in July, 1941, and demanded Japan's withdrawal from China. In their revision, the attack on Pearl Harbor was a desperate attempt to strike a blow that would lead to a spheres-of-influence agreement between Japan and the United States. Japanese subscribing to such a view believe that President Franklin D. Roosevelt had foreknowledge of the plan to attack Pearl Harbor but entrapped Japan by doing nothing to forestall it. A view popular in some circles in America is that Roosevelt allowed the bombing of Pearl Harbor to take place so that the war with Germany could begin.

"We did not fight for Japan alone," insists Professor Hasegawa. "Our aim was to fight a Greater East Asia war. . . . After all is said and done, however, the reality remains that Japan went into the Asian continent to save it but ended up fighting against it." Hasegawa has even written that if Japanese textbooks describing an "advance" into, rather than an invasion of China are to be revised, so must the West's view of Christopher Columbus: "If we wish to accuse the Japanese of an invasion, then revision should begin with accounts of Columbus's discovery of America in 1492, renaming it 'the first step in the invasion of the New World.' "

Fighting Foreigners

For centuries the Japanese have had their problems with foreigners. One anecdote indicates the mutual misunderstanding that often preceded violence. In September 1862 a British merchant named Charles Richardson was riding along the Tokaido highway near Yokohama with three friends. They encountered the procession of a powerful lord of Satsuma, Hisamitsu Shimazu. The procession was making its way from Kagoshima, at the southern end of Kyushu, to Tokyo in panoply and splendor: as Shimazu proceeded in his palanquin, mounted samurai in armor as outriders, along with foot soldiers waving banners, pikes, and spears, protected the heart of the procession. [The Japanese were on their way to Edo at the shogun's command. Powerful local lords were required to visit the shogun every two years. Gifts for the military governor were required. To guarantee their attendance at court, the lords' wives and children were kept in Edo as hostages. This arrangement demanded money— for transportation, for gifts, and for the long stay in the capital. Its cost had much to do with the relatively peaceful 250-year rule of the shoguns, for to finance the system the local lords had to tax their people heavily. Taxes on the farmers were confiscatory because of the need to maintain well-equipped armies and multiple households. The system helped to impoverish the warrior class, while the merchants, who supported them, prospered and eventually came to share power with, or even dominate, the shogunate. Today Japan's politicians shamelessly depend on modern merchants for their sustenance and advice from the business community guides both politician and bureaucrat.]

Details of the events conflict heavily. The official British inquiry states that Richardson and his friends respectfully rode their horses out of the way to let the procession pass, whereupon they were assaulted without provocation by the samurai warriors. It asserts that the samurai slashed at the Englishmen viciously with long swords while foot soldiers jabbed at them with lances as the hapless, innocent foreigners tried to escape. The Japanese version is that the foreigners haughtily refused to give way to the procession and acted menacingly toward the entourage and Lord Shimazu. An attack was therefore the only reasonable action possible under the circumstances.

An American version of the incident, published some years

later, said that it was caused by both a failure to communicate and a lack of understanding. Unknowingly Richardson and his friends had failed to show proper respect by dismounting and perhaps even genuflecting, as the Japanese would have been expected to do. They may not have known the protocol, and to get out of the way, they began riding through the procession, inadvertently disrupting it. Only then did the samurai attack.

Richardson's companions, while wounded, managed to escape, but Richardson was grievously hurt. He fell from his mount, dying at the roadside. A Japanese teahouse proprietess is reputed to have braved the disapproval of her peers by giving the dying Richardson a cup of water. The outraged British government demanded indemnity of 100,000 pounds sterling from the shogun and 25,000 pounds from the government of Satsuma. The shogunate paid off, but nine months later, when Satsuma had not paid, a squadron of British warships sailed into the bay at Kagoshima, the capital city of Satsuma province. Some guns were fired from the shore, and the British ships returned a cannon barrage that sank several Japanese ships in the harbor. The town was severely bombarded. Townsfolk were stunned, and local officials were humiliated. Chastened, the Satsuma government borrowed the money, paid the indemnity in silver, and promised to execute the murderers if they were found.

Satsuma, impressed with the British naval artillery, developed its own heavy weapons industry. Today one can see the gun emplacements in Kagoshima's downtown park facing the waterfront, installed to defend against any further foreign attacks, which of course never came.

It was a time of resistance to encroaching foreign influence in Japan, and the lesson the British visited on Satsuma was not instructive to all. Treaties had been signed, but the nation was still feudal, and after more than two centuries in isolation, some local leaders were not eager to change their ways. They vowed that the foreigners, who had exploited China and other Asian nations with unequal treaties and granted themselves extraterritoriality (under which they were answerable only to themselves and not the national authorities for crimes and accidents), would not do the same in Japan. Imperial loyalists were encouraging *sonno-ron*, reverence for the emperor, and ultranationalist, xenophobic zealots were calling for *joi-ron*, or "expulsion of the barbarians." Soon *sonno joi*—"Revere the emperor, expel the barbarians"—became a rallying cry. Foreigners became fair game for marauders, who attacked both legations and travelers. Most foreigners left their residences well armed or with bodyguards.

One of the unfortunate victims was Henry Huesken, the brilliant Dutch-born secretary and interpreter for America's first consul-general to Japan, Townsend Harris. After the bombardment of Kagoshima, a number of samurai and local lords for another region, impatient with the shogunate's inability to expel foreigners, decided to scare them away. Freebooting Japanese ships began harassing British, French, Dutch, and American vessels in the waters around Shimonoseki, home of the powerful Choshu clan. The tactic didn't work. The foreigners organized a war flotilla of British, French, Dutch, and American ships and in the summer of 1864 bombarded the forts lining the straits at Shimonoseki. They landed a small contingent of marines and demanded a peace treaty. Choshu was subdued.

To a large degree the impotence of the shogunate in the face of the foreigners' invasion led to the eventual overthrow of the long-lived Tokogawa Shogunate and the beginning of the Meiji Restoration. The decision to supplant the hatred and fear of foreigners with a policy of learning from the West proved wise; Japan was then, as now, the most advanced industrial nation in Asia at the time of its grab for territory and its entry into World War II. Japan learned fast, in less than a generation. When Japan defeated the Baltic Fleet of Imperial Russia in the Straits of Japan just after the turn of the twentieth century, many in the West could not believe an Asian power had done it on its own (one popular rumor was that every Japanese warship had a British naval officer in command).

The bloody encounters with the West show that neither side had a monopoly on valor. I stood atop Iwo Jima's Mount Suribachi one day in 1970, twenty-five years after the battle, with a former U.S. Marines sergeant who had fought there. As he gazed down at the beach, where one of every two invading Americans was wounded and almost all the Japanese defenders died, he said, "I don't know how we did it. Must have been human waves." No American newspaper at the time would have characterized the assault forces as "human waves"; that expression was reserved to describe the other side. On a second visit to the beach in 1985, I met the son of the Japanese general Tadamichi Kuribayashi, who commanded the costly, futile defense of Iwo Jima. He was filling a container with the distinctive, large-grained black sand of the invasion beach as a remembrance—his father's remains, like those of thousands of defenders inside the labyrinth of caves dug by the defenders, have not been found. "Many brave men came here," said Taro Kuribayashi. "It took many marines against such a defense." He emphasized the word "brave," and he meant men of both sides.

CHAPTER FOUR

THROUGH FOREIGN EYES

After a visit to Japan in 1934, the American historian Will Durant wryly concluded that the Japanese were "sentimental and realistic, sensitive and stoical, expressive and reticent, excitable and restrained, aboundingly cheerful, humorous and pleasure-loving, inclined to picturesque suicide—and occasionally cruel to animals and men." As World War II approached, Durant suggested that the Japanese men he met possessed "all the qualities of the warrior—pugnacity and courage and an unrivaled readiness to die." Many Allied troops were to discover that he was right.

Attempts to understand and characterize the Japanese people have continued unabated since the Chinese chroniclers of antiquity wrote of the people of a place they called Wa. These people were known to take ritual purification baths and to be fond of liquor. No theft occurred in Wa, and litigation was infrequent. The old scribes did not need to search for a reason that would explain the law-abiding nature of the early Japanese; they merely pointed out that the punishment of miscreants was severe: a light offender usually lost his wife and children, and for a more grave offense, all the members of his household and all his kinsmen were exterminated (at the time this mode of punishment was known in China as well). Justice in the land of Wa, now Japan, remains severe if not draconian.

Theft is increasing, but Japanese crime rates are still among the lowest in the world. (In a 1987 comparison of Japanese crime rates with those in the United States, Great Britain, West Germany, and France, Japan's crime rate was the lowest and its arrest rate the highest.) Civil litigation, also increasing, is still not the preferred method for settling disputes in Japan; resorting to a court battle to resolve a grievance is considered a personal failure by the parties involved, but court dockets are growing.

Jesuit missionaries from Portugal and Spain who made their way to Japan in the sixteenth century found surprisingly receptive congregants among the Buddhists and animists, including local lords. They found the Japanese a people ready for Christianity, yet treacherous, quick to rebel and shift their loyalty, easy to sin. Japanese behavior toward one another—enemies smiled and observed all the normal courtesies before attempting to kill each other—so puzzled one visiting priest, according to a 1965 compilation of early priestly reports by Jesuit scholar Michael Cooper, that he said Japanese behavior was "beyond both belief and understanding." Another marveled at their melancholic disposition, in which they delighted in "lonely and nostalgic spots, woods and shady groves, cliffs and rocky places, solitary birds, torrents of fresh water flowing down from rocks and in every kind of solitary thing which is imbued with nature and free from all artificiality."

The pioneering Portuguese priest, Father Joao Rodrigues, who became interpreter for two shoguns before Japan expelled all foreigners in 1610, found the Japanese "so crafty in their hearts that nobody can understand them." He wrote that they have one face for the outside world, another for friends and family, and a third for personal counsel, but also that the duplicity had limits: "they do not use this double dealing to cheat people in business matters, as do the Chinese

in their transactions and thieving. . . ." The Jesuit priest
Francis Xavier, noted that the Japanese "have a high opinion
of themselves because they think that no other nation can
compare with them as regards weapons and valor, and so
they look down on all foreigners." But along with their critical review of the Japanese character, these missionaries also
found the Japanese prudent, discreet, and patient. Most of
the conversions appear to have been sincere: many Japanese,
originally ordered by their local lords to join the faith, endured torture and death for refusing to recant later.

Lafcadio Hearn decided that much charm, or its illusion,
existed in Japan. Along with amiability of manners, dainti-
ness of habits, and delicate tact, Hearn asserted that the
Japanese retained "the strange power of presenting out-
wardly under any circumstances only the best and brightest
aspects of character." But he also said that no country could
hope to survive in the wider world of the twentieth century,
if it lost its capacity for aggression and could not confront
others "hardened by the discipline of competition, as well
as the discipline of war." Hearn was witnessing the end of
what he called old Japan; the year was 1904 and Japan was
at war with Imperial Russia. He concluded that the Japanese
were being hardened to withstand war, but that as a new
industrial state Japan was more likely to be damaged by
foreign capital than by foreign armies. The future of the nation now out of its long isolation "must rely upon the least
amiable qualities of her character."

What were those unfortunate qualities? Writing in 1895
to Basil Hall Chamberlain, the British scholar and expert on
things Japanese, Hearn declared: "Imagine a civilization on
Western lines with cold calculation universally substituted
for ethical principle! The suggestion is very terrible and very
ugly. One would prefer even the society of the later Roman
Empire." In writing later to Chamberlain, Hearn predicted
that: "the Japanese of the next generation will not be kind
and open-hearted and unselfish, I fear: they will become
more intellectual and less moral. For old Japan, in unsel-

fishness, was as far in advance of the West as she was materially behind it."

Rumors, Suspicions, Lies

The period of 1910 through the 1930s was replete with Western writing asserting that Japan could not be trusted. These suspicions were brought about by Japan's aggression, first in Korea, which Japan formally annexed in 1910, followed by the land grab in Manchuria and the setting up of the puppet state of Manchukuo in 1928. In 1937 Japan attacked China after manufacturing a shooting incident on the Marco Polo Bridge in Beijing. The China incident, a transparent provocation, was much like the bomb the Japanese detonated in Manuchuria as an excuse for troops to take over and create Manchukuo. In 1909 one Homer Lea, a curious and little-known military analyst, uncannily predicted details of a war between Japan and the United States in an obscure book, *The Valor of Ignorance*. The book, rediscovered and reprinted after Pearl Harbor, is written by a master of purple prose and invective. Lea asserted that the Japanese, "with their sword-girded gods and militant bonzes [Buddhist monks], are heathen in the eyes of this Republic, heathen in all the contemptuous, naked inferiority that that term in a Christian nation implies." Lea insisted that "the only conditions that may have the power of preserving peace between Japan and the United States, or at least retarding hostilities, are to be found in the political relationships that these two nations bear to the world, and the economic interdependence they have with each other."

Lea did not profess to know many Japanese, but he knew strategy and tactics and the military mind. After the Japanese defeat of Russia and the beginning of the buildup of Japanese imperial power in the Pacific, he predicted that Japan would continue to expand at the wishes of those he called "samurai opportunists." Lea correctly noted at the time that Orientals could not expect to get a fair trial on the West Coast of America because juries invariably distrusted them as heathens. Lea seemed to agree, writing that "the word of one Occidental is considered more worthy of credence than the oaths of an entire colony of Orientals." The Japanese returned the favor. In the ensuing decades Japan's depredations in China, widely reported abroad, were hardly communicated to the Japanese themselves. Instead, newspaper columns were jammed with tales of grand victories and selfless heroism as the superior leadership of Japan continued to assert its claim over the backward nations of the region. Hatred of such barbarous acts as the Rape of Nanking, in which many thousands of innocent Chinese were murdered and raped by marauding Japanese troops, turned to racial stereotyping in many American newspapers. After the attack on Pearl Harbor, newspapermen, travelers, scholars, almost anyone who had been to Japan it seemed, wrote articles and books about the Japanese that were largely steeped in race hatred.

Two weeks after the attack on Pearl Harbor, *Time* magazine published an article, "How to Tell Your Friends From the Japs." The Japanese, instructed the editors of *Time*, "are hesitant, nervous in conversation, laugh loudly at the wrong time." They also "walk stiffly erect, hard-heeled. Chinese, more relaxed, have an easy gait, sometimes shuffle. . . . The Chinese expression is likely to be more placid, kindly, open; the Japanese more positive, dogmatic, arrogant." But as victory in the war became certain, the lack of knowledge regarding Japanese mores was of concern to potential Occupation authorities. How could the "heathen" Japanese be expected to act toward an occupying force?

Nobody had a monopoly on understanding the Japanese. Many diplomats, not least Joseph Clark Grew, the United States ambassador to Japan from 1932 to 1942, and a few journalists published valuable insightful works on political Japan, but it was anthropologist Ruth Benedict of Columbia University who wrote the landmark analysis, *The Chrysanthemum and The Sword*. When published in 1946 it immediately became a virtual textbook on the Japanese for foreigners, particularly the Americans, who up to then had been immersed in wartime propaganda. Benedict noted that since Japan opened itself to the world, only seventy-eight years before, foreigners have been describing the Japanese "in the most fantastic series of 'but also's' ever used for any nation of the world." Benedict pointed out that in describing most countries, it is unlikely that the observer would say the people were "unprecedentedly polite" and then add "but also insolent and overbearing," as was common in the case of Japan. These contradictory depictions are, Benedict pointed out, the "warp and woof of books in Japan." And what is more, "they are true. Both the sword and the chrysanthemum are part of the picture."

Benedict's own list of perfectly acceptable contradictions include the binaries aggressive and unaggressive; militaristic and aesthetic; insolent and polite; submissive and pugnacious; loyal and treacherous; brave and timid; and conservative and hospitable to new ways. Less than a half century later after the book's publication, anecdotal evidence of the "but also" nature of today's Japanese persists. Some traits were identified centuries ago. Benedict said that the role of the United States as occupier and mentor of a new Japan would be fraught with difficulty, that no nation could "create by fiat a free democratic Japan." But she also recognized the ability of the Japanese to adapt to changed circumstances through an "ethic of alternatives," which continues to confound foreigners today.

Much the same way foreigners have tried to understand the Japanese in terms they are familiar with, the Japanese have tried to describe themselves in their own terms. "We have a lot of trouble understanding ourselves," says a Japanese educator. "Some Japanese are preoccupied with the subject." Over time Japanese governments, businesses, and cultural entities have assigned spokesmen to deal with foreigners bewildered by what they were looking at: an ancient civilization immersed in tradition and yet as modern in some ways as any Western nation, a nation willing to compete with the West while reserving the right to be selective in its adherence to worldwide norms. Japan's spokespersons haven't done the job very well, especially if their mission was to give Japan a new measure of sympathy. But it doesn't matter, for as Japanese economic strength has grown, a new respect for, even a fear of, Japanese capabilities is developing. Inasmuch as the Japanese never expected nor cared to be loved by outsiders, this is a suitable situation, one that they can cope with.

Promises, Patriotism, Politics

If it is true that the world is being given more information about Japan than ever before, it is also true that there is no topic as interesting to a Japanese audience as its own self. The subject of an endless outpouring of analytical books, pamphlets, lectures, and television and radio programs, the national self proves interesting to all countries. In Japan it amounts to a kind of public narcissism. Westerners and other Asians delight in noting how little the Japanese approach to outsiders has changed over centuries. Japan's expensive efforts to make the outside world understand Japan more often than not center on the notion that Japan's situation, once understood, will enable the outsider to get hold of the truth about Japan—that its moves in commerce or diplomacy are right for the country and that outsiders should make allowances.

For many years it was accepted within Japanese political circles that Japan must pursue an "omnidirectional" foreign policy. It was thought necessary for Japan to avoid offending any nation that might supply raw materials or technology or buy Japanese products. Nations along Japan's vital trade routes were also to be propitiated. But very few nations of consequence lay outside this formulation; if Japan were to refuse to adhere to the Arab boycott of Israel, the Arab oil-producing states would take offense. These were the same Arab countries from which Japan imported three-quarters of its oil. Because of Japan's need to import almost all its raw materials, trade with the apartheid regime of South Africa was condoned as well. (A grateful South African government, pleased to be able to buy and sell directly with Japan, conferred upon visiting Japanese the curious status of honorary whites.)

As Japan entered the 1980s, her banks' assets towered over those of her competitors worldwide. Once Japanese automobiles, electronic goods, and semiconductors took the lead everywhere, it was no longer acceptable, even at home, to be politically omnidirectional. Without abandoning its trading ties to the socialist world, Japan in the mid-1980s positioned itself as a member of the West. As a valuable ally of the West on the Siberian flank of the Soviet Union, Japan had tailored its defense posture to accommodate an American view of what kind of defense was needed in the North Pacific and the Sea of Okhotsk, where Soviet nuclear missiles and nuclear missile submarines menaced both Japan and the United States.

But Japan continued to maintain barriers to protect markets and producers of goods at home, at the same time depending on open markets for Japanese goods abroad. Slowly, under pressure mainly from the United States—the Europeans, much less impressed with the theories of Adam Smith, had been applying directly retaliatory measures—Japan dismantled most of the formal barriers that protected her industries. Japanese leaders almost to the man described dropping the barriers as concessions forced by foreigners on a weak and resource-poor nation.

Prime Minister Yasuhiro Nakasone, who served in the mid-1980s when American pressure was heaviest, was the first prime minister to position Japan as a member of the West. Despite his promises to reform Japan's exclusionist policy, he was unable to accomplish everything. Even so, Nakasone told a small group of foreign correspondents at lunch, the Japanese were making accommodations that they had never been forced to make before, and in fact that conventional wisdom held could not be done.

Getting the Japanese people to change long-standing habits without a major crisis is a grand challenge. Nothing Japan's trading partners were threatening, such as protectionist legislation and new tariffs, ever caused an emergency, and so the people have not been moved to change their habits. Another prime minister, the late Masayoshi Ohira, attempted to persuade people to conserve energy by showing up at work one summer day in what he called an "energy-saving suit": a modified safari suit whose short-sleeve jacket was open at the neck. He hoped to induce managers of office buildings to cut back on air conditioning and to convince citizens that they would be more comfortable in the heat if they wore this double-knit outfit. The project flopped. To many Japanese, Ohira looked ridiculous in his new clothes. At government ministries the few brave souls who showed up in the garb were ridiculed. Suit, shirt, and tie remain the required dress of Japanese salarymen, regardless of weather or consumption of energy.

Through decades of trade negotiation demands from abroad are consistently treated as military assaults. Newspapers continue to use military terms such as "invasion" and "bridgehead" to describe foreign entry into the Japanese market. Japanese readers consequently have the impression that the nation is being subjected to extreme foreign pressure. Yet foreign negotiators keep up the pressure, for only when a Japanese politician is under great stress from outside can he be seen conceding to foreign demands that significantly affect Japanese business.

Since Perry's black gunboats dropped anchor in Japanese waters more than a century ago, the economic point at issue between Japan and the United States and the rest of the world has been opening the country to trade from abroad. Some of the nation's businessmen and farmers remain a step ahead of the diehards. One diet member admits to being surprised by what the cattlemen told him on a recent visit home. "They used to be silent, these rural people from Iwate," said Motoo Shiina, "but now they talk about everything. The cattle raisers said, 'We are enterprising. We can adjust to the environment. What worries us is not whether you are going to stop the import of American beef, but ambiguity and business conditions in the future. So make a clear decision and tell us.' It was a bit of a surprise to me, but I was pleased. It makes sense."

Before the relative enlightenment of the 1980s, Japanese businessmen, bankers, economists, and government spokesmen almost unanimously insisted to foreigners that the Japanese economy was like a person on a bicycle, propelled by its momentum but certain to fall down if the peddling ever stopped. A major recession, a Middle East war, or an embargo cutting off the nation's mobile pipeline of oil tankers and ore carriers, would bring prosperity to an abrupt end. Therefore, what looked like prosperity was illusory; the fast-improving standard of living should not be considered real.

Seeing Themselves

The Japanese notion of permanent vulnerabilty is a kind of national creed, and it is partially responsible for the continued success of conservative ideas. And it also helps to account for the nation's unusually high savings rate, which once soared to about 20 percent of earned income and is now near 15 percent (in the United States the rate is about 6.6 percent). Some analysts say that savings of individuals and companies have financed Japan's phenomenal industrial growth. A people who expect the good life to stop at any moment are a people ready to sacrifice and save; it has been the lot of the Japanese for millennia.

A natural pragmatism and a belief in shared struggle helps the Japanese confront reality. American Marines fighting the Japanese in World War II were astounded by their ferocity and how few surrendered. Some of the Japanese who did surrender gave information surprisingly quickly to the victors on the strength and defenses of their Japanese units. "For them," explained a former Japanese naval aviator, "life in Japan was over, because having been captured, they had dishonored themselves and betrayed their superior officers and the emperor. They could no longer go home."

A few soldiers held out as long as twenty-five years before coming out of hiding or being persuaded to do so when they were discovered to be fighting as though the war still continued. Sergeant Shoichi Yokoi survived in a Guam jungle for twenty-eight years, and Second Lieutenant Hiroo Onoda spent thirty-three years conducting patrols in Lubang, a sparsely populated, mountainous island in the Philippines. When discovered by Japanese search parties, Onoda refused to surrender until he received the order from his old superior officer. The retired officer was located and flown to Lubang. In a small jungle clearing, Onoda stood at attention while his former leader, Major Yoshimi Taniguchi, read the official order to cease hostilities. Only then did Onoda give up his carefully preserved rifle, still in firing condition.

Sacrificing for survival, the Japanese have been put to the test often. Struck twice by oil crises, Japan recovered because the decision was made to allow the blow to strike every citizen. Prices rose dramatically at once; no attempts were made to forestall the inevitable. Japanese suffered through a time of massive inflation and readjusted to the new reality of expensive oil. Industries began a massive project to produce the world's most energy-efficient products; ten years after the first OPEC oil embargo, Japan was using less energy than it had at the time of the crisis. Makers of Japanese electrical appliances competed with one another to produce the models with the lowest consumption of power.

It is surprising to many that the only nation ever to have suffered the atomic bomb turned to nuclear power. Japan's forty plants generate a quarter of the nation's power (compared with 19.5 percent in the United States and Great Britain, 70 percent in France, and 33 percent in West Germany). By 2010 the government aims to raise the contribution of nuclear power to 50 percent. Critics say there have been minor nuclear plant accidents, including levels of radioactive gas and water, but the government has overriden protests after lengthy hearings. Citizens have been unusually passive on the subject, perhaps because they are constantly made aware of the nation's need to import virtually all its oil, gas, and coal. Energy experts lament that some gains are being lost as affluence takes over Japan. Although Japan is still a leader in energy-saving techniques, its oil consumption is rising. In 1989 it returned to approximately where it was at the time of the first oil crisis in 1973—still a remarkable position to be in.

As Japan moved into the mid-1980s, most formal barriers to trade had been relaxed. Japan had the lowest average tariff of any developed country. Reluctance to buy foreign products, for whatever reason, has become the center of Japan's political problems with her major trading partners, as well as Japan's lack of hospitality toward foreign investors. The nation's prosperity blossomed while it piled up gigantic trade surpluses with most of the world. Stung by references to Japanese as "economic animals" (Charles DeGaulle was quoted as calling a visiting Japanese prime minister a "transistor salesman"), the Japanese could not efface their image as crass mercantilists. America's trade imbalance with Japan soared as high as $60 billion, hovered around $50 billion a year, and slowly declined as Japanese began building some autos for the American market in the United States. Choosing sites away from traditional, unionized labor markets, they succeeded in producing quality cars at low cost. When I asked Shoichiro Toyoda, president of Toyota Motor Company, why his firm was so reluctant to build cars in the United States, he replied that it was not because he thought the quality of the labor was poor, but because he felt the costs of producing cars in the Midwest would be prohibitive. "I don't think we can make a profit," he said frankly. When in 1985, the advanced nations met and devalued the dollar, the equation changed; Japanese labor, with its lifetime employment and seniority-based wages, had now become more expensive. American labor was becoming cheaper.

Nevertheless, danger flags were flying. Japan was still not buying enough from the West. American trade officials demanded a broad scale revamping of Japan's built-in nongovernmental impediments to trade. They attacked Japan's interlocked corporations, its mazelike distribution system, the practice of bid rigging on major projects, and a purchasing philosophy that favored domestic companies over foreign. They argued, for example, that Japanese computer companies gave discounts of 80 percent to universities to keep foreign computers out of Japanese schools. One American approach to Japan's protectionism has been to point out that increased purchases of foreign goods will benefit the Japanese consumer. American rice is much cheaper than the highly subsidized Japanese variety, for example, and has been considered highly palatable by housewives participating in blind tasting tests. Yet to protect Japanese rice growers, no foreign rice is allowed on Japanese store shelves.

Consumers aside, the Japanese government and commercial officials uncharacteristically have begun to point fingers at American shortcomings that make continued trade imbalances inevitable: the lack of long-term planning and investment in research and development of United States firms, the low savings rate, the high budget deficit, and Americans' propensity to spend. For the first time in postwar history, the Japanese were speaking out publicly in reasonably forceful terms. "I think you have got to realize," says political historian Hans Baerwald at the University of California at Los Angeles, "that the Japanese have been listening to us tell them what they ought to be doing for more than forty-five years. Some of them are tired of it, and the younger ones resent it."

Living In a New World

Taizo Watanabe, the Japanese ambassador to Egypt, is a former Washington embassy officer who lately has served as the Foreign Ministry's spokesman. His view is that a lot of changes are taking place under the surface in Japan. "In a sense Japan is now going through the road of internationalization because we are free from some prejudices and complexes," he said recently. "We are more able to get more information about what is going on in other countries, and we can always listen more calmly to voices of criticism and expectation and discern what is really scapegoating Japan and what is the true wish of others as to what Japan ought to do."

Japanese prosperity has brought about increased visibility as well. The art world was shocked when in 1987 the Yasuda Fire and Marine Insurance company bought Vincent van Gogh's painting *Sunflowers* at Christies' in London. They paid $39.85 million, more than three times the highest price paid for any painting at auction. *Sunflowers* is a painting known throughout the world, and van Gogh painted it in the same year the insurance company was founded. Consequently, *Sunflowers* became the centerpiece and symbol of the company's art museum in a new forty-three-story headquarters building in Tokyo. The high prices the Japanese paid helped to raise figures to remarkably high levels for some art, particularly paintings of the French impressionists.

Foreign dealers today still troop to Japan with slides and paintings, hoping to interest affluent purchasers. The Japanese Ministry of Finance reports that in 1989 alone Japanese spent more than $1.5 billion for Western art. The purchases piqued the curiosity of the tax authorities, who began investigating. In 1991 it was revealed that some sales were used as tax dodges and money-laundering schemes. The use of foreign art as a commodity embarrasses serious Japanese collectors who, like museum directors and curators around the world, lament the great leap in prices brought about by enterprising Japanese. Like most fads in Japan, splurging on Western art came to a halt at the end of the 1980s, in the face of the reality of overextended loans on Japanese real estate as well as tax office scrutiny.

Although the Japanese government cautioned investors to abate their purchase of so-called trophy properties in the United States, purchases of real estate in America caused American editorialists to warn of a new peril from Japan. Japanese real estate purchases in the United States rose to

$14.77 billion in 1989; since 1990 the pace has slackened. The motion picture studio Columbia Pictures was sold to the Sony Corporation by the Coca Cola Company (that paradigm of American international salesmanship). When a portion of Rockefeller Center was sold and Matsushita Electric bought out the entertainment conglomerate MCA for $6 billion, American business grew worried. After the Columbia Pictures transaction, Sony chairman Akio Morita professed puzzlement at the negative reaction: "You know, it takes two to do something like this, a buyer and a seller. Why are they blaming the buyer and not the seller?"

Japanese diplomats posted in the United States had anticipated the reaction. Before, Japanese investors had been advised to steer clear of purchasing farmland, national totems, and landmark buildings. Now that major Japanese companies no longer have to depend on government protection and financial help, they are less willing to strictly follow government guidance.

The Japanese magnates and corporations who have spent billions in the United States, in Great Britain, and in Europe were not only seeking status, they were looking for good investments. The massive investment in North America by all nine of Japan's carmakers pivot on their confidence that they can sell automobiles built with North American labor. The electronics companies buying into Hollywood want to ensure a steady stream of software for the video hardware they build. In the process, they will most likely change the way movies are made, distributed, and shown. The investment in Rockefeller Center looks to most like a solid and safe purchase. At the same time, not all investments have been profitable. Japanese investors now own more than a third of the office space in downtown Los Angeles, much of it vacant. Plans to set up a new and expensive membership club at Pebble Beach, one of California's premier golfing facilities, stirred up a lot of political opposition. The argument was that the fees would be so high only the Japanese could afford to join.

Takashi Kiuchi, chairman and CEO of Mitsubishi Elec-

tronics America, has spent many years trying to internation-
alize his countrymen. He has run the New York, Los Angeles,
and Long Beach marathons and has climbed Mount Whitney
in his attempt to understand the United States. He says many
Japanese act badly abroad. It is "as if we Japanese have
shown ourselves into another's house, ignored the food prepared by our host, spoken a language only we could understand, had a great time among ourselves, and gone home."

The need for Japanese individuals, as well as companies,
to understand the meaning and responsibilities of the internationalization of Japan is recognized by only a few. A government campaign was launched to encourage Japanese to
travel abroad and see how the rest of the world lives; fully
10 million Japanese travel abroad each year. But whether
this travel "internationalizes" a basically insular people is
problematic. The trips offered by travel agents are prepaid
tours, and there is little or no contact with local people except
through a camera lens. Many of the complaints of the Japanese tourists' clannishness and insensitivity to local people
and customs are the same as those leveled at affluent, cam-
era-draped traveling Americans in the 1950s.

Foreign ministry officials insist that interest in foreign languages has never been so high. Demand for speakers from
the foreign ministry on international subjects is brisk. More
Japanese are being employed in United Nations Agencies,
and the United Nations High Commissioner for Refugees is
Japanese. Japan's foreign aid is reaching new heights, especially in Asia.

The debate over letting foreigners into the country to do
menial work still rages, but the opponents are losing. The
need for highly skilled workers at a time when the population
is not growing but greying necessitates that many unskilled
jobs go to new residents. Assimilation, however, is another
matter. It is likely that Japan will add another tier to its
society. Today Japan's ethnic Koreans and native *burakumin*
outcasts remain isolated. No prestigious company will hire
them, but plenty of room exists in the secondary and tertiary
levels of society, in the service industries of the nation, and

in its underworld. It may be many generations before inter-marriage between persons of different status results in upward societal movement.

But many changes are taking place in the life patterns of Japanese today. The lure of bright lights and high-paying jobs in industry and in the chic shops, hotels, and markets of the big cities continues to siphon young women from the countryside. Family farms, even small ones tended part-time, need a second pair of adult hands and preferably some children's hands as well. Japanese farmers have to seek wives from elsewhere to take over the chores. (Hundreds of young women have been imported from the Philippines for this purpose.)

Life in the countryside is lonely for the young and changing too rapidly for many of the old. Susumu Miura, a part-time farmer and cab driver from Sado, a picturesque rice-growing island off the coast of Niigata, says the old lifestyles are gone. "There is no opportunity for young people here," said Miura one day recently. "The good boys go away to university and never come back; only the less clever ones stay home." A widower, Miura raised three children and watched them all go away. His daughter married and moved to Niigata, his oldest son joined a Tokyo-based electronics company, and the youngest son left for university. "There is nothing I can do about it," says Miura with a shrug of resignation. "I am alone now. If I had had stupid kids they'd have stayed here. Sometimes I regret forcing them to study hard so they could get ahead. Look what's it's got me. I tell my friends that if you force your kids to study hard you'll only lose them in the end." At fifty-three Miura thinks he is too old for a Philippine wife.

Beyond the "Crossroads"

After a long stint in Los Angeles, a Japanese journalist lamented that so many articles on Japan see Japan "at the crossroads." Actually, he insisted, there is no new direction: Japan's long-range policy is consistent in its pursuit of self-interest and in its conservatism. It is not traveling internationally but thinking internationally that the Japanese find difficult.

In Japan's urban areas, loyalties to the old ideas have begun breaking down as new immigrants arrive from the countryside and try to fit into the complex social structure. For a time, the Buddhist sect *Soka Gakkai* and the Japan Communist Party recruited members from the alienated new denizens of the city. Millions poured into the cities and found themselves cut off from a traditional life; they resided in the cramped apartments of public housing blocks or factory dormitories. *Soka Gakkai* at one time boasted 16 million members in Japan and hundreds of thousands in the United States, principally in California. Predictions by political analysts that the movement would soon have radical influence on the policies of Japan were wrong. The *Soka Gakkai's* affiliated party, the *Komeito*, or clean government party, has proved to be generally conservative and a fairly dependable ally of the ruling party. The social changes that have overtaken Japan in its shift from a rural to an urban society are not yet fully understood. A vice chairman of the federation of the nation's major industrial companies says he was astonished to learn that nearly a third of the new college graduates who enter the giant companies switch jobs or companies within their first few years. Such movement was unheard of only a brief decade ago.

An American management specialist recently spoke of a young man on the executive track of a Japanese hotel chain. Well liked and with an assured future, he was required to spend a number of years as a desk clerk, to be followed by learning stints in the various departments of the hotel. The rise to assistant manager would take more than twenty years. He was just starting on this typical career trek when he was spotted by a foreign hotel executive who offered him a job as an assistant manager at a hotel overseas. It was a tremendous leap forward, something virtually impossible in the Japanese system. He was also offered an enormous increase in pay. He took the job almost immediately.

His mother was scandalized by his behavior—not only had he left a prestigious Japanese hotel chain to work for foreigners, he also did not ask the advice and permission of his superior. The American consultant made the following comments:

> It was obvious why he didn't do that, and could not do that. If he had asked for advice, his boss would have advised him against taking the job with the foreign company. As a good Japanese he could not have gone against the advice; it would have been an insult to the advisor. It was wise of him not to ask. That way the youth could be regarded as rude and ungrateful, but he would not have insulted his advisor or made him lose face for not being able to persuade the young man to stay.

Akio Tanaka, a section chief at the Ministry of Trade and Industry who worked for the Foreign Ministry in Brazil, sees other changes in the attitudes of young Japanese:

> When I was in the lower echelon at the Foreign Ministry we had a lot of frustration because we had to work until very late—but it was not only us bureaucrats but people in private companies too. We expressed our frustration, we wanted to spend more time in leisure; for us there was a dichotomy between working and leisure, private life and working life, there was this contradiction. Now that I am back from Brazil I notice today's young people do not express their frustration; they seem to have less of it because they don't think there is this dichotomy. . . . Also they think their work should be interesting. Not something very boring that you should do just in order to get bread—that is the thing about the younger generation.

Consistently since the 1970s, most Japanese questioned in government surveys have said that they see themselves as being middle class. A 1989 survey showed rising dissatisfaction among blue-collar workers as to income, assets, savings, and the amount and quality of leisure. Society appears to be moving toward a less work-oriented and more family-oriented vision of life. Asked when they felt they were leading a full life, the largest proportion of workers said it was when they shared pleasures with family members. Finding primary satisfaction in work came in second. Whether this is another "crossroad" or another step along the long path taking the Japanese away from the farm may come clear in time. The journey is not smooth, nor is it anywhere near over. In fact, for most Japanese it has hardly begun.

CHAPTER FIVE

THE JAPANESE MYSTIQUE

The Japanese people inhabit many Japans. Some of them are opaque, fugitive, inaccessible to the foreigner. They reserve for themselves an idea of nationhood and self that outsiders usually find puzzling. Historically, the cult of Japaneseness infused the nation with a proud, even arrogant, spirit during its growing and triumphant years. It preserved Japan in its darkest years and resides today in Japanese hearts. For the Japanese, the study of themselves as a people, what their special spirit is, and what the language means to them—the spirit of the language itself—is incessant.

Japanese have difficulty explaining to outsiders what they mean by *kotodama*, the perceived wondrous power of the Japanese language; *Yamatodamashii*, the spirit of historical Japan that infused its military with a willingness to attempt the impossible; *Nihonjinron*, the question of identity and what makes the Japanese, in their own eyes, special; *kokutai*, the unique national structure. All these translations are unsatisfactory; they are too simple. They lack the emotional content that they evoke in Japanese.

"You are too much interested in words," lamented a veteran politician, when I pressed him on the subject not long ago. The most respected public figures are not the eloquent orators; the sleepy-eyed, and fatherly speaker, who usually appears vague and tongue-tied, is admired. The rare, outspoken, dynamic politician who impresses his counterparts in the West is likely to be the least trusted at home. A prime minister such as Yasuhiro Nakasone, famous for his close relationships (for a Japanese politician) with Western leaders, especially Ronald Reagan, appeared to be an exception to the rule. But he remained in power only so long as he fulfilled the needs of the ruling party; his relative popularity overseas did not translate into votes at home. In this regard, American politicians such as Richard M. Nixon and George Bush, and even China's Zhao Ziyang, discovered that foreign policy triumphs and popularity abroad do not impress the voters at home.

The mistrust reserved for the Japanese politician by his constituents often proves to be deserved. Supporters of political candidates in Japan often pass through narrow neighborhood streets with bull horns and loudspeakers, calling out nothing more than the name of a candidate and a thank you (never an apology for the noise pollution). Verbal skills are not generally prized or learned at home. Many large companies run programs to teach their executives how to deliver a presentation in a foreign language. (At the California State University at Long Beach, run by Hugh Leonard, a former Catholic priest who spent many years in Japan, exposes Japanese executives to Western life and business methods and even prepares them to manage companies in the U.S. and deliver proposals and technical papers in their own companies at home, as well as in international meetings.)

Talk, Talk, Talk

Despite the storied Japanese respect for silence, the calmness and stillness of Japan in its most meditative moments, and the distrust of words, Japan is a nation awash in babble.

The airwaves—taken up by radio, television, sidewalk telephones, mobile car phones, pagers, and beepers of all sorts— are saturated with it. Coffee shops and bars are noisy. Although the average decibel level in Japanese restaurants is quite low, words flow liberally. Indeed, in a land where much daily business is conducted with a minimum of words, there are often torrents of words when a smile or nod would do. Ducking through the entrance curtain of a restaurant, shop, or inn, one is often bombarded with an explosive, sometimes cheery, sometimes bored, chorus of welcome, and on leaving, another chorus of thank yous. These cries of welcome and thanks are refreshing in an increasingly depersonalized world. "I don't care if they mean it or not," a French friend remarked as we left a Shibuya restaurant one night. "I like it."

Japan was the first nation to install artificial voices in automobiles to warn drivers and passengers that they have not closed their doors properly or fastened their seat belts. Conductors on tour buses, perennially pert, crisply uniformed, and excruciatingly polite young women, are notorious for nonstop talk. Very often, in the normal snail's pace of traffic, the prepared text they deliver is shorter than the trip, and the conscientious conductor will burst into song to prevent silence from breaking out. Even at some of Japan's most sublime cutural sites, such as the ancient garden of rocks and raked pebbles at the Ryoan-ji temple in Kyoto, loudspeakers annoyingly blare prerecorded information for the visitors.

Japanese take words a step further with a kind of communication they call *haragei*, literally "belly talk," which isn't talk at all. *Haragei* implies that trust in people, understanding, and sincerity are as important as the words that are spoken. It is often said that only with force of personality can some difficult deals be sealed, win which one side can win over the other to its way of thinking by sheer dint of earnestness.

In negotiations, when each side knows what the other side really wants and an impasse is nearing, it may be time for the Japanese version of talking turkey. The Japanese negotiators may not even do any more direct talking about the deal. Agreement is more likely to occur after a round of golf, a visit to a nightclub or to a favorite bar. At some point along the way, a meeting of the minds may occur. "More likely," scoffs an American businessman who has observed the process, "It's a question of who has power and who doesn't. In these tough negotiations the weaker side never seems to win, with or without words. But a satisfactory deal is crafted." For negotiations like this to work, both sides have to understand the rules of the game, and foreigners are rarely able to play.

In government-to-government negotiations, a primary strategy of the Japanese is to overwhelm the other side with data, which keeps the adversary scurrying just to keep up. A Los Angeles attorney who participated in only one round of negotiations admits to being stunned by what he went through. "I felt as though we were a high school football team playing the Forty-Niners," he says. "They outnumbered us with staff and with the quality of their research. Every member of their team was an expert in the topic being discussed. We were overwhelmed. And we lost."

One former veteran American trade negotiator, Clyde Prestowitz, Jr., has written that usually after the long trip from Washington to Tokyo, the entire American team was invariably tired and badly in need of sleep, but the Japanese hosts would cordially invite the members to dinner—not out of Japan's storied sense of hospitality, but in order to keep the visiting team groggy. "In time I became convinced," wrote Prestowitz in *Trading Places*, "that one reason we tended to do poorly in negotiations was that we were always half-asleep."

Haragei and tricks with foreigners aside, the Japanese who value long-term relationships can conduct business with few words and without formal contracts. The owner of one of Japan's oldest and biggest construction supply firms says, "I don't remember ever having a contract with any of our [Japanese] suppliers or customers. We understand each other." In general, the contracts that Japanese are accustomed to distress foreigners because they invariably have escape clauses in them that, in the opinion of foreigners, negate the concept of a contract. In such contracts a paragraph stipulates that if any factors arise that would tend to affect the ability of one party to fulfill the terms of the contract, the two sides will sit down and negotiate the necessary changes.

The conventional explanation for the ability of Japanese to understand each other with a minimum of words usually cites Japan's agrarian and village roots. The members of a small, closed society could know just about everything about each other, making words unnecessary. As one specialist on Japanese culture, Kyozaburo Dozeki, puts it, "It was considered foolish, even impolite, to explain everything from beginning to end in words, and those who could not understand unless full explanation was given were considered boors."

Quieter Japan

There is, of course, a quiet Japan. At the Grand Shrine at Ise, the mecca of Shinto, the fish swimming in the pebbled and purified streams seem suspended in space. Wordless landscapes, preferably quiet and unpolluted, are becoming harder to find, but they continue to speak to the Japanese and the contemplative visitor. The exquisite slope and swerve of the tiled roof on an ancient Kyoto temple, the stunning spectacle of a huge, blood-red sun setting behind the snow-capped cone of Mount Fuji, remain familiar symbols. Fuji's cone has served as a landmark, symbol, and backdrop in scenes of mountain, meadow, lake, ocean, city, village, and farm (some of the symbols that validate Japan's sense of uniqueness). Although Japanese culture springs from borrowed roots, the adaptation that makes it identifiably Japanese is a matter of pride.

Japanese thirst for and never seem to tire of the subject of their small and accident-prone land. Emperors real and mythical have devoted much of their lives to composing poems, mainly about nature. The Japanese aesthetic emphasizes attention to minute detail, the exceptional beauty of the small and the ordinary. In verse Japan is a bit of earth minutely observed as perhaps no other. A rigidly stylized seventeen-syllable *haiku*, or the thirty-one-syllable *waka*, or the *tanka* poems at their finest celebrate a land invested with mystical qualities. The first modern emperor, Meiji, composed 100,000 poems, and Hirohito, though a scientist by training, was adept at calligraphy and was a fair poet himself. Not for the Japanese poet is the bold epic; rather, value is placed on the small glimpse of nature, an insight so sure and apt it evokes a stunned intake of breath.

The poet or artist is helped by the surprising variety of the nation, a mountainous, wooded land surrounded by ocean. The Japanese prefer not to talk outside the family of their industrial pollution, their urban sprawl, its impacted cities and alienated residents.

Looking out over a smog-cloaked Tokyo with the chairman of a major chemical company one day I commented, perhaps provocatively, "Look what Japan's grand industrial renaissance has done for the people; they can't breath freely, the children can't go out to play when the smog alert sounds. You can see Mount Fuji in the distance only on a cold winter day, when the wind blows the pollution out to sea. This doesn't look like progress." The chairman sighed assent, and then his expression brightened and he turned prophetic: "That is true," he nodded, "but cleaning this will be a whole new industry for us." And so it was.

Japanese eyes turn elsewhere. Emperor Akihito has written a scientific tome on the fish native to Japan and surrounding waters; his father wrote many more. Today elders lament that their reverence for the land is not emulated, or even understood, by their children. In millions the Japanese are traveling abroad when once they were content to stay at home and visit to the far reaches of their own back yard. Japanese high school graduates will have been paraded through, over, or past very important historical and cultural venue in the land, traveling by bus and train and even by plane, usually in ruly uniformed groups.

Traveling abroad is one way for people to appreciate foreign lands and evaluate their own in comparison. The internationalists in Japan hoped that travel by so many people would help to modernize Japanese thinking and put the country's social shortcomings into perspective by opening people's eyes to alternative ways of living. The change is slow in coming. A social critic and friend, S. Chang, laments Japanese provincialism:

> I used to think when people went abroad and saw how cheap the food was in America, how much room Americans had to live in, how many parks and playgrounds and what good roads other countries had, they would come home and demand something better than we have here. But I was wrong. They come home convinced that this is the world's best place to live, the best place on earth.

To be sure, some positive impressions cannot fail to imprint themselves. But home is home, and after I had spent six months living in a Chinese hotel while reporting in Beijing I got a sense of what the return home must mean to Japanese. After being charmed by the straightforwardness of its people, the visitor to China begins very soon to notice the lack of cleanliness and order, the absence of simple civility in the shops and on the streets, the wilted and rotting produce, and the slovenliness and surliness of service workers. My arrival back in Japan, the sight of the pristine tarmac at the airport, the orderly handling of passengers, and the cleanliness of everything to be touched convinced me why the Japanese might feel that there is no place like home.

To some degree travel *has* sophisticated the Japanese who do go abroad. In the early 1960s, when limits on foreign exchange and innate frugality kept many from traveling, the government issued a pamphlet explaining foreign customs to Japanese travelers, cautioning them not to remove their clothes in public and not to stand on the seats of Western-style toilets. The instructions were necessary then because many tourists were from well-to-do farm families and had not been exposed to modern Western amenities. Many early postwar travelers to the West often found themselves perplexed by the Western style toilet; Japanese toilets require the user to squat, straddling a porcelain fixture set into the floor.

As the Japanese, with their strong national currency, became more familiar with Western lifestyles, they had what seemed like a brilliant idea. They proposed to buy property and settle retired Japanese in Hawaii and other pleasant climates, where their retirement income would buy them more than it could at home. The idea, reputed to have had high level approval from Japan's Ministry of International Trade and Industry, was greeted with alarm in the United States, Australia, and elsewhere; this was one Japanese export that was unwelcome. One major reason the scheme never panned out is simple: elderly Japanese were not yet ready to give up Japan.

Japanese Grown Up

What does one make of a people General Douglas MacArthur described as a nation of twelve-year-olds? A people with 2000 years of culture rightly resented the slur. For despite their pride in national culture and tradition, Japanese possess an understanding of their shortcomings and are even willing to speak of them. Sitting at the tempura counter in one of Tokyo's newest hotels, a foreign ministry official told me about investigations of histories of Japan used by nationalists to inculcate the Japanese with a sense of special origin and destiny. In fact, he said, not only much of Japanese culture, but also most Japanese people, are descended from Korea and China. The administrator asserted, "We are mongrels, and we have found that we no longer have to sacrifice ourselves for the sake of the national interest. People now feel free to express their feelings against the government and the ruling political party as never before."

Even so, the mystique of Japan as a special place; the Japanese as a specially endowed people, does not easily fade.

How could Japan, alone among all the nations of Asia, have reached the heights of power as the world's second richest economy without something special propelling its people? The cult of Japan's uniqueness is formalized and ingrained in the nation's educational system. No country invests so much time and trouble to keep the flame of uniqueness alive in language and custom. Some traditions Japanese consider to have ancient roots, such as elements of the enthronement ceremonies for the emperor, have actually been recently invented. Ethnocentrism is not the private province of the Japanese, but they have learned how to use it in nation building.

So unique are the Japanese, children have been taught that their brains function differently from all others. Scholars have spent careers analyzing this premise. The assumption of physical difference is illustrated by the story of the Japanese man who a few years ago explained to a Harvard economist that Japan could not be expected to import much beef (the United States was pressing Japan to open its markets). The reason, he explained, was that Japanese intestines were longer than those of non-Japanese and could not tolerate beef. Amused by the notion of a unique Japanese anatomy, the American expressed his skepticism. The Japanese man investigated this intestinal anomaly and reported what he had found in the largest daily newspaper in Tokyo: Such a contention was a myth promulgated by the government during World War II because there was no meat to allocate to civilians. People were encouraged instead to eat a lunch of white rice with a red pickled plum in the center; the design of the food resembled the red and white flag of Japan. It had nothing to do with medicine or anatomic fact, the professor wrote. But he found the fiction was taken for granted by virtually all his friends who, like himself, grew up during the war.

The fact of Japanese anatomic uniqueness was further elucidated by Ichiro Kawasaki, a world-traveled diplomat who wrote *The Japanese Are Like That* in 1955. "The Japanese stomach," wrote Kawasaki, "is inordinately inflated, and its position is much lower than that of Westerners, mainly because of the heavier weight which rice imposes on their stomach. Also the bowels of Japanese are, according to medical evidence, longer than those of Occidentals by a foot or so because of the inveterate diet." Kawasaki does not cite medical proof of this assertion.

"The humidity, the quality of the water and other factors," he wrote in his once popular book, "combine to make foreigners appear more and more like the natives of the locality they stay in over the course of years spent there." More likely, the author became more accustomed to seeing the foreigners. Kawasaki, who served for a time as chief of protocol for the Foreign Ministry, wasn't so amusingly off base when he concluded that: "every generalization, whether in favor of Japan or against it, can be disproved by an overwhelming mass of contradictory evidence. One can find evidence that Japanese are industrious, lazy, efficient, incompetent, kind, cruel, peaceful or warlike."

CHAPTER SIX

SEX, CENSORSHIP, AND SANCTION

Imai-san came into my office looking somewhat sheepish, holding a flimsy government form. He was embarrassed. "They want to know," he began hesitantly, downcast eyes scanning the paper, "for what purpose you are importing pornographic material into Japan?"

"Pornographic material?" I said.

"The book that arrived by air shipment of office materials from the States."

"Book, book . . . Oh, yes." The book was the catalog of the Pablo Picasso retrospective at the Museum of Modern Art in New York. Pornography? Picasso's erotic etchings are well known, and a few were reproduced, about the size of postage stamps.

As a "convenience," the Japanese customs service was offering to destroy the offending book, since it could not be allowed into the nation where it would, presumably, corrupt the morals of the youth and deprave society. Instead, many telephone calls ensued. Imai-san made it clear to the officials that the *gaijin-san* intended to make things difficult by demanding the delivery of the book. After several weeks of deliberation, a verbal judgment was issued: so long as the material was not for sale, publication, or public display, the importation would be allowed, just this once. Everyone involved was relieved.

It was a special concession, of course, one not normally offered the hapless Japanese traveler or visiting foreigner. Ordinary citizens and expatriates are usually willing to accept the judgment and lose the item in question, rather than complete the endless paperwork, endure the embarrassment, and spend the time solving the dispute. When the Picasso book was finally delivered, it had been so vigorously thumbed and bent by examining officials that I had to have its binding repaired.

Diligently censoring foreign publications for not only erotic but bloody and violent scenes as well, the customs service is aided by self-censoring publishers and printers who deal with foreign materials entering Japan. The Japanese national police take over the chore on domestic goods, though their eyes seem less acute. A few years ago Japanese customs intercepted a catalog on the late avant-garde photographer Man Ray; it was being sent to a Tokyo publisher, who wanted to issue a book about Ray's nude studies and other art. Customs refused to allow four of the 256 pictures into the country, ruling they were "articles that damage local manners" because they showed the models' pubic hair. The Japanese publisher protested, and France's external trade minister wrote an official note saying the Japanese government's attitude was "astonishing" and "beyond our understanding." Customs did not relent; the publisher did. Not long afterward, however, one of Japan's leading newspaper companies published and sold 20,000 copies of a lavish and expensive book of nudes by foreign photographers; and visible wisps of pubic hair in a small number of photographs rated only a verbal reprimand from police. Importers of possibly questionable material soon learned which customs posts were not so eager to defend public morals and shipped through them. By consensus, the examiners at Narita International Airport were considered the most censorious.

Despite official attitudes, and perhaps because of them, the Japanese appetite for foreign pornography remains insatiable. Customs officers examining baggage at Tokyo's Narita Airport find videotapes stuffed in the dirty laundry, disguised as books, hidden in false bottoms. One clever consumptive gentleman tried to hide a porno film by taping it in the cavity of his sunken chest, but the customs officer questioned his lumpy physique and confiscated the film.

Foreign magazines shipped in bulk, especially the more explicit ones, have long been examined for evidence of morally objectionable sights. If found, the offending areas were originally blacked out with marker. Platoons of housewives were set to work censoring the incoming shipments of publications, the women's only task being the deletion of any view of a hirsute crotch. But then some of the more indefatigable fans of *Playboy* and other such magazines had learned how to soak away the black ink and dry and iron out the pages. So customs turned to a device that actually scratched the image off. Legendary Japanese ingenuity was thwarted by the scarified image.

When the Japanese censors get through with some imported feature films, their clumsiness in editing amplifies the imagined offense. Cuts in imported films are obvious and jarring. When the popular film *M*A*S*H* was first brought to Japan, the censors laboriously scratched through each frame of a humorous scene that centered on a glimpse of the nurse Hot Lips Hoolihan, surprised in the shower. But instead of hiding the offensive pubic hair from sight, the scratches on the film permitted a bright beam of light to pulsate on the screen, with flashing colored edges of red, green, yellow, and blue. Foreign audiences howled with laughter, mystifying most Japanese patrons, who were accustomed to such annoyances.

Homegrown Only, Please

Sexual images are not the only ones to be censored. An issue of *Time*, printed in Tokyo for Japanese and Korean subscribers, contained a photograph of a Vietnamese soldier proudly displaying two severed heads. The picture was running simultaneously in other worldwide editions of the magazine. But the sight of the striking picture in the page plates alerted the printers and Japanese representatives of *Time* at the printing plant. Before officialdom could even see the photograph, the decision was made to cut the heads from the picture, which resulted in a photograph of a grinning soldier holding two empty white holes. The printers were acting to avoid a possible reprimand from police after publication.

This incident is consistent with an unwritten policy that photographs of Japanese depredations in Asia, including executions, decapitations, mutilations, and hangings, are grimly familiar in countries that suffered under Japanese occupation but never published in Japan's mainstream media.

Japan is awash in its own sexual, brutal, and bloody films, books, cartoons, and photos. Often the sex is a mere adjunct to the brutality and blood. Sometimes it is the other way around. And sometimes it is just sex alone, or sexual innuendo. A Japanese department store could fly a multistory banner advertisement of a completely naked young girl—without pubic hair, of course—on the front of its building with nary a complaint. The nation also supports more than its share of live sex shows, thinly disguised prostitution, and ribald evening and not-so-late-night television shows.

"My lasting image of Japan," says an English advertising executive now back in London after a long stay in Tokyo, "is that cute little office girl in her spotless white blouse, sitting on the subway as prim as you please, reading a woman's magazine and studying the detailed illustrations on how to give a man sexual pleasure." Such remarkably explicit publications are available along major thoroughfares, in bookstores, at subway station kiosks, and sidewalk bookstalls. The person who can't patronize those places, or who is too embarrassed, can do his or her shopping at vending machines at selected locations, sometimes next to those that dispense beer, whisky, and soft drinks. Rarely vandalized, these sleepless sentinels cater to the lascivious twenty-four hours a day.

Pulp comic books replete with tales of samurai adventure and lurid, modern sex are avidly read by commuters on the nation's crowded railways. Countless office workers on their way to or from their homes wile away the commute lost in the fantasy world of the comics. At the end of the line of almost any commuter or subway train, a veritable library of discarded comics is usually gathered up and recycled into pulp and used again to feed the hungry presses that spew out the 300-page magazines at an unimaginable rate—a stunning 2.5 billion copies a year. About half of them graphically depict sexual acts. Tokyo mothers have begun to demand something better for their children and have forced publishers to put the label "hazardous" on the most offensive of these publications. Some publishers have been forced to drop the business completely.

Historically the illustration of erotic tales and comic depictions of sexual contests and scatalogic subjects has been commonplace. Many serious books are also produced in cartoon versions, including biographies, books on economics, and even politics. One such, *Barefoot Gen*, which has been translated into several languages, is a vehement tract against the politicans and the political climate that brought about the Pacific War and the eventual bombing of Hiroshima.

The cartoon is an old and proud tradition in Japanese folk art. Satirical comics drew official ire from time to time before the military took over Japan's government and stifled them in the period before World War II. But the true flowering of the genre, and its broadening into a mass marketing phenomenon, didn't take place until after the Occupation. Those comics that delve into romantic tales and sexual fantasy favor explicit drawing of the human figure; nubile young girls are usually drawn from a floor-level perspective, and the depictions of rape and other sexual violence are vivid, if stylized. The taboos against the portrayal of pubic hair are scrupulously observed. But readers are seldom spared splattered blood or severed bodies and appendages. Some sexual themes are graphic through indirection. Intertwined limbs and distorted views mask the forbidden sights. A crashing surf often substitutes for sexual climax.

Casual Sex

Sex in Japan does not carry with it the sinful connotations of the Western Judeo-Christian ethic. The overtones of guilt and the echoes of the loss of the Garden of Eden do not resonate in Japan. Questions surrounding sex and reaction to it are rather questions of taste; people worry about the shame and embarrassment that openly sexual, or unmannerly, behavior might bring to one's family and friends. Discretion in personal behavior is required. What is considered correct behavior and what one should be ashamed of are now being looked at in a somewhat different light as Japanese begin slowly to see their society changing. Western norms, or perhaps Western inhibitions, have come into play. The small and poorly understood feminist movement struggles valiantly to liberate Japan's women from what they see as pervasive sexual exploitation.

In January 1857, Townsend Harris, America's first envoy to Japan, noted in his diary that his interpreter, Henry Heusken, told him he found the Japanese to have a shocking openness about sexual matters. While taking tea with a Japanese family, the husband and father began asking Heusken the English names of objects in the room, and then of his person, and finally the man "opened his dress and taking his privities in his hand—in sight of all the females—asked the names of the various parts in English!" Harris himself recalled seeing mixed bathing and asking a government official if this "was not rather injurious to the chastity of the females." The official said it sometimes happened that a woman's virtue was lost. And when Harris asked what a man did when he married a female who was supposed to be a virgin but in fact was not, the official answered: "Nothing. What can he do? I was once serviced in that way myself, but what could I do? It was not my fault."

There is today an openness and tolerance of sexual expression rare in the Western world. Homosexuality, for example, has long been accepted as a private fact of life. In some forms, it has been romanticized as the purest of loves, particularly when associated with innocent youth and brave samurai. The literature of Japan abounds in tales, from the feudal period onward, of love between men. The comic book romances are often centered on beautiful androgynous persons involved in grand adventures.

In Kabuki theatre men play all the roles, and the *onnagata*, who play women, are popular heroes to real women. The most glamorous of the Grand Kabuki *onnagata*, Bando Tamasaburo, descendant of a long line of Kabuki actors, says, "We personify women in an age of elegance. Many of the manners and movements we have perfected are lost in today's society. Actually, many women come to Kabuki to study us so they can understand how they should act." The fluid grace of an *onnagata* such as Tamasaburo is indeed envied by women. During an informal lecture session in Tokyo, Tamasaburo, a slender, handsome young man in an elegant suit, was asked playfully if he ever got confused by being a man offstage and a woman onstage. "All the time," he answered with a mischievous chuckle.

Homosexuals are not harrassed by police in Japan as they are in some other countries, though they are sometimes viewed with some curiousity. Occasionally a weekly magazine will run a wide-eyed picture story about transvestites to titillate the readership, but generally speaking, Japan has been a haven for foreign homosexuals, who find partners, peace, and official indifference. Western travel guides for homosexuals list many places for gays to find acceptance in Japan. To most Japanese, homosexuality is not an issue. Many homosexual Japanese men marry and have children, as they do elsewhere.

For the affluent heterosexual male, the practice of keeping a mistress is beginning to go out of fashion. Changing attitudes toward sex in high places forced the resignation of Prime Minister Susuke Uno, when Mitsuko Nakanishi, a forty-year-old geisha, revealed that Uno had paid her $21,000 during their five-month liaison and then tossed her aside. Uno and his political party, the ruling Liberal Democratic Party, had other, seemingly more significant scandals vying for attention at the time, but when the geisha told her story it became the major outrage, and Uno's term as prime minister was finished. It was an interesting sign of the times that the scandal story broke in a major Tokyo newspaper, whereas political scandals have habitually been printed abroad or in the scurrilous weekly press.

Uno's failing was not only that he had indulged in the affair, but that he had tossed her aside in a peremptory way. Worse, he had allowed his peccadilloes to become public. In Japan people who can afford to take on mistresses are expected to abide by an unwritten code of conduct in breaking off the affair. One device for an amicable parting is the financing of a small shop, so that the woman can support herself. For Uno's mistress, a payment of $21,000 was not nearly enough. It was felt Uno, a politician, should have known the rules of the game.

In 1896 Japan's first prime minister Hirobumi Ito went to Taiwan on an official visit and secretly brought his mistress aboard the Imperial Japanese Navy vessel. He managed to keep her out of sight during the voyage, but at the destination his manservant made the mistake of unloading the woman's distinctively nondiplomatic luggage along with the prime minister's. Reporters accompanying the prime minister had great fun with the story.

Early in this century another important conservative political figure, Bukichi Miki, was running for reelection, when he was accused by an opponent of having not one but three mistresses. According to the respected financial daily *Nihon Keizei Shimbun*, Miki responded explosively, "What are you talking about? I have five mistresses, not three. I take care of them because they need me. I just can't kick them out. It's my duty to provide for them." Miki won the election in a landslide. A Japanese writer who follows the social activities of the political elite says, "Politicians stopped parading their women at parties about thirty years ago. Today the electorate takes a dim view of hanky-panky, and legislators are more discreet than in the past."

Although Japan banned prostitution in 1956, the image of the call girl has changed from the famine-poor days of the 1930s, when desperate rural families sold their daughters into servitude in the giant geisha houses, restaurants, bordellos, and bathhouses of the cities. Today sex for money, still big business, has gangland connections, and the number of women imported illegally from the Philippines, Thailand, and elsewhere for the purpose is estimated to be more than 100,000. Police occasionally find warrens of these pathetic women, lured by Japanese *yakuza* gangsters to come to Japan to earn easy money, only to find themselves trapped, without their passports, afraid of turning to the police, and kept in near starvation for months on end. Japanese prostitutes, according to a police survey, say that their choice of vocation is based on the need for money and lack of training for any other career. Many are runaways and outcasts.

But many ordinary young Japanese girls find prostitution a simple way to make extra money and do not mind talking about it. Recently the owner of a "mistress bank" described her business to a Tokyo newspaper. Her work consists of acquiring college girls to agree, for a monthly sum, to spend a specific number of hours each month with a specific client. "It's sort of a part-time job for me," said one school girl, casually. Her patron had installed her in a small apartment near her university, and she found it convenient and profitable.

Such casual attitudes do not seem unusual, considering the way sex oozes from late-night television. (In Japan "late-night" can mean as early as 9 P.M.) It is not surprising to see talk show hosts leeringly interviewing bare-breasted dancers or showing video camera excursions into "no panty" bars in the Kabuki-cho section of Tokyo's Shinjuku entertainment district. On one talk show, a woman with large breasts weighed them on a scale to the delight of the host and hostess, and presumably the home audience; the show's ratings were very high.

Misnomers, Mashers, Sexual Gods

In 1984 a visitor from Istanbul asked his taxi to take him to the Turkish embassy. He was surprised and outraged when he found himself delivered to a *toruko*, the Japanese version of the so-called Turkish bath, where massages and sexual favors are sold. Later, on hearing the story from his irate countryman, the information attaché of the Turkish embassy embarked on a lone crusade to extricate his country's name from the cheap world of the baths. In less than a year the association of bathhouse owners agreed to a linguistic if not an occupational change, a remarkably rapid turnabout that gave a lot of publicity to the establishments as a sort of consolation prize. The police suggested the new name might be *koshitsu tsuki yokujo*, which means bathhouse with attached private rooms. The association members stifled their chortle; they were going to have something shorter, a bit more catchy and less antiseptic. They settled upon a hybrid English combination, Soapland. Whether the baths are called *Toruko* or Soapland, the menu of sexual favors is the same, though prices have risen. A slippery, writhing wrestle in the suds—glimpses have been shown on television, naturally—can run as high as a thousand dollars.

Second-hand sex and the Japanese equivalent of the Italian pinch is a common topic among female riders of Japan's crowded commuter trains. The Japanese magazine *Yukan Fuji* reported that a Tokyo company surveyed one hundred of its female employees, and more than 95 percent said they had been molested on their way to or from work. A railroad official who responded to the survey said that most grievances are made during the morning rush hour, and that the complaints keep increasing each year as the trains get more and more crowded. Why do these assaults take place only on the morning trains? Presumably the mashers are too exhausted after a long day's work to ply their trade. Too, many men are out drinking after work or putting in overtime in the office, while working women are rushing home to feed the children. But the railroad official also said he was sure only a fraction of the incidents are reported. *Yukan Fuji* gave "Tips on Masher Bashing" solicited from women who know how. One said: "Jab him with a pin. Make him pay for his fun with a little pain." Another asserted: "I have found it effective to grab the guy by the arm and pull him from the train. He will begin to lose his cool. That's when you slap him as hard as you can, then jump back on the train before he can pull himself together."

Keio University professor of psychiatry Keigo Okonogi says that older Japanese men live lives full of male bonding experience. They have difficulty relating to their wives and families because they spend so much time away from them. Younger men have a different problem: being too dependent. Their problems are equally great:

> Rejected by a woman, men grovel and throw themselves on her mercy. They come to me for counseling when they find the woman is not interested in them anymore. A man who shamelessly tries to play on the emotions of an independently minded woman very quickly becomes a burden to her. She wants to live her own life and rejects him. But such men do not give up easily; they resort to various ploys that cause the woman much pain. Many females say, 'My husband is a Peter Pan. He just won't grow up.'

This is the other side of what Okonogi calls the "samurai-wimp generation gap." Whereas older men, particularly those educated before World War II, tend to be afraid of being emotionally involved with women because it might damage their own sense of masculinity, the new generation wants too much from women who are beginning to discover their own capabilities and career opportunities.

Men accustomed to thinking of their society as male dominated, which it still is, are professing surprise at the assertion of women's rights, long guaranteed but rarely honored. Government and corporate offices are notorious bastions of sexual harrassment. Recent reports from Tokyo women's groups say awareness of women's rights is growing rapidly as more and more women move into the workplace. Interestingly the experience of Japanese firms in the United States in regard to such subjects as sexual harrassment has been edifying. The former head of the American unit of Honda Motor Co., Soichiro Irimajiri, now back in Japan, told the *Wall Street Journal*, "I was sensitive to these problems in the United States. But back in Japan I didn't think I'd have to think about it. I guess I'm wrong."

Dr. Yasushi Narabayashi, noted as Japan's earliest modern sex therapist and marriage counsellor, laments that Japanese have been deficient in taking a sensible attitude toward sex education. Despite myriad sexual images and an agrarian culture replete with fertility gods, the Confucian ethic has suppressed discussion of the subject. Phallic cults and many of the countryside festivals of such cults were outlawed in 1868, when the Meiji government decreed the modernization of the country. Nature worship of this kind was considered embarrassingly primitive to the new arbiters of culture, who were Western oriented.

The British scholar W. G. Aston wrote of an 1871 trip north of Tokyo toward Nikko:

> I found the road lined at intervals with groups of phalli, connected no doubt with the worship of the sacred mountain Nan-tai. . . . I once witnessed a phallic procession in a town some miles north of Tokio. A phallus several feet high, and painted a bright vermilion colour, was being carried on a sort of bier by a crowd of shouting, laughing coolies [sic] with flushed faces, who zig-zagged along with sudden rushes from one side of the street to another. It was a veritable Bacchic

rout. The Dionysia, it will be remembered, had their phalli.
A procession of this kind invaded the quiet thoroughfares of
the Kobe foreign settlement in 1868, much to the amazement
of the European residents.

Today, at the Tagata Shrine near Nagoya, regular festivals
are held in which models of male and female genitals are
paraded and genitalia-shaped souvenirs are sold to visitors.
The shrine usually has a contingent of foreign tourists on
hand during festival days, enticed there by articles in visitors' guides. The evidence of the roadside gods of fertility
Aston referred to can still be found in rural areas of Japan;
they represent a last vestige of a natural religion that probably predates Shintoism and Buddhism.

But there is much about Japan's primitive religious past
and its sexual overtones that is not understood by the scholars, even today. Even so, ambiguity does not bother the Japanese as it seems to bother Westerners. Japanese gods, the
kami, are ill defined, and nobody tries to draw pictures of
them. They are, as is often explained, gods with a small "g."

Among the mysterious practices handed down from antiquity is the ceremony in which a new emperor, such as
Akihito, enters a holy Shinto site, a hut built especially for
the occasion. He partakes of symbolic rice specially grown
for the occasion and communes with the ancient sun goddess.
In some readings of the meaning of the ceremony, which
takes place out of sight, the new emperor has intercourse
with the mythical goddess; in other versions he enters her
womb. Some interpretations indicate that he is reborn as a
god, whereas in others he becomes a man-woman. What actually happens during the long night an emperor spends
alone in the hut has never been revealed. And no one gets a
chance to ask, for only one person knows the answer. Certainly the new monarch, now officially relegated to the legal
status of symbol of the nation, gets a night of meditation.
Like much of what happens in Japan, the ambiguity is what
fills such events with awe.

In contrast to the conservative adherents to the ancient

ideals of a disappearing rural Japan, the modern young
urban Japanese are less concerned about these beliefs. Freed
from nationalistic obligations of state-run Shinto and less
connected to the land, the Japanese are evolving psycholog-
ically. Some researchers such as Dr. Narabayashi think it is
not necessarily to the improved well-being and stability of
individuals. The Japanese young executive, says Dr. Narabayashi, is very often impotent, dominated by a frigid mother
and frightened of a seldom seen father who keeps a mistress.
The sexual despair he finds typical of his patients is occa-
sioned by the husband who takes up mistresses and neglects
his family. Although the doctor counsels many wives to leave
their husbands, few do it, fearful of being ostracized by both
community and family and worried about the support and
education of their children.

According to Dr. Narabayashi, their frustration turns into
"an almost abnormal concern for the education of the children" (thus the celebrated "education mother"). But not all
the children: the mother's attention tends to focus on the
son—daughters tend to be less pressured. The overprotected
sons are pushed to succeed in examinations; a government
study in 1986 showed that 73 percent of Japanese women
wanted their sons to graduate from university, but only 27.7
percent wanted the same for their daughters. In this scenario,
Dr. Narabayashi says, the mother sees sex as a barrier to the
boy's career. She tries to stifle it, lest it interfere with the
boy's studies. "It is just impossible for him to create a joy-
ful relationship with a woman because she has never been
anything but an enemy while he was chasing academic
excellence."

Recent studies reported in the Japanese press indicate that
sexual awareness is increasing among youth, but there is a
large gap between Japanese sexual experience and that of
Western children. The Ministry of Education carefully re-
stricts what can be taught at what grade level, holding off
teaching about contraception until senior high school. Parents say they are fearful of the teaching, but in the absence
of it, comics and magazines, movie posters, and word of

mouth suffice. Evidence of changing mores is found in changing statistics: teenage abortions have almost doubled in a
decade, and venereal disease is rising steadily, though the
numbers are still relatively small.

The new studies show that 7 percent of Japanese children
have had intercourse by age sixteen, compared with as many
as 30 percent of American children and 22 percent of British
children. Japan has the lowest incidence of reported forcible
rape among advanced countries—only 1.4 per 100,000 inhabitants. (The figure for the same year was 37.6 per 100,000
in the United States, 11.3 in England and Wales, 6.8 in
France, and 8.6 in West Germany.) But how much rape is
reported to police is still not certain. Japanese social critics
suggest that the reported figure for Japan is far from accurate, considering the shame connected with the crime.

Longtime foreign observers of Japan often note the change
in public behavior of young people. For generations, mothers
have been making a priority of etiquette. Today you can still
see mothers constantly shoving children's heads down,
teaching them to bow when meeting other people. Girls are
taught particularly polite manners, posture, and general attitude, not to mention a largely subservient language.
Strictly segregated for many years, now boys and girls are
beginning to share more and more experiences in school.
Says a Tokyo junior high school teacher, "The boys and girls
tend to keep themselves separate in the earlier grades, but
by ninth grade, especially those who participate in school
plays, they mix and even touch each other." Touching each
other is the newest behavior. Whereas Japanese manners
used to dictate strict decorum in public, today in urban areas
the old manners are missing. Boys and girls sometimes hold
hands, find themselves more or less at ease with each other,
and, to the dismay of their elders, can be found embracing
in places such as the manicured public areas near the Imperial Palace.

On a Saturday evening in one of the newer, trendier entertainment districts of Tokyo, such as Shibuya, there is a
certain charm about the thousands of boys and girls together

and in their separate groups, dressed expensively, amusing themselves in innocent pursuits. On the last trains out of Shibuya station just after midnight, there is a kind of flirtatious naiveté abroad as these eager, well-dressed youngsters gather, chattering and giggling and making jokes. The lack of sophistication of Japanese youth worries some social critics, who feel they mature too late and lack the experience and poise needed to get along in the modern world. Girls are still expected to live at home after finishing high school or college, and then to marry in their middle to late twenties. The high cost of housing makes it extremely difficult for young women to move away from home. The dormitories large Japanese companies still maintain for single workers is a lure for some of the more adventurous. It is in this setting that many find husbands among their male coworkers.

Geisha, Courtesans, Prostitutes

If adult Japanese men are, as is often charged, immature, frustrated, and impotent, it does not stop them from pursuing sex, or the pleasant associations of sex, in a headlong way. An evening with a geisha can be an extremely costly, aesthetic experience, which may (or may not) have little to do with sex except some gentle teasing. The geisha is not forbidden to have sex, but it is usually under very special— and expensive—circumstances. The less-expensive substitute, the bar hostess, will rub her client's thigh, feed him peanuts and whisky, talk seductively, play finger games, laugh at his jokes, and allow herself to be pawed. She knows he's going to be drunk by 10:30, possibly sooner; he'll stagger off into the night, or into the cab that has been waiting for him for the past half hour. The business of drinking and playing at sex in cabarets and bars with one's colleagues is a way of life in Japan's cities. In Tokyo's upscale Ginza district, Chuo-dori, the central street, is literally blocked at closing time by hundreds of idling taxicabs assigned to pick up tipsy clients and take them home. The uncontracted citizen

who tries to catch a rare empty taxi after about 10:30 or 11
P.M. must signal the driver with his fingers raised to show
what multiples of the metered fare he is willing to pay for
the ride home.

But that cabfare expense is likely to be mere pittance compared with the cost of his enjoyment. Privacy is part of that
cost. The old geisha houses and traditional restaurants of
Japan, such as *Nakamura-ro* in Tokyo's vanished Yoshiwara
district, housed political intrigue as well as pleasure. Exquisite meals, limitless pleasure, and absolute discretion prevailed, secrets of state and of company were scrupulously
kept. (Today many companies have their own bars and night
clubs accessible only to company employees. Bartenders,
waiters, and busboys are also employees, and no secrets leak
to an outsider.)

Also very old is the myth of the geisha. The last of the great
genro, or imperial advisors, Prince Kimmochi Saionji, was
said to have fallen for a spectacular geisha named Tama over
many visits to Nakamura-ro. In his fictionalized 1938 biography of Saionji, subtitled *The Man Who Westernized
Japan*, Bunji Omura describes Tama's seduction of Saionji:

> She came close to Saionji. She sang light, popular songs, then
> classical tunes; her delicate fingers drummed on the tabors,
> one on her shoulder, the other in her lap. Her melodious voice,
> perfect rhythm, enunciation and control enchanted her lis-
> teners and transported them to other scenes. Tama saw that
> Saionji's head was bowed; he was lost in her music. At the
> conclusion of every song, Saionji and Tama drank together.
>
> Saionji awoke with a heavy head and found the star geisha
> lying beside him. . . . He sat up on the mat; the geisha was
> still on her side. Her face clouded. 'I have never rested with
> any man. No matter how drunk I was as part of my enter-
> taining patrons at this house . . .'

Romanticizing the geisha has been more than a cottage industry in Japan, especially the storied top class of courtesan,
called *tayu*. This rank was conferred only on those "most

adept in music, terpsichorean and poetic exercises," as it was once written. *Tayu* literally means person of many arts; the term can refer to a Noh or Kabuki actor as well. The great ukiyo-e artists painted them—indeed these women *were* the "floating world" of the woodblock print. When a *tayu* walked abroad in the daylight to keep a date with a wealthy patron—he had to be wealthy to afford her attentions—she was accompanied by at least one hefty male attendant with a paper parasol to protect her from the sun. Wherever she went with her towering lacquered hairdo, brocaded kimono, and tall wooden clogs, she was also followed by a platoon of attendants.

Today few *tayu* remain, and they are never seen parading in the streets. In Tokyo and in Kyoto's Shimabara district, a few black-lacquered, enclosed *jinrikshas* and their ancient pullers still deliver the ladies to their clients, but the ancient customs are giving way to less traditional behavior. The secluded, muted restaurants on Tokyo's Akasaka district side streets continue to play host to political intrigues and to once forbidden gatherings of World War II veterans, who reminisce and sing old war songs. At most establishments there is little sex involved beyond the comforting presence of comely kimono-clad young women who pour drinks and serve food. Liaisons are, of course, arranged, but discreetly. Nostalgic war gatherings may be mostly sexless, but chilling wartime realities were admitted officially in 1992, when the Japanese government said many thousands of women, mostly Korean, were shipped overseas during the war years as comfort "girls" for the pleasure of the Japanese troops.

Today's establishments of pleasure are called love hotels. They are built to resemble everything from ships to enchanted castles. The well-known Queen Elizabeth sits right along a busy freeway, while the Emperor is perched, crennelated parapets and all, in a residential neighborhood of Tokyo's Meguro district. Love hotels vie for originality: each room is designed in a different motif or dedicated to a different sport. The Emperor has a room simulating a golf green, and most rooms in the elaborate establishments feature mirrors, deep bathtubs, video cameras, revolving, vibrating, and otherwise mobile beds. The client, however, is expected to bring his own partner, as prostitution is illegal. In actuality, many of the clients of Japan's love hotels are husbands and wives who find their own homes so small and so crowded with family that they cannot have the privacy they crave. There are drive-in love hotels for the true privacy seekers, where the fees and all necessary exchanges are handled automatically, where even the car is left in a closed garage during the rental of the room.

But in the seventeenth century, wealthy samurai found splendor at Sumiya, one of Kyoto's more famous bordellos: fifteen rooms of varying size, each decorated differently. The Blue Shell Room was decorated with exotic seashells inlaid everywhere. A damask room had all the appointments covered in rarely seen damasked cloth; another room was patterned with folding fans. There were peacocks painted by an exceptional artist on the walls of the peacock room, plum blossoms for the plum room. It was enough to turn a swordsman into a poet. Swords had to be deposited in a special chest before entering, just as American gunslingers had to check their guns at the door of similar establishments in the Wild West. Sumiya's patrons were the provincial feudal lords on their way to and from their alternate year's compulsory residency in Edo.

Despite male domination and intense interest in sex, in one survey as many as a quarter of the men who were in the managerial class admitted they experienced impotence. Forty percent of them ascribed it to the stress of work. It is certainly no compliment to Japan's warrior tradition that 33 percent of the women respondents said they were not aroused by their men but merely "quietly put up with it." The joke in Japan that sex stops after the second child reflects a traditional scenario in which men tend to find their companionship and sexual fulfillment outside the home, leaving the wife to have her own life, raising the children and managing the family finances. But recent studies reveal that housewives, long thought to be uninterested in sex after marriage, do indulge in extramarital affairs.

For a time in the 1980s thousands of Japanese men fanned out across Asia, to Korea, the Philippines, Thailand, and elsewhere, where the sole object was to drink and have sex. So blatant were some of these tours that in Korea, for example, the men would be bussed from the airport to a hotel where the women could be seen lined up in the lobby, waiting with room keys in their hands. Many excursions were labeled golfing tours, and often the men would arrive at the airport with golf bags that were never opened as the men caroused through several days of drinking and fornicating. The hotel in Seoul was next to a police station, where it is said disgusted police finally prevailed on the proprietor to keep the women out of public view. Complaints from citizens and church groups brought a halt to the more overt aspects of the situation in Korea. In Thailand and the Philippines, church and citizens groups rose up and picketed the Japanese embassy. So much pressure was placed on the activity that the Japanese government itself clamped down on the tour operators.

One day I asked my friend Yuki Ishikawa about Japanese travelers. "How many of these millions of men who go abroad each year expect to have sex with foreign women?" I asked. Yuki looked at me indulgently: "Why, all of them, of course."

CHAPTER SEVEN

GOOD WIVES, WISE MOTHERS

The woman came peddling a child's bicycle down the steep roadway toward Tokyo's bustling Azabu Juban, a narrow street lined with shops, her knees pumping furiously, her hair flying. As she turned I saw her fall, her knees scraping the rough asphalt. Despite the accident she immediately got back on the tiny bike and continued her frantic peddling.

As I came to the corner I saw she was racing for a big yellow school bus. A group of second- or third-grade boys were boarding, and each mother bid her son goodbye with a smile and a bow. The woman on the bicycle arrived just in time, panting and grinning with embarrassment and bowing hurriedly to the other mothers. The last boy was anxiously waiting for his mother, the woman on the bicycle. He had forgotten his hat, and she fitted it on his head as he climbed aboard the bus. The mother smiled to no one as she limped past me on her way home pushing the child's bike, still breathing hard.

The woman in Azabu was doing what Japanese society expected of her, and she of herself. The boy could not go to school without the hat; he might be taunted. Worse, his mother might be insulted, a dreadful challenge to a young Japanese boy. Such a display of motherly sacrifice it is still considered proper for a Japanese mother.

The traditional Japanese mother makes a career of guiding her children through the intensely competitive arcana of Japanese education. In doing so she is more than a homework nag, she is the prototype *kyoiku mama* or "education mother." She becomes directly involved in and identified with the child's success or failure. At many of Japan's music schools the mother must accompany the child during the lesson, not only bringing her into the picture but making her a responsible party. If the child has not progressed satisfactorily, the mother shares the shame, and of course she also basks in the glow of childhood success. Sometimes the involvement is even more direct: as many as 23,000 Japanese housewives hold daily after-school study sessions for neighborhood children in a system devised by teacher Toru Kumon. They want to increase the children's skills outside the professional cram system of after-school schools. Some Japanese children are enrolled in more than one after-school study program.

The Japanese home is very often ordered around the activities and needs of the children and their school work. The father, more often than not, commutes long distances, is often expected to go out drinking with the boys after work and is only seen by his children on weekends and holidays. Although Japanese mothers may be the hardest working in the industrialized world, life is easing up. Today, several households in Japan have the usual trophies of modern advanced civilization: 65 percent have air conditioners, and 22 percent have pianos, a popular instrument and a sign of culture. There are 197 color television sets in every 100 homes, 104 automobiles for every 100 homes.

The conventional Japanese housewife maintains the finances, doling out an allowance to her husband who brings home his pay envelope dutifully untouched. She normally gives him a modest allowance for his lunches—his evenings out with the boys are usually company financed. (An obedient, hard-working friend once confided to me that to have his own money he lied to his wife about the amount of his semiannual bonus, which was paid in cash.) She also diverts herself in her spare time with education for herself—lessons in cooking, economics, decorating. Some even manage to pursue extramarital liaisons, as the weekly press likes to detail.

The picture postcard vision of the deferential, submissive, long-suffering Japanese woman is deceptive. Visitors to Japan, especially men, are often charmed by the subservience and delicacy of the women they meet. Many women still conform to the stereotype, masking a girlish giggle behind a manicured hand, bowing lower than human anatomy would seem to permit, eating after everybody else has been served, speaking in a defenseless, squeaky tone with eyes averted, or whispering acquiescence almost inaudibly.

The image is misleading. Generations of adversity and discrimination have created resourceful women who make most families' major spending decisions, push their children ahead to success, and invest in the family's future. In ages past some of them fought beside their warrior husbands, and until 1643, with the death of Empress Meisho, female emperors were not uncommon. As recent figures show, when women are unhappy with the way their married life is going, they are not averse to divorce. Although Japan's divorce rate is still low (about 1.29 per thousand marriages, compared with 4.80 in the United States, 2.81 in Great Britain, and 1.95 in France), single-parent families, primarily led by women, are on the increase. Under such circumstances the question arises, What is to become of the children and their education?

In Japan's feudal period, ordinary women were officially relegated to a life of servitude. But in the late nineteenth century, when Japan opened to the world, the mission of women broadened. The nation's intellectuals argued that women had new obligations: to bring Japan into the modern era, to play a role in educating the children, and to help mold the modern Japanese man.

Under the Occupation, there was no compulsory education for women beyond sixth grade until 1947. All schooling above the elementary level was segregated by sex. Education for women consisted largely of preparation for motherhood and a study of the accepted arts and occupations. In 1930 only 13 percent of eligible young women went on to secondary education. The Ministry of Education established Tokyo Girls' school in 1872, and it was not until 1900 that Tokyo Women's Medical School was founded. Thirteen years later, the Department of Science of Tohoku Imperial University became the first Imperial university to admit women.

Despite the lack of educational facilities and their restricted nature at the time, Meiji era intelligensia expected their wives to hold their own in polite conversation, even with foreigners. "Ah, the duties of women are so difficult and their responsibilities so heavy!" lamented scholar Mori Arinori in 1874. In the years leading up to World War II, Japanese women were extolled as vessels of virtue—especially those who gave birth to sons. During the war, their labor was crucial in forging the arms and maintaining the farms and factories at home. Women and children were pressed into service, making everything from bombers to blankets. For many children there was no schooling, only work, for able-bodied men were overseas fighting the war. The women persevered. The wife of a senior Japanese industrial executive recalls her wartime work making wooden wing ribs for bombers. Her duties have made her fluent with tools: "I can do all the plumbing around the house," she declares, though she is wealthy now and doesn't have to.

In postwar Japan, women's labor was a crutch to be leaned on. It was not until recovery that Japanese women could consolidate their position and begin to demand recognition of their rights. The Occupation forces abolished licensed prostitution, did away with polygamy, and introduced women's suffrage. In the first postwar general election for seats in the House of Representatives, thirty-nine of seventy-nine women candidates won. The voter turnout was 67 percent for women, 78 percent for men. One newspaper columnist suggested that the women would have come to the polls in greater numbers had they been able to believe suffrage was really happening. The next year, in the first election for members of the upper house of parliament, half the women candidates won. In elections for local assemblies throughout Japan, 789 women took seats.

Images, Realities

It remains true that the role of older women in today's Japan is still rooted in the Confucian tradition of service and obedience to father, husband, and firstborn male. The expression "Good Wife, Wise Mother, for good or ill" remains in the minds of most adult Japanese. Despite considerable change in the thinking of young Japanese women and their moderately progressive young husbands, Japanese women have made little progress so far toward the liberation and equal rights the national constitution grants them.

The constitution says, "All of the people are equal under the law and there shall be no discrimination in political, economic or social relations because of race, creed, sex, social status or family origin." Subsequent labor law ruled that there must be equal pay for equal work. "But what good is a law that grants equal pay for equal work when a woman can't get equal work?" asks a progressive female legislator. That was a few years ago, but even now, despite the passing of a law requiring equal opportunity in employment, women are skeptical that much will change without continued pressure. The law was passed, cynics say, only because Japan has participated in the United Nations' Decade for Women. At the event's conclusion in 1985, Japan had to pass some kind of statute doing away with discrimination against women to sign the treaty. But the law carries no prescribed penalties for violators. At the same time, some see the new law, which does away with preferential treatment of women, as a setback; for example, menstrual leave is abolished, as is the prohibition against late hours of work. In any case, the law does establish some sense of direction. Companies are periodically queried as to their hiring and training practices, and although there arc no penalties involved, the companies certainly do not wish to antagonize government officials, on whom they must often depend.

Like women in the West, Japanese women still feel the pull of domestic responsibility, despite work-filled days. Unaccustomed to liberation, those women successfully manage to blend the obligations of parenthood, housekeeping, and observing the complicated rituals of holiday observances. But the action of some is opening wider fields for the many. It has been noted how farmers are finding it difficult to attract young women to the drudgery and the physical stress of the agricultural life. The same female reluctance is being discovered by marriageable age men who inherit family shops normally run by women, and by men who have elderly parents to care for.

The entry of Asian women into Japan to marry these men raises a moral issue among Japan's liberated women, who tend to see the marriages as exploitation. But traditionalists such as Shigehiki Toyama, a professor at the esteemed Ochanomizu Women's University in Tokyo, reacts to the situation by saying, "farmers take foreign brides because Japanese women are afraid to do a real day's work. The mothers of today's dainty debutantes, a generation whose diligence and dedication helped create Japan's affluence, should teach their daughters the value of honest labor." A matchmaker of Professor Toyama's acquaintance confided that it is extremely difficult to find a bride for an eldest son whose parents own a small but prosperous store. "A family business just isn't chic," he explained. "Many women now have college degrees. They don't want to spend their lives tending shop and they cringe at the thought of serving customers." If current female taste in husbands are any indication, according to Professor Toyama, writing in a Tokyo newspaper, "the family enterprise seems headed the way of the family farm."

So too is motherhood in decline. It is ironic but not surprising, considering the shrinking birth rate, that birth control today is officially frowned on in Japan. Use of the birth control pill is still strictly controlled by physicians, who are reluctant to prescribe it except for regulating menstruation, the only use the Ministry of Health considers safe. Condoms, sold door to door by housewives—many women are embarrassed to purchase them in public—are the most common method of birth control. But abortion, an estimated 1 million a year, has become the defacto means of birth control for large numbers of Japanese women.

This does not mean abortion takes place without a rearward glance. Quite the contrary—at temples and shrines in Japan women atone for abortion and pray for the repose of the lost souls by attending religious services, frequently decorating small statues in a separate part set aside for such children. In some religious sects the mother who has aborted, or who has lost a child by stillbirth or miscarriage, carries with her for a time a small wooden tablet inscribed with the child's name. The custom is widespread. Tablets left behind at shrines and temples, written by mothers of aborted babies, tell of their anguish. It seems only natural in the context of Japan's Shinto religion, where all objects are imbued with a purpose, where there is even a service of thanks and good wishes for broken sewing needles.

A low birth rate, along with the relaxation of societal pressure to have many babies early in life, has enabled more women to postpone marriage until their thirties. By 1990 the population rate had sunk to 1.57 children per family—numbers that spell a disastrous decline in Japan's population and an increase in the percentage of aged people who must be supported by the younger generations. One government official, Finance Minister Ryutaro Hashimoto, on hearing the news of the low birth rate in a cabinet meeting, ruefully told the press that it was a direct result of higher education for women, who were distracted from their rightful roles in the home. The reaction among politically and socially active women was immediate and vocal. Hashimoto's comments even drew adverse editorial comment from some of the nation's conservative press.

The new birthrate is the lowest since 1899, when the government began keeping count. But the new information was certainly no revelation. The birth rate has been dropping for twenty years. The trend was widely noted in 1979, when the birth rate was reported at 1.77 by the Statistics and Information Department of the Ministry of Health and Welfare. Ministry officials say that the population of the nation cannot remain constant, let alone grow, without a figure of at least 2.1 children per family. Women do not seem to be concerned enough to wish to reverse the trend. In 1988 a new national holiday, "Conjugal Day," was proposed, a day on which husbands and wives could do something about the falling birth rate. The idea failed from the start.

Author and commentator Atsuko Fujitani pointed out a decade ago that "until now predictions of the future have been based on male ideas and viewpoints. Such factors as the changing situation of women have been ignored, for these visions of the future have been constructed in minds that believed beyond any doubt that the role of the woman is to bear children and keep the home fires burning." Those who cared to investigate have known for a long time that Japanese women had many interests and that working and earning money was high on the list. The evidence seems to show that education does indeed open women's eyes to new possibilities beyond, if not exclusive of, the home. A survey of university women made by Ms. Fujitani's Women's Studies Society of Japan showed that of those Japanese women holding jobs, 96.7 percent wanted to continue, while 82.5 percent of those who weren't working said they wanted to find work. Seventy-five percent said they wanted their husbands to help with the housework, a wish that statistically bears little hope. A 1990 Labor Ministry report of a survey of working couples reveals that working wives spend three hours and thirty-one minutes a day doing housework. The husbands devote an average of eight minutes.

Politics, Scandal, Sumo

Women now represent two-fifths of the Japanese work-force, earning about 70 percent the pay of the average man in a similar job. It's not a properly recognized role in Japanese society, says Sociologist Yoriko Meguro of Sophia University. As she sees it, women are being used as "convenient tools." Despite the considerable strides that have been made, "women are still not full members of the society because they are not in the circle of decision-makers."A survey of 1000 companies by the British journal *The Economist* revealed that no more than 150 of them had any women at the level of section chief, and less than twenty had any women above that level.

Yet in business and politics, Japanese women are beginning to make their first widely noticed marks. "Full-time housewives are a rarity today," says Mayumi Moriyama, a former member of parliament and labor vice minister, who served as chief cabinet secretary in the government of Toshiki Kaifu. In politics she says, "the number of women who stand for public office is small, but they are writing a clear message."

Only a few years ago, in the House of Representatives, less than 2 percent were women. In the upper house (the less powerful of the two), the House of Councillors, women held only 7 to 8 percent of the seats. But by 1990, women held 2.3 percent of the lower house and 13 percent of the seats in the upper house. The upper house roster is sprinkled with the names of famous novelists, television and film personalities, former athletes, and other social notables who are known throughout the country and run for national office rather than for office in their home district. The electorate seems to bestow membership as a kind of gift upon celebrities who want to run for the office, though few are practiced in politics. The seats are considered harmless by serious politicians since the main work of governing takes place in the lower house. But it is a step to power for women because it gives them visibility and enables them to raise issues that might not otherwise get any attention. Furthermore, when the ruling party lost its majority in the upper house after more than three decades in power, every vote, including the women's, was important and needed to be courted for the approval of legislation.

Moriyama, who has spent her professional life in the nitty-gritty of politics and the lower house, was one of two women appointed to the cabinet of Prime Minister Toshiki Kaifu after money and sex scandals shook the political establishment. Newspapers editorialized about corruption, and change was in order. Activists and reformists spoke boldly about the sex scandals, and women's groups took up the cudgel and campaigned against the ruling party's new consumer tax, which for the first time taxed foodstuffs. The party took a drubbing in the election, but managed to survive with a slim majority.

In deference to the women's activism, after an election in which more women ran than ever—143 candidates—Kaifu named Moriyama to replace chief cabinet secretary Tokuo Yamashita, who resigned after the revelation of his involvement in a scandal. But after handily winning the next election, Kaifu named a new cabinet with no female members, dropping Moriyama and another woman he had appointed. Moriyama was unhappy. But looking back on it, she said, "To be honest, I was surprised by my sudden and unexpected elevation." She knew she had been appointed primarily to stop the hemorrhaging of public confidence in the Liberal Democratic Party, especially among women. Some time after she was dropped from Kaifu's second cabinet she said in Los Angeles, "We took two steps forward yesterday. We have taken one step backward today. Kaifu used two women in his cabinet as a token of respect for women's votes. It is a fresh sign of change. . . ."

The brief political success of Takako Doi of the Japan Socialist Party in becoming the first woman to lead any political party even impressed rival political candidates. For a time the Japanese were ahead of both major American political parties in this respect. Female politicians give Doi good marks for what she accomplished in capturing the leadership of the party. Knowing that the party was in a shambles and was losing membership, Ms. Doi came along and faced the difficult time.

In candid moments, the conservative Moriyama says she would like to make some of the changes in her party that Doi tried to accomplish in her party. In particular she would like to amend old attitudes and revamp the party platform and its entrenched structure. The platform calls for disarming Japan and abandoning the nation's security treaty with the United States. These are not widely popular views in Japan and keep the socialists from gaining strength. After five years as the party's leader, Doi found she could not turn the party from its traditional path: when the great gains made in the election of 1989 were lost in 1991, Doi, a former professor of constitutional law, admitted defeat and resigned.

"There is a remarkable upsurge of women's interest in politics," says Moriyama. "Unfortunately, the male majority seems not to be aware of the change that is taking place." Women continue to win political contests for seats in local and prefectural assemblies—13 percent of the seats in Tokyo's Metropolitan Assembly are held by women. In the election of 1989 after which Moriyama got her job, 17 percent of the women who ran for contested seats won.

It was Moriyama's lot to dramatize the fact that some institutions of Japan are not yet ready to accept women in traditionally male roles. She made headlines when, as chief cabinet secretary, she attempted to do what her male predecessors had done: present the Prime Minister's Cup to the winner of the Grand Sumo tournament in Tokyo. Sumo, an ancient Shinto-influenced sport, takes place on a consecrated mound of hard-packed clay, the *dohyo*. The combat surface is strewn with purification salt by the giant wrestlers, clad only in colorful loincloths, as they prepare for each short bout. The sport has many women fans, and in fact the giant, pot-bellied wrestlers are popular sex symbols and celebrities.

When Moriyama announced that she intended to fulfill her

duty as chief cabinet secretary by presenting the trophy, the all-male Sumo Association was scandalized. The purists of the sumo world had always kept women off the *dohyo*, and they didn't intend to change tradition. Moriyama withdrew her request in the face of pressure from within her own party, later explaining that what she was after was change, not a fight. "In this country," she told reporters, "it is not clever to push as hard as possible if you really want to have a good effect." Perhaps the "good effect" was to show the hidebound nature and intransigence of the establishment, both in wrestling and politics, over the incident.

In some equally unenlightened but less organized places, battles are being won. For example, the first cases of sexual harrassment in the workplace, translated into Japanese phonetic pidgin as *sekushuaru harasumento, seku-hara* for short, are now being played out, and they are shocking men, who have long been accustomed to dealing with subservient women. When the Tokyo Bar Association announced a telephone line for victims of sexual abuse at work, 138 women called in within the first six hours. Most were from women who had been pressured for sexual favors by their bosses, and one in five had lost their jobs after rejecting the overtures. An insurance agent reported a common attitude among many clients is that "in the insurance business a saleswoman goes to bed with a prospective client to get a new policy."

A study found that half the seventy-one respondents had been fired for rejecting bids for sex by their superiors. One boss, rebuffed in his advances, is accused of pasting pictures of the woman's face on pages from pornographic magazines and then posting them around the office. The nation's first widely noted sexual harrassment lawsuit was filed only in August 1989, by a thirty-two-year-old editor against her boss and his publishing company, charging that he had spread rumors that she had been promiscuous. To the surprise of many, a ten-year-old suit against a government agency by ten women for sexual discrimination in promotions finally ended in mid-1990, with a $640,000 award for the women.

Says Moriyama on *seku-hara*, "I would advise Japanese businessmen to learn what the term means." The times are changing, she says, and she sees it even in her own family. "The husband of my daughter cooks at home. That was not possible in my time. Today's young parents are more enlightened than my parents were." Even so, tradition has its say. A young graduate of an American university working in a Japanese architectural firm was shocked to find that women graduate architects were expected to make the tea and did it without complaint. In the Japanese Self Defense Forces women are finally to be admitted to the academy; the services do recruit women and women do parade in their own units, but they are still primarily military office personnel. During recent maneuvers on the rolling plains at the foot of Mount Fuji, I noted that a female private in olive drab delivered the tea to officers at the command post.

Fighting Words

The first woman to be named editor of the prestigious *Asahi Journal*, a periodical once published by the national newspaper *Asahi Shimbun*, Mitsuko Shimomura, says the demand for change is real but the nation's business leaders and politicians are still not yet convinced of it.

"They don't understand women," Shimomura says. "They tell us we have created this economic giant, but so what? We don't want to have a big GNP, we want to have a better quality of life. The women want their husbands back home. They want to share their life together. They don't want more and more money." Shimomura says the movement has been a long time in coming: "There is an underground, quiet movement that has been going on among Japanese women for a long time; women's consciousness has been dramatically changed.

"But the way we change, the way we do our movement is different from the way American women did it." There is much less confrontation, fewer mass meetings, rallies, and overt challenges. Lecturing around the country before she took over the editorship, Shimomura found groups of women seeking ideas that will point them toward a more fulfilling life. "They are ready," says Shimomura. "The younger generation of women, up to about forty, married women, some working, some part-time workers, they ask all the questions on how to educate their daughters in breaking traditional ways. They want to make sure they know how to handle their husbands and solve their problems when they are working. The men never seem to realize what is happening." The wife of a Japanese bank manager graphically described her life with her inattentive husband a few years ago to Japanese journalist Shigeo Saito. She said: "My husband and I seem to be riding a pair of separate escalators."

One reflection of the unattentiveness of Japanese men to the changes taking place is found in the newspaper headlines. Writers seem to have only two ways to refer to women— either as OL, for office lady, or *shufu* (housewife). Says Shimomura: "The *shufu* is now in the minority, just sitting home and cooking and cleaning."

The term "OL" refers to the young woman who works only to earn money and who expects to find a husband and get married and quit work. Career women, ambitious women, now entering the work force do not fit the tight old mold. Says Shimomura, "Even young women feel they are career women now. But *shufu* can also feel the same thing; some *shufu* are even doing volunteer work or going to the cultural center to study or going back to school. Some housewives are in between tradition and the new culture. You can't put these women in a box, or in an old headline."

Politicians meanwhile, according to Shimomura, "don't understand any better than the headline writers. And unless and until they do, the political parties that don't will continue to decline." Women, after all, outnumber men among registered voters in Japan, and traditionally a greater percentage of women vote than men.

New Careers, Old Slogans

Japanese women have made steady career progress in traditional service industry specialties such as design, public relations, and retailing. The industrial companies still need an influx of young women workers and returning housewives to keep the assembly lines running, and now college educated women are finally being accepted in elevated positions such as money traders and banking specialists. But in the nation's most prestigious companies the doors to the executive suite and the board room are still closed. Entrepreneurial women, on the other hand, are attempting to build their own firms.

Foreign firms in Japan, with the exception of IBM and one or two other giant venture firms, find it hard to attract the best male graduates of Japanese universities. But as Jackson Huddleston points out in his book *Gaijin Kaisha:*

> Japanese parents are now often willing to let their daughters work in foreign corporations as an internationalization experience, a chance to use the English they have studied for so many years and to work prior to getting married and settling down to raise a family. It is particularly attractive to girls from upper middle-class and wealthy backgrounds.

Huddleston quotes a foreign employer as saying, "The women are absolutely outstanding. We are using them as chemists and in research and are beginning to break through some barriers. Two are now in management. We are bringing them in slowly but surely."

But even in foreign firms that have found Japanese women to be effective in executive jobs, sooner or later a rising young Japanese woman is likely to have to deal with her counterpart, the Japanese male executive. Few companies are willing to gamble away business opportunities by using women in all situations, as they use their men. Women argue that too much Japanese business is transacted on golf courses (where traditionally only the caddies are women) and in hostess bars. Many progressive Japanese agree. But the system is not changing rapidly, and so generally speaking, even the

Japanese women who move up in foreign companies bump against the familiar glass ceiling.

Huddleston, who as a banker introduced the American Express credit card in Japan, says he has found that some women will stay on for careers in foreign firms, and "despite protestation on the part of Japanese men, they can also be effective in interacting with clients outside the office." Entertaining clients has been exquisitely refined as a way of life in Japan. The Japanese tax office reports the nation's businessmen spent $37 billion dollars on entertainment in 1990, more than the nation spent on defense, about $29 billion. In today's tougher economic times, these traditionally bloated sums are being deflated.

The image of women as hosts to Japanese customers is in its infancy. Some thirty prestigious golf clubs in the country do not accept women players, and although Japan has produced some world-class women golfers, the idea of an afternoon of golf with a woman is not yet a concept that appeals to many male clients. A round of golf in Japan is generally a daylong event because the courses are so remote from the population centers, and the idea of a Japanese businessman spending an entire day in the company of a woman is daunting (perhaps to his wife as well). Nonetheless, foreign women have made the breakthrough in dealing with Japanese clients, and progressive women think they will become more and more successful. Government ministries are recruiting women, and political parties are getting used to the idea of women in positions of power. But the likely change will come in increased numbers of women dealing with men and increased numbers of men becoming more comfortable with the idea. An eventual decrease or elimination of the tax deductibility of sporting events and drinking marathons could help stimulate change.

There are those who feel change will come sooner than the panjandrums of Japanese business realize. After all, female business acumen is an accepted fact in Japan, where the laws have until now protected the small, family-owned but female-run stores that pepper the nation. Anybody dealing with a female Japanese proprietor knows how shrewd a bargain she can drive. The enthusiasm, however, of younger Japanese women to take over the store is dwindling as opportunity for more interesting work, and the benefits that go with it, presents itself. Along with new experience comes new knowledge: as women make progress in the larger business world, they are finding that the place is not as wonderful as it is cracked up to be, and its denizens not the wizards they have painted themselves to be.

An anonymous woman recently bared her soul in the letters column of the newspaper, *Asahi Shimbun*. The twenty-eight-year-old Osaka resident confessed that she thought she was getting a superb spouse when she married her husband, graduate of a prestigious university and an employee of a major corporation. But she is unhappy, because her husband has been groomed for success from childhood and nothing has deterred him; he has never experienced a setback, and so he lacks compassion for people less fortunate or lucky than himself. He thinks everybody else is a fool, and any comments from his wife are greeted with an automatic, "You don't know what you're talking about, dummy."

Author Seiko Tanabe, born in 1928, wrote recently that "women of my day were taught to defer to masculine pride and authority. Thus I was all the more disappointed to discover the truth: the giants were actually pigmies." In an article in the intellectual monthly *Chuo Koron*, she recalled a conversation with the vice president of a large corporation:

> I expected a man in his position to be urbane, interesting, a raconteur. What a shock when his entire conversation consisted of bragging about his alma mater. His equally brilliant son, he pointedly added, had also attended the same school. The preening arrogance of this corporate peacock! I thought to myself, 'If a dope like this can make it to the boardroom, you would have to be brain dead to fail in business.'

Tanabe sees chilling implications beyond the realm of business:

In 1945, the average citizen blamed the disaster on the Army, Navy and the Tokyo Imperial University, whose graduates entered government service and planned and led the war. The masses still resent the prewar best and brightest who brought the nation to ruin. But women retained their illusions about men. They worked hard alongside their husbands to rebuild society, helping to achieve Japan's phenomenal postwar recovery. Today, our faith in men has been strained to the breaking point. Many women have given up on finding personal fulfillment in the marital relationship. The pampered, emotional eunuchs they have for mates don't even realize the marriage is collapsing. When the inevitable blowup occurs, the perplexed husband will wonder, 'What's got into her?'

Strong talk from a member of the graying generation. But her comments are echoed by those who have been decrying the stolidity of Japan's male politicians. Even Mayumi Moriyama, a team player if there ever was one, is sounding the alarm. She says that the nation's ruling political party, her party, has implemented a wide range of farsighted social policies, "but now, having failed to grasp the consequences of these innovations, the party is the victim of its own success." It is no surprise to realize that the nation's leaders move toward change only when they are forced by the weight of foreign or internal pressure to do so, and that very few political spirits are lifted by change. Says Moriyama, "The male-dominated LDP's perception of women has changed little over the past three decades. The enlightened legislation [the party has passed] was intended to secure female votes, not to raise women's status."

Recalling the diet debate on an equal employment opportunity bill in the mid-eighties, Moriyama, then chief cabinet secretary, says, "I secretly worried whether the Cabinet understood women's issues well enough to handle the opposition's questions." To her relief, both the prime minister and the labor minister "spoke knowledgeably and persuasively, emphasizing women's increasingly important role in the labor force and the need to eradicate discrimination in the workplace."

A diet member asked the prime minister to state his personal view of womanhood. Moriyama, among others, was holding her breath. On an earlier occasion Nakasone had infuriated more women than he amused by saying that when he is on the campaign trail, women remember the color of his neckties but not the content of his speeches. And his agricultural minister, Hisao Horinouchi, shrugged during a campaign speech and rhetorically asked his audience whether women really had what it takes to be in politics.

Nakasone answered the question as most of the skeptics among his female constituents expected him to. "Women," he said, "should be good wives and good mothers."

CHAPTER EIGHT

GANGS, GANGSTERS, SHORT FINGERS

On a spring afternoon two small schoolgirls were playing in a tiny park near downtown Tokyo when the car stopped nearby, virtually blocking the street with its sheer bulk. It was an American-built limousine, a long and wide Cadillac, with reflective black windows screening the passengers from public gaze, the kind of car that attracts attention in Japan for its presumed ownership. A gangster's car. To the chagrin of Detroit, the biggest Cadillacs and Lincolns have for years been the flashy vehicles of choice for the nation's swaggering gangs of *yakuza* extortionists, gamblers, smugglers, and all-around bad guys. The bigger and more conspicuous the better.

Law-abiding citizens call the *yakuza* wastrels, hoodlums, rascals, or good-for-nothings. *Yakuza* see their groups as clans, families, brotherhoods, and their individual selves as descendents of the masterless samurai who roamed Japan in a romanticized bygone era doing good, fighting evil and official corruption, protecting the lowly and dispossessed. In actuality, many of those unemployed and wandering swordsmen were hungry freebooters and extortionists, which perhaps makes the analogy more apt than most of Japan's modern hoodlums realize.

No romantic notions seemed to attend the small group that arrived in that little park in the Azabu section of Tokyo. While the limo remained parked at the curb, three men in dark pin-striped suits got out and walked hurriedly to the smelly cement block public toilet a few meters from the curb. The children saw the men emerge minutes later, the short man in the middle with a cloth wrapped around his hand, holding his right forearm with his left hand, sweat on his brow, a grimace on his face. All three reentered the car, and it moved away slowly, threading its way through the narrow street toward the nearby expressway. "We could see the blood," one child later reported at our dinner table with a shiver.

The children missed the gory part but they had seen the gangsters in an act of *yubitsume*, finger cutting, in which an errant gang member atones for a transgression against his *oyabun*, or "boss," by sacrificing the end joint of his little finger. It is an old ritual, and in some gangs it is also practiced as a sign certifying the member's submission. Japanese police say as many as 40 percent of the members of some gangs are thus mutilated. For those so permanently marked, the mutilation is something to be proud of. The full-body tattoo, that painful-to-acquire human tapestry, is another proud and powerful symbol of commitment to an unconventional life. Tattooed men vie with each other for the artistry of their enveloping designs—cranes, dragons, and rising suns rather than anything so mundane as arrowed hearts, a flower-bordered "Mother" or slogans such as "Born to Die."

The practice of *yubitsume* is said to go back to the feudal era, when it was a truly effective and yet only slightly disfiguring punishment. The loss of the little finger joint made it more difficult to wield a sword, and therefore the sacrifice was literally disarming. Now the sight of an otherwise ordinary gent reading a paper on the subway, with one or more fingers shortened, elicits a measure of trepidation, awe, or just plain curiosity from other passengers. Some Japanese gang leaders, who periodically hold press conferences, have said they want to do away with this old custom, but such customs die hard. There is a story, perhaps apocryphal, that an enlightened gang leader chastised one of his old lieutenants for forcing one of his subordinates to commit the act; full of remorse, the lieutenant only knew one way to perform a penance: he chopped another joint off his own finger.

The gangs of Japan, sometimes called *boryoku-dan*, or "violence groups," are something akin to the Mafia in the United States. But they are much more visible to the public and police than American mobs have been since the 1930s. Japanese gangsters flaunt their flashy trademarks, caricaturizing themselves. They make a mockery of the widespread notion that little crime exists in Japan.

On the contrary, there is a lot of crime in Japan and it is growing. But except for the *yakuza*, and bloody crimes of passion and madness, very little of it is seen to be violent. Ordinary citizens are aware of establishments assumed to be run by the mob—not just sex clubs and striptease parlors, but money-lending companies, restaurants, bars and nightclubs, and even construction companies. The *sokaiya*, mob people who disrupt the annual shareholder meetings of companies that refuse to pay for their silence, get considerable newspaper coverage when they harrass a meeting. When American corporate raider T. Boone Pickens made his failed bid to get a seat on the board of directors of the Koito company, *sokaiya* disrupted the meeting with heckling and shouted epithets at Pickens: "Remember Pearl Harbor!" "Go back to America! Yankee go home!" "Japan has already defeated America in the economic war!" "Go away, you dirty pig!" Pickens gave up his quest not because of mob harrassment, but the unpleasantness made the decision easier.

Recently more than a thousand Japanese companies agreed to hold their annual meetings on the same day, hoping to thwart the gangs and their disrupters, *sokaiya*, by sheer numbers. The companies met with only moderate success and have not broken the gangs' grip. So common is the practice of disrupting meetings that the *sokaiya* have made it into the lexicon. Editors of modern Japanese-English dictionaries feel it proper to define the term *sokaiya* as "a person who holds a small number of shares of stock in a number of companies and attempts to extort money from them by threatening to cause trouble at the general meeting of the stockholders."

It has been a tradition for companies to pay a fee to *sokaiya*, who then attend the meeting and, acting like company employees, stifle any dissenting voices by intimidation. Companies that refused to pay saw their annual meetings drag out with long-winded complaints, embarrassing innuendo about the private life and peccadilloes of company executives, arguments, even fisticuffs among shareholders, all of which is likely to be reported to the local press. Pickens is convinced that the *sokaiya* who harrassed him in the Koito meeting were hired by persons within the corporation who were vocal in their disapproval of Pickens' presence on the board. It is a common tactic, called "company work."

Sporadic murderous clashes take place between rival gangs over turf and the lucrative gambling, prostitution, extortion, smuggling, and the manufactured illegal drug trade. *Yakuza* activities are being more widely noticed in Japan in the past few years because they have become so blatant. Some emissaries of Japan's biggest gang were arrested in Hawaii attempting to refit themselves with a fresh arsenal after a breakaway segment of the gang took most of the gang's firearms.

Guns and Gang Wars

Doing "company work" is only one of the more visible aspects of gangland activity. Sometimes it's just plain murder. Elements of the nation's largest gang syndicate, the storied 22,000-member *Yamaguchi-gumi* of western Japan, were locked in a struggle for territory with twelve gangs affiliated with the upstart *Hatani-gumi*, and a *Yamaguchi-gumi* foot soldier was murdered. At that point, the police knew there was a lot of trouble ahead.

The word *gumi* can mean association, company, club, or gang; even respectable construction companies traditionally use the word. *Yamaguchi-gumi* was founded by a tough organizer of Kobe dock labor, Noboru Yamaguchi, before World War II. He died of natural causes in 1946, an unusually placid departure for a Japanese godfather. Yamaguchi's favored lieutenant, a burly young thug named Kazuo Taoka, took over the gang as its new *oyabun*. Taoka had endeared himself to Yamaguchi in 1937 by killing, with one stroke of a sword, a rival on the docks who annoyed Yamaguchi. Taoka, nicknamed "The Bear," went to jail for the murder and thus sat out the war behind bars. In a rare interview in 1973 Taoka insisted that his organization was "a friendship and mutual assistance society," a relief organization designed to rehabilitate what he called "social misfits and dropouts." He said that if the government were willing to take care of these needy people, he would gladly disband his benevolent association.

It is true that the gangs give jobs to outcasts and minority members of Japan's society, such as some among the *burakumin*, or "village people," who are shunned because of their historically unclean occupations (cattle and horse slaughtering and leatherworking, for example) and the Japanese-born Koreans who are rarely, if ever, employed in responsible positions by major Japanese companies. They are also good to some old folks and widows, especially those of good *yakuza* foot soldiers. A motley assortment of hoodlums, thugs and ne'er-do-wells find access to money, position, and protection in the gangs. Allied with right-wing politicians, Japan's gang leaders traditionally did the bidding of rightist leaders before the war and reemerged during the Occupation. The leadership of the gangs managed to stay just on the cusp of the law, and their connections protected them from police interference so long as they didn't step too far over. Although he was shot at more than once and seriously wounded, Taoka survived until 1981, when he died in a Kobe hospital of cardiac insufficiency. In the local papers, the benign manner of his death was frequently compared to the similar peaceful demise of Al Capone.

Japan has strict gun laws; generally speaking, only the cops and the crooks have guns. But recently guns have become something of an obsession. The crooks smuggle them in by sea from Thailand and the Philippines through the myriad ports of the Japanese islands. Realistic replicas were on sale in Japan less than two decades after the end of the war, and they became popular with model builders and amateur war historians. Some weaponry, such as the fine handcrafted swords once carried by samurai and latter-day military officers, is regarded as high art.

Guns—handguns, especially—have always been the subject of tight police control in Japan, but there has never been a popular movement toward private ownership of guns. The Japanese learned to make firearms patterned on the Portuguese harquebus matchlock, but the sword was always the weapon of honor for the nation's warriors. The Japanese military, which proved to all too handy with guns during the expansionist era, no longer brags openly of its prowess, and a general of the Ground Self Defense Forces once lamented to me that the young recruits are frightened by their weapons. Many of them go through an entire military career without firing a shot. Lacking the space for a practice range, members of the Air Self Defense Force learn to use aerial weapons in the United States, and missile defense crews do the same.

The underworld, playing out its own drama, has been only too eager to embrace the gun. They have also lately taken to the hand grenade as an easily concealed and convenient device of destruction to be used against enemy offices and vehicles. The 1990 gang battle began with sixteen shooting incidents, including several murders. After a few weeks of violence, the gangs agreed to a ceasefire, which was duly reported in the nation's press, but minor incidents recurred. Several citizens were wounded in cases of mistaken identity.

Police say Yoshinori Watanabe, *Yamaguchi-gumi*'s fourth leader since the founder's death, sent out fax messages to all his affiliates calling for adherence to the truce. It didn't work. There were too many grudges to settle, too much territory at stake, and much too much money involved. Police tried to stave off further vendetta violence by arresting a dozen men. After a regional *Yamaguchi-gumi* boss in Hokkaido was killed, 800 officers from forty Osaka police stations swooped down on sixty-two *Yamaguchi-gumi* offices and the headquarters of affiliated gangs and arrested many more.

The increasingly bloody public activity of Japan's gangs has been attracting a lot of attention in the past several years. Three members of rival gangs shot it out on the Hiroshima train station platform, wounding three innocent travelers who were caught in the crossfire. The three gangsters are being tried for attempted murder, and their gang a year after the incident agreed to pay $100,000 in compensation to the victims. In a civil suit the three shooters were ordered to pay $3500 to the victims and $1400 for damages to the station. But such small sums are negligible, indeed laughable, to the *yakuza*, whose nationwide take is estimated by police to be well over $10 billion a year.

The Metropolitan Police Agency reinforced its Tokyo gang units when news arrived that the *Yamaguchi-gumi*, which until recently had confined its major activities to its traditional territory in Kobe, Osaka, Kyoto, and parts west, was beginning to move some of its affiliated units, in the form of real estate and money-lending or loan-sharking companies, into the Tokyo area. *Yamaguchi-gumi* has long had a nonaggression and nonpoaching pact with the main Tokyo syndicate, *Inagawa-kai*, but it was breaking down.

The Tokyo area bloodshed began in a western suburb called Hachioji. There were ten shootings and a dozen other assaults by *yakuza* in one week, including two stabbing deaths. A housewife was wounded by a gangster who mistook her home for that of a rival and peppered it with gunfire. One gang boss ducked and saved his life when five shots came crashing through a window of his home. A truck rammed into a flimsy wooden house in another case of mistaken identity. Children in a part of town near the headquarters of the local gangs were advised to take a circuitous route to school; some merchants closed their shops early in the evening. Police say that because *Yamaguchi-gumi* has not been able to score a decisive victory over its rivals at home, other challenges will likely develop. In turn, *Yamaguchi-gumi* cannot afford to lose face or territory by shrinking from a challenge.

Despite a natural reluctance to get involved in the affairs of gangs, one neighborhood in the town of Hamamatsu, 120 miles southwest of Tokyo, rebelled when a gang moved in and built a double-thick-walled, six-story building with steel mesh over tiny windows. Intending to use the building as its headquarters, gang members painted the hulking structure black and hung the geometric symbol of *Yamaguchi-gumi* over the entrance. But neighbors draped banners of protest on their houses, encouraging the head of the regional organization, Tetsuya Aono, to go away. They trained floodlights on the front of the building all night long and got a grant from the city to build a command post where citizens and police could document all comings and goings from the building. The gang didn't appreciate the attention and struck back: several neighbors were harrassed, their car windows were bashed in; homes were vandalized; and one man was stabbed.

Local merchants retaliated. They refused to sell to gang members. The city stopped garbage collection to their building. Finally Aono brought an $80,000 lawsuit against the neighbors for the distress they had caused him, his lawyers declaring in court that Aono had the right to live wherever he chose. The neighbors countersued to evict him as a nuisance. Aono painted the building white in a fruitless gesture of appeasement; he finally moved away and the building fell vacant.

Despite losses like that, about 3,300 gangs remain in Japan. Members number 100,000 or more, and the gangs appear to be growing. Recent investigations brought to light the terror tactics of *yakuza* hired by real estate speculators to acquire property from reluctant homeowners, which included physical violence, threats, and harrassmeht. Elderly widows were assaulted, badgered to sell by *yakuza* making incessant phone calls, setting up noisy stereo sets next to the thin walls of their houses or apartments. Pets were killed. Gangs also run a lucrative trade in prostitutes, recruiting young women from Thailand and the Philippines. Entering Japan as tourists, they have actually been sold into prostitution. Their passports are confiscated by their bosses, and the women become virtual slaves. *Yakuza* also are a major supplier of illegal workers from places such as Bangladesh and Pakistan to do menial work in the construction industry, jobs that newly affluent Japanese now find distasteful. The construction industry has long had a close association with the gangs, some of which began as labor contracting agencies for construction businesses.

Equally interesting are the ties between gangs, the right wing, and the police. From time to time, the gangs have been useful in maintaining order and protecting unpopular figures from enemies at events where police might be outnumbered. The gangs also proved handy during the student/leftist riots against the United States-Japan Treaty of Mutual Defense and Security in 1960 and again in 1970, when the treaty was up for renewal. Police also find that the gangs, with their cohesiveness and code of obedience, act as a brake on unorganized, free-lance crime. A crook inside the fold, disciplined by unyielding authority, is less likely to strike out unpredictably on his own. This is true in the case of the wild young motorcycle gangs, the *bosozoku*, the "wild tribe," as they like to be called, many of whom are subsumed into the *yakuza* as they graduate from hell-raising on the street.

The gangs have a long history of strikebreaking. They have contracted with right-wing nationalist supporters to assault and intimidate liberal and leftist political candidates and unions. They are known to the police to have occasional ties with some major corporations, which have used members of the "associations" to convince recalcitrant landowners to sell property, or to elicit contributions for worthy causes. Police accuse the gangs of being the primary gun smugglers and manufacturers of methamphetamines.

A reporter for the *Mainichi Shimbun,* one of Tokyo's biggest newspapers, recently got an anonymous interview with a local *Yamaguchi-gumi* boss, who told him: "If you are aiming for the big time these days, the thing to do is to get yourself a company connection. Even top corporations find they need protection. Plenty of companies approach us and ask for a syndicate 'advisor.' "

The National Police Agency's organized crime chief at the time, Hisahiro Kawabata, told Mainichi, "When a major company needs to take care of a problem discreetly it seeks the help of a gang; the mob's take is good, and the risks are nil." As an example he told the story of a Tokyo construction company that was harrassed after it sold an unprofitable property to a realtor. The deal eventually forced the realtor into bankruptcy, and he went to the *yakuza* for help. After a visit from the *yakuza,* the construction company bailed out the stricken realtor at a cost of $1.3 million. According to Mainichi:

> The construction company is a major corporation. It advertises regularly on television. . . . When it paid up, the firm made it clear that the recipients would not have to worry about [paying] taxes on the gift. The money was most likely disguised as an operating cost. Such stories are common, yet they never surface in the media. Large sums of money continue to disappear every year from the books of major corporations into the tax-free pockets of organized crime. And the law is never the wiser.

Solicitations of money for the funeral of an important *yakuza* are gigantic bonanzas. One mobster has boasted that the funeral of a don can bring in condolence contributions of as much as $350,000—at a 1992 exchange rate, the sum in dollars would be double. The more important the personage, the higher the fee. The service fee to the temple and the cost

Emperor Hirohito in 1987, just before his eighty-sixth birthday. At that time he was the longest-reigning monarch in the world.
(AP photo by Sadayuki Mikami.)

*Hiroshima's land-
mark Industry Pro-
motion Hall, before
the atomic blast.*
(Unless otherwise noted,
all photographs courtesy
of Edwin M. Reingold.)

*The ruin of the In-
dustry Promotion
Hall, now the sym-
bolic "Hiroshima
Dome," as it ap-
pears today in Peace
Park. It was near
the epicenter of the
atomic explosion.*

Ryoichi Sasakawa, Class A war criminal suspect, now Japan's biggest philanthropist.

Memorial to victims of the atomic bomb at Peace Park in Hiroshima. Students fold a thousand cranes in origami paper and hang them in this shelter in memory of those who died.

Dedication of memorial to both Japanese and American soldiers who died in Iwo Jima, one of the bloodiest battles of World War II.

Maritime Self Defense Forces on annual maneuvers in Sagami Bay.

The new army: women on review for the prime minister at Saitama military base.

Demonstrators in Sasebo protest the arrival of the nuclear warship U. S. S. Enterprise.

Riot police prepare to do battle with demonstrators in Sasebo.

Politicking, Japanese style. Candidates travel through countryside and cities in vans equipped with loudspeakers.

Street entertainer and his dog in the old Shitamachi (downtown) section of Tokyo.

Taking family pictures at the most popular venue in Tokyo, before the double bridge, Nijubashi, which leads to the Imperial Palace.

Two women in period costume enjoy a contemplative moment at the Meiji Shrine.

Burning these sacred arrows at the end of each year insures good fortune.

Children in traditional dress on Children's Day.

Women sort mikan, *a cross between an orange and a tangerine, in a small plant in Kyushu.*

An old Imperial Palace storehouse contrasts with modern Tokyo business-center buildings.

Busy Honda motorcycle assembly line in a giant but spotless plant.

Japan's experimental magnetic levitation (Magalev) train test track and vehicle in Kyushu. The train is designed to attain speeds of 500 km/h.

Japanese houses are often not much bigger than Japanese cars.

Main entrance to the holy of holies of the Grand Shrine at Ise, where the Amaterasu Omikami, the sun goddess, is said to visit, and where the emperor traditionally reported to her on major events.

Mt. Fuji.

Japanese sightseers touring temples in Kyoto, the ancient capital.

New Year's wishes are written on white paper and deposited at the Meiji Shrine.

*Modern practition-
ers of traditional
archery get a bless-
ing from a Shinto
priest before the
tournament at Yasu-
kuni Shrine, Tokyo,
dedicated to the
souls of the war
dead.*

*Parade in traditional
dress before festival
of traditional sports.*

A Sumo match, the ancient traditional sport, at the Sumo stadium at Rokugikan in old Tokyo.

Young men carrying portable shrine in Tokyo matsuri (festival).

The new Emperor Akihito dressed in formal attire.
(AP Photo.)

of distributing invitations is minor compared with the take. Said the mobster:

> It used to be that about $45,000 of this money went to the dead man's family; the rest was pooled at headquarters. But three years ago we decided to give the family the whole amount. There aren't any retirement benefits or pensions for godfathers, you know. And it's not a good idea to leave that much money lying around the office. The tax people might sink their teeth into it.

Contacts between mainstream gangs, politicians, and businessmen are known to the public and certainly to the police, not to mention journalists, historians, and political scientists. Japanese leaders, including the late Showa Emperor Hirohito, have appeared in public with some of the most frequently accused leaders of organizations known or widely suspected to be involved in corrupt affairs.

In the late emperor's case it was during a colorful pageant of volunteer fire fighters from all over Japan at Tokyo's Korakuen Stadium. Ryuichi Sasakawa, an early fascist and one-time Class A war criminal suspect who became the nation's czar of motorboat gambling, was at His Majesty's side—just the two men in the royal box. Sasakawa finances many civic causes, including volunteer fire fighting. Despite unsavory activities and associations, he has been decorated twice, in 1978 and 1987, by the Japanese government.

The link between public figures (including prime ministers, one of whom sent congratulations to the wedding of Mitsuo Taoka, another one of whom kept an unofficial *yakuza* bodyguard) and gangsters is occasionally commented on in the press. In 1987, before a serious financial scandal among government and ruling party officials toppled two successive prime ministers, 478 people were arrested on bribery charges, among them government officials, including several city mayors. The "black mist" of political corruption clings to many prominent members of Japan's ruling party. The political system makes huge financial demands on Japan's politicians.

Psychiatrist and novelist Inada Nada complains that "despite a law-and-order reputation, Japan is remarkably tolerant of organized crime. Top hoodlums, recognizable by their crewcuts, flashy clothes and huge, U.S.-made cars, operate openly." The *yakuza*, he says:

> have center-city offices and are listed in the telephone book. In other countries, criminals belong to secret societies; Cosa Nostra denied its own existence for decades. But Japanese hoods proudly display their crest and nameplate on the door. Nowhere does the mob operate as flagrantly as in Japan. Sometimes a United States politician is ruined when his secret ties to organized crime are revealed. Japanese society is less rigid about the underworld.

Dr. Nada believes public tolerance is much too high, especially in the case of the trafficking in women: "People regard it as a dirty business," he wrote recently in *Tokyo Shimbun*, "but since it is not technically illegal, nobody cares very much." The tolerance among the general public is often viewed as a typical lack of interest in people outside the group, or responsibility for them. Prostitution is illegal but of course must be proved. Since the women usually come in as tourists, their main official transgression is overstaying the period of their visa—that is, if they are caught and if their boss produces their passports for the police to examine. It is a poorly kept secret that certain flights into Tokyo and Osaka are favorites of gunrunners and prostitutes; the flights arrive at the busiest times of day when airports are jammed and customs officials are overworked. In Nada's opinion, "Although crime syndicates are behind all these activities, it is public patronage that makes them profitable. It is time for a change of attitude and a crackdown on organized crime."

There has never been a Japanese effort like the U.S. Justice Department's organized crime task force, which was responsible for rooting out, charging, and convicting the leaders of organized crime. From time to time Japanese mobsters cross the line and are arrested and convicted, but the big bosses, who are public figures, do not suffer such ignominy. Publications of the major gangs list their jailed members and their release dates, and important gang figures, when released, are always greeted and feted. The weekly magazines publish photographs of the lineup of big cars and of the crew-cut members of the brotherhood waiting in tight suits and sunglasses outside the prison.

Common Crime, Common Criminals

Despite the depredations of the *yakuza*, Japan's crime rates for the more common offenses are still the lowest among industrialized nations. There are probably no cities elsewhere in the world where a lone citizen can walk the streets at night without fear of being mugged, raped, or killed. Except for the gangs, the use of firearms is miniscule, even in bank robberies, of which there are few. A desperate police officer, heavily in debt to usurious *yakuza* moneylenders, recently robbed a bank in Osaka, but he used a toy pistol instead of his service weapon.

This anecdote, however, does not gainsay the surge in serious crime—kidnapping, torture, and murder, not just the traditional intimidation of classmates—by juveniles. As the good life beckons to those with money and as more women are moving into the workplace, many children are left alone to grow up with babysitters. Fathers working late hours rarely see their children, and there is little familial socializing except on holidays. While this situation is similar to that of the modern upwardly mobile Western family, it is fairly new to Japan. Critics say that traditional familial and group restraints on antisocial behavior are collapsing at a time when affluence and leisure time are on the increase.

There is a detectable increase in cocaine addiction and trafficking as more and more Japanese travel abroad. Cocaine brings at least three times the world price in Japan, which may explain why the amount confiscated by police leaped from 13.6 kilos (about thirty pounds) in 1989 to 70 kilos (about 155 pounds) in the first half of 1990 and is rising. Police say there may be connections between the gangs and Colombia's Medellin Cartel. Some of the cocaine seized in the port of Kobe was taken from Colombian ships, and Latin Americans have been arrested in connection with the seizure. There is no official tolerance for or leniency toward illegal drug use in Japan—marijuana is viewed as a hard drug— and first offenders are given stiff sentences. The former Beatle Paul McCartney, his wife, and four children were once detained at Narita Airport when he was found to have 219 grams (about a half-pound) of marijuana in his possession. He had come with his entourage of fifty musicians and eleven tons of equipment for a nationwide tour. McCartney was interrogated for eight hours—his wife and children were released—and then thrown into a Japanese jail overnight. Japanese papers carried front-page photos of McCartney the next morning, handcuffed and roped together with other suspected miscreants as he was taken to court. It was just the kind of case the police were pleased to get: treating a celebrity as they would a common drunk or addict sent a sobering message to the drug users of the nation, young and old, famous or not. McCartney was expelled, and the long anticipated tour cancelled.

Ethnocentric Japanese authorities often refer to the rise of drug offenses unfairly as the Americanization of crime, or the American disease, brought about by the exposure of Japanese youth to Western films, music, and pop culture. Local origins of the problem are not admitted. It is still quite common for a foreigner who reports a crime to be told that the perpetrator was most likely another foreigner. This feeling was given some highly publicized credence a few years ago, when a seemingly respectable American student was found to have been the cat burglar who had preyed successfully on a central Tokyo neighborhood. The Japanese remember the Vietnam War, when American servicemen visiting Japan were one conduit for narcotics from Southeast Asia.

But contemporary Japanese fiction of the period depicts a homegrown, as well as GI-induced, source of drugs. The chemically produced methamphetimine ("speed") drugs are said to be the province of the *yakuza*, as well as much of the smuggled cocaine and heroin, now that the number of American servicemen has dwindled.

In most crime categories, like murder, rape, and robbery, Japanese figures are much lower than those in the West. But at least one kind of criminal seems to stymie the efficient Japanese police. It is the pickpocket, a breed that infests the train stations of the nation, whose arrest rate was a disappointing 25.9 percent. Many of these are freelance dips unconnected with organized crime. The police reported that the famed *Tokaido Shinkansen,* or Bullet Train line segment between Tokyo and Osaka, is a particularly ripe venue for pickpockets. Of 163 cases aboard the trains in the September-November period of 1989, only two arrests were made.

There are plenty of theories as to why most other crimes are so low. For one, it is generally agreed that the lack of handguns among ordinary people has a lot to do with it. It is just more difficult to kill somebody with a sword, unless one is practiced and adept at it, than with a handgun. Gangsters prefer guns, but daggers and swords are used frequently by nonprofessionals. The lack of ordinary weapons has led to some bizarre crimes. During the Occupation era, one Masamichi Hirasawa strode into a bank, identified himself as a health inspector, and announced that he had been sent to administer a preventative dose of medicine for a raging disease. He mixed up a lethal cocktail, which the submissive bank staff obediently quaffed. As twelve of them died in agony, he walked off with the money. He was caught and spent the rest of his life in jail.

One can't overlook, as a crime prevention tool, the presence everywhere of the local uniformed police. They maintain small substations in every neighborhood and, like old-fashioned beat cops in the West, know every household and every person in the neighborhood. The police aren't perfect, as we have seen, but there is no doubt that they are a deterrent.

Police routinely set up traffic roadblocks to make sobriety

tests. They sometimes shove an alcohol detector wand into the car and ask the driver a question. As the motorist breathes onto the sensitive part of the instrument, it determines whether alcohol is present. The police, who take traffic accidents very seriously, confiscate the driving licenses of drinking drivers.

Legitimate auto-body shops will not repair a damaged car, I discovered to my annoyance, without a police report detailing the damage and how it was caused. One Sunday I had inadvertently backed into a concrete-and-steel utility pole while leaving the home of an artist in the Aoyama district of Tokyo. The rear bumper was dented, and I sent the car for repair the next day. But the body shop would not touch it until I had taken the police to the scene of the accident, where they could match up the scratches and determine that there was no other damage for which I should be held liable.

Auto accidents of all kinds are taken seriously. The Ichihara Prison, not far from Tokyo, was established in 1969 just for traffic offenders. Almost all of the inmates have had a previous traffic offense of some kind. About a third have been convicted of negligent homicide; about half, of driving under the influence of alcohol. The average sentence is nine and a half months. During that time, the inmates take driving aptitude tests, analyze traffic accidents in classes, undergo driving simulation, have psychological discussions about right living, attend "introspection therapy" sessions, and watch documentaries, some of them heart-rending stories of the victims of traffic accidents. New inmates are housed in a semiopen dormitory, to make sure they don't decamp at night, and after a period are moved to an open dormitory. When it is time for prerelease orientation, they move into the "Dormitory of Hope." During their stay the inmates are subjected to lectures on self-control and accountability. There is also a "Monument of Atonement" at which the inmates can pray and seek expiation.

Prisoners held in standard prisons for felonies are given much harsher treatment. They have little privacy and few

privileges. But amid a spare life of discipline they are nevertheless given counseling and job training. The death penalty
still applies and about two persons a year are executed by
hanging, but the government does not reveal any information about the condemned prisoners, not even the number
executed.

Japan has a trial-by-jury law, but it has been in suspension
since 1943. In the meager twenty years during which juries
heard cases in Japanese courts, exactly 25,192 cases were
tried. Only 484 cases actually went to jury deliberation. In
many cases, defendants plea bargained, pleaded guilty, or
were persuaded to waive their right to a jury's deliberation.
But with the acquittal rate running 17 percent, the authorities became restive and abandoned the system. Under the
jury law, certain crimes, such as political activities pros-
cribed by the Peace Preservation Law, were not subject to
jury trial. The court was free to change the members of the
jury at will and, most significant, the court was not bound
by the verdict of the jury. The prevailing sentiment among
the populace is that the system is stacked against the suspect.
It hasn't eliminated crime in Japan, but certainly plays a
part in keeping most people on the safe side of the law.

Even so, skeptics suggest that the Japanese authorities
underreport crime and that Japan is not the law abiding
place it seems to be. Much of the extortion and strong arm
activities of the gangs is not reported, but every year there
are suicides—sometimes committed by whole families—
hopelessly in debt to *yakuza* money lenders. When the late
photojournalist W. Eugene Smith was beaten and nearly
killed by hired hoodlums for documenting the plight of the
sufferers of corporate pollution in Minamata, it was no shock
to most Japanese. This kind of intimidation by hired brutes
on behalf of companies and even political figures is not unusual.

Yet if the incidence of crime seems different in Japan, and
it is, it also strikes the observer that the nature of the criminal
is somewhat different from the Western stereotype. The
swaggering gangster, often portrayed in films as a kind of

Robin Hood, is a popular stereotype, and ordinary citizens give him a wide berth. The world of *mizu-shobai*, literally the "water business," or the saloon and night-club world, is shot through with shady characters, fast-buck sharpers engaging in illicit activity such as illegal gambling, prostitution, confidence games, and extortion. It is a world few foreign visitors penetrate, or wish to.

Foreigners encounter simpler crimes. Charles d'Honau, an American businessman then living in Japan, arrived home one evening to find a Japanese man rifling through the family possessions. Having heard similar tales from foreigners and Japanese alike, and having been warned against doing any violence to the intruder, d'Honau ordered the criminal to stop and then commanded him to take a seat and wait until the police arrived. The burglar bowed, then resignedly took his seat until the police arrived to take him away. No force was used; it is widely understood in Japan that injuring a burglar is as much a case of battery as it would be to assault a person at random on the street, even if it occurs in your own living room.

Ordinary law-abiding Japanese do not normally sleep with guns or other weapons at hand. Traditional Japanese house construction is so flimsy that breaking and entering would be a misnomer. Some Japanese never lock their houses, and in traditional homes, it is customary for a visitor to enter the *genkan*, or foyer, to announce his or her arrival. But in today's modern, faceless, reinforced-concrete apartment blocks with fireproof metal doors, locks are used. The modern Japanese, now blessed with a plethora of worldly goods— computers, pianos, stereos, giant-screen televisions—but fated to live in cramped quarters, have plenty of things to be stolen. But Japanese footpads are selective. Even in Japan's sprawling cities, really conglomerations of distinct neighborhoods, disposing of stolen goods is a problem. It is also difficult to conceal anything from the alert eyes of the police.

Professor Eiichi Kato, who spent nineteen years with the Ministry of Home Affairs, many of them watching public officials for evidence of having received bribes, says nothing escapes the eyes of neighbors and the police in Japan's neighborhoods. Some 15,000 police substations blanket the country and constantly check on who is in what house, what their normal habits are, and provide what some call twenty-four-hour protection (others call it spying). Whatever it is called, it is unlikely that a criminal could pull a truck up to a house, as is sometimes done in the United States, and matter-of-factly haul away the contents. Thievery from warehouses and distribution channels is another matter, and goods that "fell off the truck" can be found being traded in some Japanese back street markets. Footpads robbing someone's home look for cash, credit cards, and signature seals with which money can be withdrawn from bank accounts.

Perhaps the Japanese craving for new goods accounts for the discriminating taste of Japanese burglars. Used goods are not desired, and in fact, the scrapping of old appliances and furniture helps to keep the wheels of the industry turning. The periodic collection of such goods, called *sodai gomi*, or "rough trash," yields a bonanza for many poor Japanese and foreigners, who cruise the streets inspecting what well-off Japanese throw away. And at parties it is not unusual for a host or hostess to show off what pieces of furniture or what television or stereo and accessories were picked off a neighborhood *sodai gomi* pile.

Having spent more than a decade living and traveling in Latin America and Africa before coming to Japan to live, my family had never had the experience of being burglarized, except for one bungled attempt in Nairobi. But on a warm spring night in Tokyo, coming home earlier than expected, I noted a light in the bedroom as we entered the apartment. I was about to say something to my wife or the children about wasting energy when I caught a glimpse of a small person darting past the bedroom door. Remembering the experience of d'Honau and others, I shouted—in what language I cannot remember—and ran to the bedroom, only to see the person disappearing through the open balcony door with a pocketful of cash. He left behind the jewelry because of the difficulty of fencing it, the police said later. The room was a wreck, clothing spilling out from every drawer. When the police arrived they fingerprinted all ten fingers of every member of the family, thoroughly blackened all the possible points of contact with a tenacious powder, but never found the burglar, one of the rare ones to get away.

Little cases of burgled cash notwithstanding, the arrest rate in Japan fits the expected pattern—higher than any other country's. Japan has an arrest rate that averages around ninety-eight per hundred homicides, versus about seventy in the United States, eighty-one in Great Britain, eighty-three in France, and ninety-four in West Germany. In the case of robbery, larceny, and theft, Japan's police are far ahead of their counterparts in the West. They make seventy-eight arrests per one hundred robberies, versus twenty-six in the United States, twenty-three in Great Britain, twenty-five in France, and forty-six in West Germany. Japanese police make an arrest in fifty-six of every one hundred larcenies, compared with a rather anemic seventeen arrests in the United States, thirty in Great Britain, sixteen in France, and twenty-nine in West Germany.

Untrue Confessions, Con Men, Avengers

Perhaps it is a legacy of Confucianism or Fascism. Perhaps it is Japan's isolation, the high population density, a lively sense of propriety or the certainty of being caught, but serious crimes yield conviction rates that normally run just a hair under 100 percent. And most of these offenses are solved by confession. Police are constantly accused of using subtle and not so subtle forms of torture. White-collar crime suspects are often the victims of a kind of psychological warfare, in which the police seem to ignore them at first or take a long time to make their moves. A businessman suspected of falsifying customs declarations or some such illegality will suddenly find himself surrounded by policemen or tax agents, or both, who box up every scrap of paper in his office and his home and carry it away. The analysis of the paper and the questioning can go on for months, but the victim is free to go about, wondering when he will be taken.

Those finally arrested are treated to harsh interrogation at odd hours of the day and night; the lights in their cells are never turned off. A quirk in the law allows police to keep prisoners at the local detention center for three weeks at a time. After being held for the preliminary period, the suspect may be released only to be rearrested and put through another period of interrogation without benefit of a lawyer. In one recent case the suspect was held for nearly a year without being charged.

Another bit of unofficial harrassment a suspect often undergoes, if his case is interesting enough to the press, is his public relegation to the status of nonperson. It happened to Prime Minister Kakuei Tanaka when he was arrested in 1975 for taking bribes from Lockheed Corporation to buy L1011 Tristar jetliners for All Nippon Airways. Immediately newspapers stopped referring to him in an honorofic way, calling him merely Tanaka. The dropping of any honorific telegraphs a sense of disrespect and disdain. And even though the case had not come to trial—it would take several years before the conviction and the upholding of appeals made it through the courts—the press seemed to be declaring itself certain of Tanaka's guilt. This is typical of Japan's press and its relationship with authority; the press accords the police a presumption of virtual infallibility in major cases.

One reason the conviction rate in Japan is as high as 99.91 percent, say some social critics, is that cases do not make it to court until the prosecutors are certain they can get a conviction. One way they can be more assured of a conviction is to elicit a confession from the suspect; thus the long and tedious periods of interrogation and investigation, a war of nerves. This process is being changed as more and more victims have been able to detail the torture they endured— not being allowed to sleep, to visit the bathroom, to wash, to eat, or to have a lawyer present until they have confessed. A half-dozen death row inmates have been reprieved since

1983, when the first prisoner was granted a retrial and was subsequently acquitted. One of them, Masao Akahori, had spent thirty-four years in prison, twenty-eight of them on death row, after he falsely confessed to the strangling of a six-year-old girl. Akahori confessed because he was told that if he did he would get a light sentence, and that if he didn't he would be kept in jail forever.

One of the most common crimes is the swindling of the credulous. Women, who traditionally manage the family finances, are frequently quite successful in playing the stock market, but they are often swindled by unscrupulous brokers who do not share with these small investors the tips and inside information that is routinely passed to bigger and more significant investors. The system in Japan has long been criticized for unfairness and outright fraud by foreign bankers, securities dealers, and analysts, and there has been considerable outside pressure on Japan's Finance Ministry to correct inequities. One British arbitrageur complained bitterly to the Foreign Ministry of a practice whereby new stock issues were made available immediately to Japanese investors but not to foreigners until later, when the price had climbed. The common problem of insider trading shocked the world's financial markets when it was revealed in 1991 that the four most prestigious brokerage houses in the country had reimbursed favored clients for losses. When the scandal cooled down, the companies were partially suspended from trading for a number of days.

Many housewives still spend much of their time dabbling in the market. At one point NHK, the government television and radio network, took note of the phenomenon and ran a serious course over its educational channel called "Economics for Housewives." The subject matter of the program was not home economics, but real world stuff, taught by university professors. It would follow, in light of the sizable amount of money that passes through the hands of women, that women are often the victims of the most audacious confidence schemes.

Kazuo Nagano, thirty-two years old and a smooth talker,

was a prototype of the kind of go-getting swindler that seems to succeed almost anywhere in the developed world. The bush-haired, hotshot salesman built a nationwide company based in Osaka by selling gold bars that did not exist; at least the police were never able to find any. But Nagano used the nonexistent gold bars to support a pyramid of forty-three companies, many of them mere money movement fronts. Nagano's scheme was not very imaginative, but for the credulous and greedy housewives he swindled, it looked like a dream come true. A customer paid one million yen for a *"junkin* (pure gold) family contract," but did not receive the actual bar of gold. Instead, the company (which Nagano called Toyota Shoji to cash in on the name of the automaker, though not related in any way) immediately paid the client 10 percent of the investment in exchange for the use of the "gold" to make further investments. The gullible clients got a check for Yen 100,000 per each million yen invested. With this up-front 10-percent payment, they thought they were now well ahead of the game. Actually the clients were being swindled out of nine-tenths of their investment. When the scheme unraveled in 1985, Nagano was broke; his own investments went sour and his liabilities were $1.6 billion. He had ensnared 30,000 people, most of them senior citizens.

Police questioned Nagano in Kobe and in Tokyo, but didn't immediately arrest him. They sealed his offices, froze his bank accounts, carted away all his records, began investigating every facet of his personal and business life, turning him into a penniless, friendless, nervous wreck. He was reduced to living in a shabby apartment in downtown Osaka, a place the Japanese press had staked out as only the Japanese press can, with at least forty cameramen and reporters squeezed into the narrow corridor of the building. Nagano was page one news.

One afternoon two men, who described themselves later as an unemployed construction worker and the manager of a small ironworks, shoved their way through the crowd of reporters, tussling with the security guard of the apartment building. One of them told the guard gruffly, "We've been sent to kill him." When the guard resisted, the men shoved him aside and grabbed an aluminum lawn chair that one of the newsmen had been sitting on. He began bashing the door, trying to get in, but the locked steel door wouldn't yield. Then one of them smashed the small corridor window next to the door and climbed inside. The newsmen rushed forward with the cameras. Few had noticed that one of the two intruders was carrying something wrapped in newspaper. There were sounds of a scuffle and cries of pain.

Shinichi Ito, a cameraman for the Tokyo daily newspaper *Mainichi Shimbun*, poked his camera through the window and got a dramatic photo of a blood-spattered Nagano being held in an armlock grip while one of the assailants brandished an already bloody sword. A few moments later both men emerged from the room, both blood-spattered, one still carrying the dripping sword. "We stabbed him," one of them shouted. The two men then calmly went outside and waited for the police to arrive. Nagano, stabbed thirteen times, was dead on arrival at a local hospital.

The videotape of the event was flashed nationwide. One viewer was the sixty-three-year-old mother of Nagano, bedridden in a Nagoya hospital at the time. She went into shock. Television stations were flooded with calls from viewers protesting the showing of the brutal images. But just as many demanded to know why among all those newsman witnesses, not one of them bothered to call the police. Japan's largest daily paper, *Yomiuri Shimbun*, in an editorial titled "Terroristic Vigilantism," concluded that "the reporters should be subject to public criticism for their failure to restrain [the killers]. The reporters placed too much emphasis on their professional duties in the abnormal situation." Using a classic Japanese admonition, the editorialist intoned, "The mass media in this respect should search their souls."

Bloody, vengeful killing is not uncommon in Japan, especially in the tight, heavily coded underworld. It even has a romanticized historic precedent. For nearly 300 years a play called *Chushingura*, or *The Treasury of Loyal Retainers*, has been undisputedly the most popular single story in

Japan. It is the historical tale of forty-seven loyal samurai who lost and then avenged their master.

Chushingura is a story based on an incident from Japan's feudal era, which immediately became the subject of a puppet play, then a Kabuki theater drama, and, in latter days, films. Though altered and embellished over the years, the kernel of fact remains and belies the transparently altered names. *Chushingura* is the story of the revenge killing of Yoshinaka Kira, a haughty, cruel, and merciless chamberlain in the palace of Shogun Tsunayoshi in 1702. Kira had taunted the countrified Lord Naganori Asano for his lack of manners and the paucity of his tribute when he came to make his obligatory call on the Shogun in 1701. Legend has it that Kira was angered when Asano, through ignorance or guile, failed to give Kira the appropriate bribe for teaching him the protocol necessary for presenting himself to the Shogun. At one point Asano was so angered by Kira's taunts that he drew his sword against Kira and wounded him slightly.

It was not the wounding of Kira that drew the Shogun's wrath down upon Asano; it was the mere unsheathing of a sword inside the palace, which was outlawed and for which the penalty was death. If the shogun and his advisers were lenient, the death could be by the offender's own hand, *seppuku*. The death sentence was duly handed down, and Asano accepted it. His men were angered, incensed, and mortified that they had not protected their lord properly. In Professor Donald Keene's translation of the original puppet play, Asano goes to his death regretting that he had been held back and had not killed Kira. "It rankles in my bones," he says, and tells his retainers, "I vow that I shall be born and die, again and again, until at last I am avenged." The narrator intones, "His voice vibrates with wrath."

Asano's head retainer, Kuranosuke Oishi, arrives just as the ritual suicide begins. Asano, who is renamed Enya Hangen, has just plunged the dagger into his belly. "I leave this dagger as a memento of me. Avenge me," he says as he withdraws the dagger from his belly and plunges the point into his windpipe to breathe his last.

In real life, the samurai of the dead Asano publicly renounced their allegiance and became *ronin*, masterless samurai. They did it to absolve Asano's family of any blame
for their revenge, which they were secretly plotting. To throw
Kira's spies further off guard Oishi sank into a life of drun-
kenness and debauchery. But the following December 14, on
the anniversary of Asano's death, the *ronin* quietly gathered
in Tokyo (then called Edo) and made their way through the
snow to Kira's residence. There they attacked suddenly, surprising Kira's guards. They killed Kira and cut off his head.
The solemn entourage then walked to Sengakuji, where they
washed Kira's head in a stone basin that remains there to
this day, and then presented it before Asano's tomb, having
fulfilled his wish for vengeance. The *ronin*, led by the sober
Oishi, turned themselves in to the authorities and in due
course they were ordered to commit *seppuku*. The deaths took
place at several venues in the Takanawa area, and the many
students of the tale can point out the places where each group
of *ronin* killed themselves.

In Takanawa, not far from the center of today's Tokyo, two
short blocks from a busy thoroughfare that funnels traffic
along Tokyo Bay to Yokohama, is the cemetery at Sengakuji
where the tombstones of the forty-seven men stand. The
moss-grown stones bear their names. They were as young as
fifteen—Oishi's own son—and as old as seventy-seven. A
small museum has preserved behind glass the artifacts of
the incident: armor, banners, maps, weapons, lacquered
boxes, and other paraphernalia the entourage used on their
1701 trek to Edo. At one end of the two-story building stands
a gallery of wood-carved likenesses of the doomed men.
Every year, tens of thousands of Japanese come to place
incense at one or all of the headstones. The pungent aroma
and whitish cloud of incense hovers continuously over the
place, and to be there alone at any time when the gate is
unlocked is very rare.

The values that so impress the Japanese about the retainers of the country bumpkin who was Lord Asano, and their
revenge for his death—loyalty, self-sacrifice—are accom-

panied by values that might not find favor in a perfect world. They include a large measure of deception, dissembling, duplicity, and cruelty, but they are set against a backdrop of injustice, or imagined injustice. And although the blood soaked story is pretty horrific, it might be remembered that it came at a time when such behavior was not so uncommon in the world. But in Japan there was order of a sort, and rigid rules were enforced unremittingly. The tenets of obligation and loyalty, in conflict with the strict rules of courtly behavior, prevailed in *Chushingura*. To the tale's contemporaries, their horrific act was a noble one.

CHAPTER NINE

IMPORTS, OUTCASTS, STRANGERS, STEREOTYPES

It sounded like a childish attempt at humor, but my inter-
locutor was serious. "When," he asked, "is a Japanese not a
Japanese?" I shrugged. My friend didn't smile: "When he is
burakumin."

Then I knew he wasn't kidding. *Burakumin,* village person
or village people, seems like a harmless name, but is, in fact,
an insidious euphemism for a class of Japanese who have
been stigmatized. The stigma has something to do with the
hierarchical system set up during Japan's feudal period, a
system that mocks the notion often put forth that the Japanese are a homogeneous people. In fact, Japanese are often
bedeviled by class distinction. This does not mean they cannot and do not work together for a common goal, but neither
does it mean that because they do they are not separated by
class.

The *burakumin* were originally called *eta,* a word that
means "much filth." So objectionable was the word that in
the 1920s it was officially dropped from Japanese dictionaries. But these oppressed people did not cease to exist, nor
did the discrimination against them. *Eta* continued to exist,

and Japanese privately used the word; some still do. But once the word was officially expunged, to officialdom it had no accepted meaning and therefore couldn't be used formally. A euphemism was found for these people, who lived in segregated communities.

Ancestors of today's people of the outcast villages in Japan were somehow cursed by the feudal administration in the seventeenth century for the menial and bloody work they did—slaughtering animals, tanning hides, working with leather. Some *burakumin* families have not been involved in these occupations for many generations and yet are stigmatized by it to this day. Unless they can slip the official lists of residents of every ward in the nation, they are marked people. A 600-page blacklist containing information on 5600 Burakumin communities was revealed publicly in 1975, but was not banned until 1980. Some critics say the list is still being used surreptitiously by employers and the parents of prospective brides and grooms to make sure no *buraku* people get responsible jobs in what are considered to be respectable firms or marry into respectable families.

Although the village people do not bear any physical characteristics that would separate them from other citizens, they are marked on the official records by the places where they live and notations that indicate their station in life. For a time the outcast villages did not even appear on official maps of the nation. Historian Naramoto Tatsuya recently explained in an *Asahi Shimbun* article that the rulers of Japan in the Edo period tried to keep the classes—samurai, peasants, artisans, and merchants—in their place by urging them to despise every one lower in the social hierarchy. "Outcasts were considered subhuman, not part of the official order. This attitude persists today."

A government body surveyed the nation on the status of the hierarchy during the Edo period and reported there were two classes within the outcast circle:

The outcasts are the lowest class of our society, being very near animals. . . . Those of them who are engaged in still lower occupations most repulsive to human feelings, such as the burying of dead bodies found by the roadside, disposition of the bodies of executed criminals and supervision of beggars, are called *hinin* [nonhuman].

The two bottom classes, *eta* and *hinin*, did not associate with each other by choice but were often thrown together. The authorities often ordered *hinin* to move into a *buraku* after having committed some crime. The upper classes treated them both atrociously. *Hinin* could sometimes obtain the status of *heimin*, or "commoner," by paying a fee called "feet washing" money.

Eta were not permitted to enter the house of a commoner, but had to kneel at the entrance and call out. "Commoners regard the giving to or receiving from *eta* such things as fire and water as in a sense tabooed," wrote the feudal commissioners. "When commoners buy things manufactured by *eta*, they throw the money to them and never take change from them. *Hinin* are, on the contrary, hired by commoners as servants ... and sometimes give to or receive from *hinin* such things as fire and water."

In one district the survey members found some *eta* who had emerged from their status after three generations and had become prosperous farmers, also engaged in the lucrative business of lending money to commoners. In another district they found a class of outcasts that ranked between *eta* and *hinin* who "manage theaters and shows and do not associate with commoners." In one locality *eta* were considered so unclean that farmers would not use the night soil from *eta* homes for fertilizer, "which in consequence is thrown into the rivers; thus the odor around the *eta* colonies is unbearable." In some towns *eta* were not allowed to use umbrellas or wear the customary high wooden clogs when it rained, but were forced to slosh around in straw sandals.

The life of an *eta* was considered valueless. In 1859, a magistrate of Edo heard the case of a mob that killed an *eta* who had tried to enter a shrine. In a now famous ruling, the magistrate declared that the life of an *eta* was worth only one-seventh that of an ordinary commoner. He concluded that unless seven *eta* had been killed there could be no punishment for any single commoner. It was only a few years later, in 1871, three years after the reign of Meiji began, that the people of the village were technically freed of official discrimination by decree. But as we have seen in the United States and elsewhere, a declaration of emancipation does not reform bigoted minds or change old habits.

A "special integration measures" law was passed in 1969 appropriating money to eliminate the *buraku* slums and build new housing, in cooperation with the cities. The law was aimed at moving the nation's 3 million *burakumin* closer to the stated ideal of integration into the mainstream of society. That, as we have noted, is a rather elusive circle. The national government has spent many billions so far, but there is fear that when the current appropriations run out, the cities alone will not be able to take on the costly burden of cleaning the slums.

Over the years groups of *burakumin* have become politicized. Some groups have allied with the Japan Socialist Party, and others with the Communist Party. In the 1930s, most *burakumin* social organizations turned toward Marxist ideals, only to be suppressed by the militarists then ruling the nation. In the first postwar election during the Occupation, a *buraku* leader, Jiichiro Matsumoto, was elected to the Japanese parliament on the Socialist ticket. Nine other *burakumin* were swept into office in the upper and lower houses.

In those heady days of liberal assertion Matsumoto was even elected vice president of the upper house. In that capacity he became the first *burakumin* to have an audience with the emperor. He scandalized the establishment by refusing to make the customary withdrawal to avoid turning one's back on the august presence of the emperor. Matsumoto reasoned that inasmuch as Emperor Hirohito had renounced his mythical divinity, it was no longer necessary to perform these demeaning rites. There were outraged cries for his ouster, and worse. He soon lost his seat through election.

The majority of *burakumin* remain segregated. In the Kobe and Osaka regions a great deal of government money has gone into improvements in housing and amenities for the *burakumin* and for educating the children. Professor Juichi Suginohara of Kyoto University estimates that nearly half of the young *burakumin* who wed today intermarry. Eventually the problem may dissolve as younger people continue to shed their prejudice. Too, some families are simply moving out of the nation's 6000 villages or city areas so stigmatized, although it is difficult to find landlords who will rent to them.

Britain's Minority Rights Group, in a 1983 report on Japan's minorities concluded that "majority Japanese continue to consider *burakumin* as intellectually dull, disorderly, rude, sexually promiscuous, violently aggressive and physically unclean." The group also estimated that despite the effort at integration and education the government and the *burakumin* organizations have made, there are approximately thirty suicides a year attributable to anti-*burakumin* discrimination.

The director of the Buraku Liberation Research Institute, Sueo Murakoshi, lamented to a Tokyo newspaper recently that "the brightest people leave the community, depriving the movement of young leaders. By 'passing' they not only give in to discrimination but tacitly condone it. It's a defeat for all of us." Since 1953 classroom prejudice has been a target of a national research council sponsored by *burakumin* organizations, but the national government in 1987 reported that more than 900 firms were found to be violating government guidelines by asking questions about social background, place of residence, and occupation obviously aimed at identifying *burakumin*. A Labor Ministry spokesman noted, however, that most of the firms violating the rule were in the heavily populated *burakumin* areas of Osaka; the number of companies asking such questions in other cities appears to be declining.

More than 70 percent of the employed *burakumin* males in the Osaka area are working for local government or private companies. But the newspaper *Asahi* discovered in a study of *burakumin* employment in Osaka that most of those public employees from the ghetto work for the sanitation department, and that more than 90 percent of the *burakumin* employees of private companies work for small- and medium-size firms. *Asahi* quoted Yoshihiko Yamamoto of the Osaka Burakumin Liberation League as saying, "Nowadays no company or local government is going to come right out and refuse someone a job because they are *burakumin*. Employers are more subtle than that. They are adept at finding excuses for not hiring us, such as schooling or aptitude. It's the same old game, but they have become much better at playing it."

Under pressures of the society, many members of the outcast minority, which now numbers about 3 million, have struck back against what they perceive as discrimination and the spreading of falsehoods. The approach of the Burakumin Liberation League has been one of confrontation and often public denunciation, threats of boycott, or worse. Dutch journalist Karel van Wolferen, author of a pioneering study of the Japanese system, *The Enigma of Japanese Power*, alluded in his book to the Buraku Liberation League and its tactics of intimidation of people and organizations it deems discriminatory. When van Wolferen's study first appeared in Japanese translation in 1990, his publisher was immediately threatened with serious consequences if he did not withdraw the books already on sale and remove the parts that offended the BLL. The publisher immediately withdrew the books from the top fifty bookstores, but after consultation with the author, sent the books back to the store shelves unchanged. Most often, publishers, alert to the possibility of reaction, obviate the problem by voluntarily removing possibly offensive sections from translations of the foreign works they publish.

Since Japan threw off its feudal system, the appetite to learn from the West has been voracious. The sometimes frenzied mania for foreign ideas and goods was a product of the Charter Oath, a Meiji declaration of 1868, which proclaimed that "knowledge shall be sought throughout the world in order to strengthen the foundations of Imperial rule." The idea was not new to the Japanese. Before isolating itself from the world for over two centuries, Japan was a grand importer of cultural ideas as well as scientific knowledge and practical techniques. The importation has always been a process of adaptation, of taking foreign ideas and giving them Japanese character. As much as Japanese wanted to use outside ideas, foreign ways were never merely imported whole into the country. Foreigners who were hired to teach were kept segregated and apart from Japanese culture.

Japan's written language, adapted from the Chinese, is a necessary and important early example. Japanese is a much more grammatically complex language than Chinese. The Chinese written language enabled primitive Japanese to express abstract concepts such as filial piety and loyalty. Before the importation of the Chinese ideograms, Japan had no written language. Among the early Japanese intelligentsia, the Chinese characters were used exclusively for official texts and serious works. Japanese women were dipping writing brushes into ink, too. Edwin O. Reischauer, the late Harvard scholar, author, and former United States Ambassador to Japan, wrote that "while the men of the period were pompously writing bad Chinese, their ladies consoled themselves for their lack of education by writing good Japanese and created, incidentally, Japan's first great prose literature." Two premier tenth-century examples of this are *The Tale of Genji* by Lady Shikibu Murasaki and *The Pillow Book* by Sei Shonagon.

It was the use of simplified elements of the Chinese characters that enabled Japanese to be expressed fully. The language has changed so much over the years since it was imported that students and scholars puzzle over the ancient texts whose language is more arcane than Middle English seems to modern students of English. Old complex Chinese characters in little use today—including the archaic language of the Imperial court—often appear in print with tiny phonetic symbols next to them to assist the reader in pronunciation.

There were those Japanese who, during the Meiji enlightenment, wished to go further. They advocated making English or French the lingua franca and abandoning the use of Chinese characters and the Japanese syllabaries adapted from them. Those movements were never taken seriously by the established educational authorities in the new government, and their plans came to naught. Yet Japan imported thousands of loan words as it sought to learn from the outside world. It should be no surprise that any speaker of English already knows as many as 1500 Japanese words, from *adoresu*, for "address," to *zebura*, or "zebra."

Western Modes, Japanese Style

During Japan's first attempt at modernization following the liberating Charter Oath of 1868, wearing of morning coats and top hats by elite Japanese men was more than an affectation; it was an attempt to throw off the old cloak of feudalism, to experience what others had learned while Japan had been isolated. Bowlers, lace-up shoes, and cloaks became an obsession. Englishmen joked about the affectation and the wholesale purchase of apparel by eager Japanese. Some Japanese never returned to the custom of wearing kimono. Western clothing for most businessmen, bureaucrats, and government officials gradually became the preferred attire. Emperor Hirohito, for example, wore Western dress exclusively.

The fancy dress balls at the elegant *Rokumeikan*, the international gentlemen's club established in central Tokyo in the late nineteenth century were, for those who attended, more than a night out; they were an attempt to learn foreign manners so that foreigners could be met on their own terms.

Some even hoped to profit by the association. Traditionalists and ultranationalists at the time were scathing in their denunciation of this aping of Western dress and behavior. The upper-crust dancers at *Rokumeikan* were on the crest of a new wave of interest in other cultures, but they were by no means a majority.

This sudden turn to the outside world was a strange endeavor, coming on the heels of Japan's hermit centuries. Die-hard traditionalists saw the moves toward modernization and internationalization as attempts to dilute Japanese culture. In their view it would weaken Japan at a time when the first treaties with the West, signed under duress by a weak and crumbling shogunate, were in need of revision. The trick was for progressive Japanese to absorb Western ideas as a means of modernizing, without absorbing too many Western ways and crude Western social practices.

Along with the Imperial restoration came widespread public education, a court system, and a European-style bureaucracy. The reforms established a conscript army that would eventually end the automatic privileges of the samurai class. At the same time, although Japanese were eager to learn from foreigners, foreigners themselves were still considered dangerous.

Outsiders, *gaijin*, are seen still as different in a way foreigners in Western countries are not. Conspicuous by their very appearance, Westerners are simply beyond the Japanese social web. There is no entrance to it for a non-Japanese. It seems incongruous, then, for a society which has modernized its economy and its diplomacy, and which has even taught the West something about managing economies and industries, to be so wary of allowing the outside world in. It distresses some foreigners to be pointed at and viewed as curiosities in outlying precincts of Tokyo and in Japan's countryside.

It is worthwhile, however, to reflect that while it is not generally in the nature of Westerners to stare at foreigners, ignorance of the outside world is not a Japanese preserve. Provincialism is not unusual anywhere in the world, and ignorance of the world, while regrettable, is not a vice.

Even though foreign travel is becoming fashionable among Japanese, encouraged increasingly by government agencies, tourism isn't internationalization. Japanese who do manage to take on the manner of the world traveler are often viewed as somewhat odd. There is still an edge of distrust of Japanese who have been abroad for a long time, speak foreign languages too fluently, or have many foreign friends. It is an open secret that some diplomats who return to Japan after their foreign assignments, drop their fluency in foreign languages quickly, lest they appear to have gone over to the other side.

In recent times, America's longest-tenured ambassador to Japan, Mike Mansfield, was often accused by the American business community in Japan as being the ambassador *from* Japan rather than *to* Japan for his seeming lack of interest in publicly demanding Japanese concessions on trade.

Westerners are generally appreciative and proud of their fellows who manage to survive, succeed, or prosper in other cultures or do their nation's work abroad. Few, save the odd spy, have been pilloried for understanding the outside world too well when they return home. It may be the lessons of Christian missionary zeal, or colonialism, or both, that have done this; the Japanese didn't try colonialism until it was out of fashion and then were very bad at it, to put the kindest possible face on historic Japanese imperialism.

But Japanese have never welcomed foreigners into their midst for any lengthy period. Unaccustomed to strangers in their strange land, recent Japanese governments for decades dragged their feet about offering a home to refugees, boat people, from Indochina. One prime minister, exasperated by many questions from reporters as to why Japan would not take but a handful of the refugees, replied that foreigners would find it very difficult to learn Japanese and adapt to the Japanese culture. Finally, under the barrage of questions

on the subject, he said, "They would not be accepted." A visit
to one small camp for refugees in Kamakura illustrated the
half-hearted attempt Japan was making to help these unwelcome guests. There simply was not enough of anything
at the facility, not enough sleeping space, not enough textbooks, not enough instructors. The obvious object of the
camp was to house these refugees until they could be shipped
to the United States. Instead of welcoming the refugees,
Japan became the major financial supporter of the United
Nations Commission on Refugees, using Japanese yen to re-
settle refugees elsewhere. This use of money, instead of heart
and helping hand, remains a constant criticism of modern
Japanese governments when they approach problems that
have to do with the outside world.

But the prime minister was wrong about the ability of
refugees to prosper in Japan, and today's government only
grudgingly admits it. An increasing, though still small, number of refugees have come to Japan, and these strangers have
confounded those who thought they couldn't succeed. They
are far from the mainstream and they face considerable discrimination, but they have shown that they can fit into a
comfortable niche in Japanese society if allowed, by working
mainly in labor and the service trades. The question of equal
rights and fair treatment is one that will soon have to be
faced. The immigration of strangers into Japan's midst is not
accepted with equanimity by Japan's right wing and other
conservative factions, who see the dangers of intermarriage
diluting Japan's vaunted sense of homogeneity. Yet the
government estimates that more than 100,000 Asian aliens
now reside in Japan illegally, working in menial jobs and
seemingly protected from expulsion as long as their labor
is needed. Other sources estimate the number may be closer
to 300,000.

Among new concerns for Japanese facing the eventuality
of a changing population is a growing Islamic community.
This new population, which may number as many as 30,000,
is composed primarily of Pakistanis and Bangladeshis, but
includes many Iranians and a number of converted Japanese.

Intermarriage of Islamic men and Japanese women is beginning, and some who disapprove charge that some Islamic men marry only to get a visa and will eventually desert their Japanese families. This may be true, but the social situation has turned out to be less difficult for these illegals than the prime minister feared. Although many of the Islamics do not learn the language and stay within their own groups, the adaptation of many from Thailand and other Southeast Asian nations has been swift, and their acceptance has been surprising.

Members of Japanese minority communities and women know where the lines are drawn against them. Young persons of Korean ancestry need not apply for executive training positions at the nation's major companies, although there is no formal discrimination against them. Yet it is possible for some well-connected persons to be given opportunities that prove the rule. A woman may be promoted to an editorship or a managerial post in an advertising agency. An exceptional Japan-born, well-educated, and well-connected Korean may get a minor executive position with a major firm. But exclusivity, ethnocentrism, and old-fashioned xenophobia is common.

A Korean who becomes a nationalized Japanese is still known as a Korean despite his Japanese name, and in instances where such persons are involved with the law, the press usually manages to drop the hint that this person is not a natural Japanese. When the Hotel New Japan in downtown Tokyo's Akasaka entertainment district burned spectacularly with a fearsome loss of life—the worst in postwar history—all the major newspapers reported that the owner had neglected to install enough sprinklers on the floors where thirty-two people died. Word passed through the press that the hotel was Korean-owned, as though that made any difference. It may have: the management said it could not secure large enough bank loans to install a needed new sprinkler system. But the inference being drawn at the time was that the hotel was mismanaged, unlike a purely Japanese company, and was not creditworthy.

Speaking Inside and Outside

Many simpler forms of antiforeign behavior seem ingrained. Foreigners long resident in Japan or scholars who have mastered the Japanese language and much of its cultural complexities often find themselves in situations where Japanese refuse to respond to them. It is as though a veil has descended between the foreigners and Japanese, preventing the Japanese from hearing their own language issuing from a foreign face.

"Many Japanese have the preconception that anything coming out of a white foreigner's mouth is English or some other foreign language that they cannot understand," writes Japan's most popular language educator, Osamu Mizutani. "Even if those foreigners should be speaking Japanese, they will deny this fact because they think a foreigner cannot possibly be speaking Japanese."

Sometimes the in-group attitude backfires. From time to time a foreigner fluent in Japanese will find himself with a foreign-born Japanese who speaks little or no Japanese. Invariably, although the foreigner will initiate the conversation with, say, a sales clerk, the replies will be directed toward the Japanese face, not the foreign one. It depends, according to Mizutani, "on whether one looks Japanese or not."

There is also a widespread language snobbery. A former Japanese colleague of mine who was growing up in Canada was sent to Japan as a teenager to visit his grandparents in Japan in the middle 1930s. As luck would have it, he was drafted into the Japanese Imperial army. In the army in China he suffered vilification and beatings because his Japanese was bad and his English was good; one memorable beating was inflicted after he was discovered reading a book of English poetry. After the war he stayed in Japan, married, had two children, and successfully practiced journalism in Japan—in Japanese and English—for thirty-five years. When he died at the age of sixty-six, an office secretary who had worked with him said to me, "You know, until a few years ago, his Japanese was not so good."

The Japanese and their language have constructed what Professor Roy Andrew Miller, in his book, *Japan's Modern Myth: The Language and Beyond*, characterizes as a maze. Language and race and fitted together in a self-validating circle. There is no way for outsiders to work their way into the circle. Foreign language scholars, translators, and collaborators can be honored with decorations, toasted, and feted, but they are always outside the maze.

It is not only to foreigners that Japanese remain stand-offish; within the maze of the so-called homogeneous population are other mazes. Even the classes above the *burakumin* had their own problems. During the feudal era, not surprisingly, the warriors, who had no trade but were expected to lead exemplary and upper class lives, very often became dependent on the merchants. The samurai often were so deeply indebted that the merchants developed a smug and subversively defiant attitude toward the warriors. The merchants also often financed the politicians who didn't have private wealth. Even today, Japan's business establishment and the nation's bureaucrats and politicians consider themselves coequal in deciding the fate of the nation; politicians look to businessmen for financial support, and businessmen in their councils tell politicians what they wish them to do. In an interview with Norishige Hasegawa of Sumitomo Chemical on the political power of business in Japan, he remarked that coincidentally he and some of his old classmates were having dinner that night with the prime minster. The men, all presidents and chairmen of large industrial companies, were going to give the prime minister their recommendation for the important post of governor of the Bank of Japan. When I asked what university this powerful alumni association represented, Hasegawa said, "Not university, high school. I'm wearing my old school tie." When the prime minister announced the name of the new governor of the Bank of Japan, no one in the business community was surprised.

Homegrown Strangers

In 1841, the five young men who cast off from their dock in Shikoku on a day's fishing trip were anything but outsiders. They were unschooled Japanese peasant boys from simple, hard-working families. One of them, Manjiro, had lost his father as a child and had to abandon his education so he could work to support his family.

The catch was good but as luck would have it the ship lost its steering and was blown out to sea. After drifting for several days the boys managed to beach their boat on a deserted island and were stranded there for several months. An American whaling ship, the *John Howland*, passed by, giving a wide berth to Japan, which was in the habit of fatally discouraging foreign whalers who landed on their shores. The crew spied the boys on the island, hove to, and brought them aboard. There was no question of returning them to Japan. As the voyage's whaling mission was finished, the skipper, William Whitfield, continued on toward Hawaii. He dropped four of the boys off in Hawaii in the care of missionaries, but brought the most inquisitive of them back to the Howland's home port, New Bedford, Massachusetts. There, and in a nearby town, over the next seven years, the unschooled Manjiro, temporarily to be called John Mung, learned English and got an elementary and middle school education. Although only sixteen, he was an apt pupil of English, astronomy, mathematics, and later, navigation. He was soon able to qualify himself as a seaman. He shipped out on a whaling voyage around the southern tip of Africa, and by the time the ship made home port, this little schooled foreigner had been promoted to second in command.

Manjiro decided it was time to go home, but he didn't want to return home as poor as he had left it. He headed for the gold fields of California, where he worked in a mine for a while to learn about gold and then staked his own claim. Manjiro made a modest strike and headed home richer—via Hawaii, of course, where he could pick up the homesick friends he had left behind ten years before. They bought passage on a whaler heading toward Japan and when the vessel neared Okinawa on February 3, 1851, the young men were dropped in a small boat to make their way to shore, while the whaler headed out to sea to avoid any official contact.

If Manjiro and his companions were expecting a grand welcome, they were rudely disappointed. Instead, he and his companions were summarily tossed into jail as suspected spies, treated like foreigners, interrogated for many weeks at the local level, and then transferred to Kyushu for even more intense questioning by the Shogun's not so gentle minions. The records of the interrogations show Manjiro to have been a keen observer in the United States, with some rather wry opinions about the contrast between the two nations. He pointed out to his interrogators that in America the political "lords" did not live protected in high castles but walked in the streets like common folk. There were many subjects he did not understand clearly, Christianity being one. Toward the end of the questioning, it appears he made up answers to satisfy and impress his interrogators. Manjiro and his colleagues were eventually granted grudging release, but were never able to evade the suspicion of divided loyalty. They had broken out of the circle and were not being admitted back in. The shipwrecked fishermen were not returned home until 1852, and even then they were still under suspicion as American spies.

When Commodore Matthew Perry arrived in 1853 to open Japan's ports to trade, Manjiro was called upon to serve in the background of the negotiations by the Shogunate because of his knowledge of America and of the English language. Although he was named an official and was given the samurai's privilege of carrying two swords, he was not accepted as a samurai by true samurai, but he was given the privilege of using a surname, a privilege denied to peasants.

When the first Japanese embassy sailed for the United States in 1860, Manjiro was in the party on the *Powhatan*, but was watched closely for signs of disaffection. He was

careful not to return with any printed or written material
that might appear to be evidence of spying. But he later made
the mistake of an impromptu visit to an American ship in
Tokyo harbor and was reprimanded severely for it. It was
more than a minor infraction in the eyes of the authorities:
Manjiro had been out of sight and may have committed some
sort of treason. He never regained status.

A century after Manjiro's fall, just after World War II, a
clever young physicist named Akio Morita cofounded a small
company that was to become the electronics giant called
Sony. Morita is the fifteenth-generation head of a wealthy
family of sake brewers, but he stepped out of that maze to
enter a field already filled with famous Japanese corporate
names. Leaving the sake business in other family hands, he
struck out for new fields. Such moves were becoming more
common in the aftermath of the war, but in some tradition-
alist eyes, this was extraordinary behavior. By the end of the
World War II, seeking markets in the West was a perfectly
understandable practice; there was virtually no market in
war-stricken Japan.

Morita chose the brand name Sony for the company because it had no concrete Japanese or foreign meaning, only
a remote link to the Latin word for sound. It would be spelled
in Roman letters and would be pronounced the same in every
country in the world in every tongue. At home Sony was
considered an upstart company, and its foreign dealings
viewed with some suspicion in official circles. In 1952 Morita
and his politically well-connected partner, Masaru Ibuka,
applied to the powerful Ministry of International Trade and
Industry for permission to export $25,000 to the United
States to buy the technology from which to develop a transistor for use in radios. The request was denied. Morita's
company was unknown (it was then called Tokyo Tsushin
Kogyo, or Totsuko for short), foreign currency was insufficient, and what's more, why would this company, and not
one of the old electrical giants, be seeking this technology if
it was so promising? Morita's cofounder Ibuka, a respected
engineer, persuaded the bureaucrats that they should go

ahead and trust this new company with its international ideas.

By dint of marketing genius, an outgoing personality, and optimistic determination, Morita moved his company into high local and international esteem. Subsequently, he has risen to become a vice chairman of *Keidanren*, Japan's Federation of Economic Organizations, voice of Japan's industrial establishment. Acceptance at that level took four decades. Morita now advises prime ministers on foreign policy matters and constantly lectures abroad on his views of international economic affairs. An inveterate traveler, he has befriended musicians, artists, businessmen, and political leaders in the United States and Europe. But many Japanese still consider Sony a foreign company, and Morita to be a special case, outside the normal industrial maze. Indeed, when Morita was named to the vice chairmanship of *Keidanren*, it was rumored that he had been chosen because he knew how to talk to Americans and Europeans and could relay the official line through his vast network of important foreigners. Morita's fate was not Manjiro's. And yet the notion that he is somehow not in his right circle persists. The assumption is that he will never become chairman of the organization.

In some fields acceptance abroad can on the other hand become the key to acceptance at home. A few years in Paris is a prerequisite for the Japanese artist working in a Western technique such as oil painting, if there is to be acceptance of his work at home. This prerequisite for aesthetic fame has a great deal to do with Japanese insecurity of the era. With Japan's emergence as a world power, a sense of appreciation for homegrown talent is growing. But Japanese collectors are still willing to spend millions for the work of foreigners while they ignore some of the stunning avant garde work, particularly much of the recent sculpture rooted in Japanese cultural values, that impresses foreign critics and collectors.

Among some of the homegrown Japanese outside of their accustomed maze is Japan's brilliant conductor Seiji Ozawa.

Maestro Ozawa has led the Boston Symphony on tour throughout the world and has conducted the world's major orchestras. But he has had to create his own podium in Japan. As a young man Ozawa eschewed the closed system under which musicians follow a prescribed route of decades-long obedience to an established master. Ozawa did not wish to follow the long route from instrumentalist to conductor; he felt his instrument would be the orchestra. But there was no way in Japan for him to learn his instrument. The rigid system of teacher and devoted disciple would not bend to deal with his idea.

Consequently, Ozawa went abroad, and the late Leonard Bernstein of the New York Philharmonic was impressed with Ozawa's talent. Bernstein gave Ozawa the opportunities he could not find at home. But in Japan, even after he was a critical success in America, displeasure with Ozawa's refusal to follow the prescribed path denied him the podiums offered to him in the West. In reaction he founded the New Japan Philharmonic, composed of young players, which he sponsors and often conducts when he is in Japan.

Architects, designers, filmmakers, musicians—even businessmen with new and unorthodox ideas—have their battles with a society that does not relish individuality and in some cases finds it threatening. The old proverb, which asserts that the nail that sticks up gets hammered down, is still operative, although many young Japanese insist that they see change coming. Japan is still a place where insiders can make themselves outsiders, and where outsiders are unable to make themselves insiders.

Becoming Jewish

There is no Rabbi *of* Tokyo, but there is a rabbi *in* Tokyo who ministers to a small and internationally eclectic flock: American and European business persons based in Japan, a dwindling number of aged, long-resident Russian emigrés, students, and traveling Jewish tourists. There are some Japanese Jews, converted spouses of Jewish men and women, but unlike China, which claims an historic enclave of Chinese Jews at Kaifeng, Japan makes no such claim.

Periodically a Japanese gentleman will telephone the Jewish Community Center to inquire how he can become a Jew. To one of these requests, the young rabbi asks, naturally, "And why would you want to become a Jew?" The answer, with few variations, was straightforward: "I want to become a Jew so I can learn how to make a lot of money."

The stereotypes that Japanese accept about foreigners are legion and are perpetuated by a rigid educational system. The early Meiji leaders were looking Westward for the qualities that made other nations great. They adapted aspects of the German educational system, selected parts of a French system of civil law, and established a quasi-British style parliament and cabinet system. But despite their respect for and adaptation of aspects of Western culture, the common stereotypes about foreign groups—the Scots are stingy, blacks are lazy—linger.

Unfortunately, for those who would like to see the Japanese divest themselves of their stereotype of the Jew, the national educational syllabus is against them. One of the four Shakespeare plays that Japanese school children study is *The Merchant of Venice,* with its portrayal of the ultimate usurer, Shylock. Jewish organizations lament the selection, but have been reluctant to attempt the task of convincing the Ministry of Education that with thirty-eight Shakespeare plays to choose from, "Merchant" might be no loss to the curriculum if it were replaced with another.

Eve Kaplan, an American scholar who has done considerable research in Japan, translated Japanese dictionary definitions several years ago and found many to be highly pejorative. For example: "Jews covet money very much . . ." She was able to persuade many publishers to consider revisions in subsequent editions. Some Japanese scholars pointed out to her that their definitions were, in fact, taken from English language dictionaries. Occasional flurries of anti-Semitic literature erupt in Japan, as happened in 1987, and Japanese dictionary definitions are still unflattering, if not downright disparaging. Their definitions of the word "Jew" routinely contain such antagonistic words as usurer, dishonest merchant, miser. Japanese anti-Semitism seems rather passive though, in comparison with that of the Germans during the war. When Hitler was urging his Japanese allies to persecute Jews, nothing of the kind happened. "Japan has not had a tradition of religious or cultural anti-Semitism," the Anti-Defamation League of B'nai B'rith noted in 1987, while warning that the issue should not be ignored lest tacit approval be given this evil.

To many who know Japan and its people, the sporadic surge of popular books that blame Jews for all the world's, and Japan's, ills, are unfortunate anomalies. As one wise member of the Jewish community of Japan put it, "To the Japanese, for the little they know of the world and its people, all foreigners are Jews." During World War II Japan became a haven for several thousand Jews who escaped from Lithuania through the courtesy of a Japanese consular official. The consul, Senpo Sugihara, granted them transit visas to Japan knowing there was no place they could transit to from Japan. The Jews managed to make it across the Soviet Union and to land in Kobe, a trading port in western Japan. There, all through the war, a *yeshiva,* (full-time Hebrew school) thrived with no interference from the Japanese.

Marvin Tokayer, a former rabbi to the Tokyo Jewish community, has studied the era and interviewed many of the survivors of those years. He says that midway in the war the Nazis were increasing their demands that the Japanese imprison the Jews. Japanese authorities ordered two elders of the community to travel to Tokyo so that the Japanese could interrogate them and see for themselves why the Jews were so hated by the Germans. As Rabbi Tokayer has reconstructed it, when one of their interrogators asked what the Jews had done to make the Nazis hate the Jews so much, one of the elderly, bearded Jews peered patiently across the table and explained, "It is because we are Orientals; look at your partners, the master race: Aryan, blond hair, blue eyes, tall, and strong." After all the Jews are destroyed, he told his Japanese hosts, the Nazis will come after the Japanese. It was an audacious performance, but it sobered the Japanese. The Jews were sent back to Kobe, not to be bothered again. The Nazis also attempted to persuade the Japanese to persecute the 17,000 stateless Jews who had found their way to Shanghai and who were under Japanese control there, but beyond requiring them to move into what was to be the only ghetto in Asia there were no pogroms or confiscations of property.

The stereotype of the wealthy European Jew, the consummate businessman and moneymaker, had so intrigued some Japanese that, according to Tokayer's research, a scheme was formulated to bring the persecuted Jews of Europe to Manchuria to help develop commerce and take some of the international opprobrium from Japan for seizing the territory. Tokayer detailed the Manchurian scheme in his 1979 book *The Fugu Plan*. The Japanese could get no support for their rescue plan, not even from the World Jewish Congress based in the United States, which was vainly seeking other ways to save Europe's doomed Jews.

Today, as it did during those war years, a rash of anti-Semitic books periodically appears on the Japanese market that causes concern among sophisticated Japanese and, of course, Jewish residents and visitors and Israeli diplomats. The phenomenon seems to run in cycles.

In 1970 a Japanese scholar of religion, Shichihei Yamamoto, pseudonymously wrote a million-seller, entitled in Japanese *Nipponjin to Yudayajin* (*The Japanese and the Jews*), a bold attempt to compare cultural and religious practices and beliefs of the Japanese with those of the Jews. The book and its mysterious origins—it was said to have been written in Japanese by a foreigner, which was considered amazing—bemused the press for many months while sales mounted. Jews were likened in many respects to Japanese, and there was a short-lived period of philo-Semitism. Years later a successful Japanese businessman, who had teamed up with Ray Kroc to bring Kroc's McDonald's restaurants to Japan, wrote a book called *The Jewish Way of Blowing the Million-aire's Bugle*. Some readers viewed it as a certain route to financial success, although the author knew nothing about Jews, only heresay. A potboiler entitled *The Secret of the Jewish Power That Moves the World* was written by Eizaburo Saito, a respected Japanese parliamentarian of the mainstream Liberal Democratic Party. The book descended to the libel of asserting a worldwide Jewish conspiracy.

In the late 1980s, as Japan struggled through a difficult financial period, the time was ripe for another bout of accusation against the Jews. The 1986 onslaught of anti-Semitic publications was largely the work of Masami Uno, the leading author of such works. His accusations were usually based on the fictitious and discredited *Protocols of the Elders of Zion*. By mid-1987 Uno had sold more than 650,000 copies of his books. The sales of his latest work, *Understand Judea and the World Will Come Into View*, soared to 850,000 copies before petering out. As other authors climbed onto the bandwagon, some Japanese bookstores set aside special sections for books on Judaism and Jews.

There may be an economic reason for such fads. Shelf space in Japanese bookstores is at a premium; consequently, a book that doesn't take off quickly, usually within a week, is soon replaced by another that will hopefully pay its way. Thus, most books fail financially. Shichihei Yamamoto, the man who wrote *The Japanese and The Jews* under the pseudonym Isaiah ben Dassan, once lamented the situation to me in his tiny, paper-choked office in Tokyo. There is no secondary market for books that do not make it, no discounting, by agreement among the publishers and booksellers, he said. What happens, then, to the books that don't make it first time out? He shrugged, "We must take them back and sell them for scrap." For this reason, when a book scores brisk sales, imitators are fast off the mark to cash in on the fad.

In Uno's latest book, not only Franklin Roosevelt, but Marco Polo, the Rockefeller family, Matthew Perry, Columbus, and Mike Mansfield were all named as Jewish agents of the international Jewish conspiracy. The author also implicated such giant multinational corporations as AT&T, IBM, Exxon, General Motors, and Ford. Some of the titles found in the special Jewish sections reveal the Japanese preoccupation with mercantilism. In a book like *Make Money with Stocks the Jews Aim For*, there is admiration for imagined Jewish business acumen, amid what one might generously call a lot of misunderstood history and unconscious anti-Semitism. Others deal with the conspiracy theory so familiar to Jews elsewhere; they include *Japan: Blueprint of Jewish Conspiracy. How Japan's Nucleus Has Intercepted Freemasonry* and *The Jewish Plan for the Conquest of the World*. Another, entitled *Scenario for Annihilation*, rehashes the denials of the Holocaust popular in anti-Semitic circles in the U.S.

At the time of the latest rash of anti-Jewish books, some popular and serious magazines joined in. One respected journal, *Chuo Koron*, published the translation of an article by Grace Halsell, an American freelance writer called *How the Jews Control the American Media*. Though the rise of anti-Semitism should not be dismissed lightly, its acceptance in Japan shows how far behind the curve of sophistication today's Japanese find themselves. Put in context, many observers, including Professor Masao Kunihiro of Sophia University in Tokyo, suggested that the books show a Japanese resentment toward the United States over trade wrangles. "Many Japanese erroneously associate Jews with America," said Kunihiro.

Professor Shuichi Kato, an astute critic of Japanese society, put it this way in an Asahi Shimbun article:

> Most Japanese have never talked to a Jew. They haven't sat next to one on the Bullet Train from Tokyo to Osaka, for example, and chatted for a few hours. Most Japanese don't take a Jewish conspiracy seriously but think it's an intriguing thesis. Anti-Semitism is the only way Japanese can safely vent their anti-American feelings. We know our prosperity depends on the United States. That's why there is little criticism of the administration's attempts to appease Washington. Frus-

tration at kowtowing to Uncle Sam is converted into anti-Semitism. Jews are the scapegoats for Japan bashing.

The popular image of the Jew, Kato wrote, "is a cross between Einstein and Shakespeare's Shylock, the epitomes of intelligence and greed."

A lot of the writing seen by outsiders as being derogatory actually carries quite a bit of misplaced flattery; Uno insisted he intended no anti-Semitism. Said one member of the Jewish community in Japan jokingly, "If everybody here thinks I'm a brilliant businessman because I'm Jewish that's all right with me." The fascination with the Jews continues, although politically Japan is only slowly beginning to increase its trade in Israel in the face of the Arab boycott, to which most major Japanese firms sedulously adhere. Japan maintains full diplomatic relations with Israel, and Israelis sometimes boast, correctly, that Israel is one of the few countries in the world that has a trade surplus with Japan.

Japan's dependence on Middle East oil and merchandise trade with the Arab world has prevented the full commerce natural between nonbelligerent nations. The presence of a Palestine Liberation Organization office in Japan rankles the Israelis, and visits to Japan by PLO Chairman Yassir Arafat always include an anti-Israel lecture. Major Japanese firms refrained for many years from dealing with Israel rather than suffer a cutoff of Arab-controlled oil. Certain second-line companies were tacitly given the assignment of trading with Israel while goods with some of the biggest Japanese brand names remained unobtainable. But despite the boycott and attendant political problems, relations are improving.

Concerned about the anomalous situation, American Jews are now raising money to set up a Jewish cultural center in Tokyo independent of the Israel Embassy and the established Jewish community. They hope to educate Japanese about Jews and Jewish culture. It is an ambitious undertaking to change attitudes of people who can cling to centuries-old prejudices. "But Jews are optimistic," shrugs one of the organizers. Perhaps a bit too optimistic.

CHAPTER TEN

THE HONEY BEE SOCIETY

Japan's success at the industrial game, dominated for so many centuries by nations of the West, is still imperfectly understood. Could cold pragmatism, discipline, and resourcefulness alone have propelled Japan to the forefront of trading nations without Western technology? Japanese themselves often admit that the linkage to outside technology was necessary, and that it continues to be necessary. There are signs that the old dependence is decaying—many young Japanese already think it's gone—and in some fields the students are now teaching the masters. Yet the image of Japan as a nation of copiers lingers in many quarters, and not least in Japan.

I was reminded of this while browsing with a friend in an expensive boutique in Tokyo. When my friend, a visitor, scanned the price tag of a French silk necktie, he dropped it as though it had bitten him. "A hundred and fifty bucks!" he exploded. "Why is everything so damned expensive here?"

I was about to give him the standard reply about tariffs and trade problems and protection of local markets, as well as a lecture on snobbery and greed. But before I could begin, our Japanese acquaintance shrugged and volunteered, "We're so good at imitating things that the only way the average Japanese can tell the difference between the genuine and the imitation is by the price." He put the necktie back on the rack and added with a sly smile, "I'm glad you weren't looking at Baccarat crystal."

It seemed too casual an admission, though a revealing one, of the charge that the Japanese are at best imitators. Ingenious, clever, efficient, and practical perhaps, but still copiers. The Japanese have often denigrated themselves in this regard. Nearly one hundred years ago, the president of Japan's United Chamber of Commerce, and the father of modern Japanese business, Eiichi Shibusawa, lamenting the slow growth of exports, confessed, "The trouble is that while the Japanese can imitate everything, they cannot, at the present time, invent superior things."

Today's Japanese don't like the lingering charge, but they are not uniformly defensive about it. They have innovated and invented many superior things, and as everybody knows, they certainly have learned how to export. Japanese innovation in automotive technology, for example, has helped them earn the respect of their overseas rivals, and in fact, the new Japanese cars are fast becoming the benchmark for American and European makers. It is true that the Japanese have had their flops in just about every field, including autos. But with a tenacity born of confidence—based on integrated, well-financed companies whose bankers work with them as partners and whose projects do not have to yield quarterly dividends—they have been able to take chances. Freed of the need to produce quick profits, and aided by tax laws that made it more sensible for investors to stay with the company for the long haul rather than to invest for dividends, they could take the time to grow their companies. They could also plough back profits into new equipment and into research and development.

Japan's high technology exports are soaring, but the nation's government funding of research and development is officially only half that of the United States. The number is low because most research and development is carried out by Japan's companies. And with certain tax advantages and low interest loans, Japan's company labs are subsidized more than they would appear to be. Furthermore, the high technology laboratories the United States supports are devoted to military projects, whereas the Japanese have been spared the necessity of doing a lot of military research. Nevertheless, the U.S. Department of Defense concluded in a recent report that Japanese research leads the United States and Europe significantly in aspects of five critical technologies that have both civilian and military implications for the future. They are semiconductor materials and microelectronic circuits, machine intelligence and robotics, photonics, superconductivity, and biotechnology materials and processes. Some research in those fields is being done by Japanese scientists and advanced degree students in Western laboratories and campuses, where results are shared.

There are few technical secrets today; the spread of technical data is inevitable. It is increasingly difficult for creators to keep to themselves the value derived from their findings. Japan's critics in the scientific community say the Japanese do not share their research as they should, even though Japanese are eager and contributing members at many international technical meetings and subscribe to the international conventions on protecting the developers and owners of so-called intellectual property, such as software and other original research. Most research in Japan occurs not at universities or government-financed institutions, but in the labs at private companies, where proprietary information is guarded jealously for competitive reasons.

As many as 25,000 Japanese researchers and graduate students study for advanced degrees in United States universities, most of them technical, but, surprisingly, thousands are receiving Master's degrees in business administration. As for Americans, less than a fifth of that number are studying at Japanese universities.

Even at home in the United States, it is not uncommon

for American student researchers to find themselves outnumbered in their university laboratories by foreign students. A former Massachusetts Institute of Technology student researcher says he looked around and was surprised to find that ten of the twelve recent research affiliates in his laboratory were from Japan. One analyst points out that Japanese companies have endowed more chairs at M.I.T. than they have at Japan's own University of Tokyo. Beyond endowing chairs and funding scholarships, Japanese companies are willing to go farther to tap the possible benefits of research from the United States. For example, the conglomerate Hitachi, Ltd., has financed a research laboratory on the campus of an American university, the Irvine campus of the University of California, a leading biomedical research center. Any patents originating with joint staff or equipment in the laboratory will be owned by the university and will be licensed to Hitachi. But the top two floors of the building will house Hitachi researchers only, and their results will belong to Hitachi. Of course there will be a free collegial interchange of ideas among all the researchers, which should benefit all.

The laboratory's construction—and attendant regulations—seemed a fair deal to the university, strapped as it is for funds, but its announcement raised cries of "free ride" against the Japanese company. Hitachi officials, who were approached by the university to establish the lab, bristle at the criticism of the operation, saying they thought they were doing the university a favor. A few years ago Shiseido, the leading Japanese cosmetics company, entered an $85 million joint venture with Harvard and the Massachusetts General Hospital, its teaching hospital, to set up a skin research laboratory. The patents from research go to Harvard, but only Shiseido will have the right to license any new technology developed there. Other American universities have been eager to take Japanese corporate money because funding from the nation's foundations has shrunk.

The reach of Japan's global technology-hungry companies is expanding. NEC followed Hitachi and decided to invest $75,000,000 in a laboratory for artificial intelligence research near the town of Princeton, New Jersey. A subsidiary of Kobe Steel, Ltd., has planned a multimillion dollar investment in a computer research facility in Palo Alto, California, near the Stanford University campus.

The Sincerest Form of Flattery

Physicist Makoto Kikuchi, who once headed the Electro-technical Laboratory of Japan's Ministry of International Trade and Industry and the research laboratory of Sony, accepts the criticism that Japan is, in Western eyes, a copycat. But he insists there are different cultural approaches to the labeling of originality. "Before we began to use Chinese characters," he explained not long ago, "the original form of the Japanese verb 'to learn,' *manabu,* came from the word, *maneru,* which means 'to imitate.' " Kikuchi went on to explain this notion of imitation:

> The first step to learning something is to imitate something. For example, in learning flower arrangement, or Japanese fencing, or almost any art or craft, the students are ordered to imitate everything from the teacher. They are told to discount their own way, they are told just to imitate. After the first year they can try their own way. We shouldn't imitate for a too long time, but only until the student has learned the fundamentals well. Then the student can innovate.

In the traditional crafts and arts, that first step can take years of apprenticeship, years of discipline. A potter's apprentice today will spend years kneading clay and making the same simple kind of pottery vessel over and over again, until his master is pleased that it is being done properly (which often means that he or she is imitating the master's work). An American potter learning the craft in Japan recently wrote that she made 200 tea bowls before she was allowed to try anything else. The method itself may have been a learned system taken from the Chinese, who lent so much to the culture of Japan. Traditional actors and artisans still take the name of their familial predecessor. A carpenter's apprentice may spend months pulling a spokeshave on practice pieces of lumber until he can create a perfectly controlled cut.

In today's high-powered world of modern science and technology, the skills are learned faster, but the entire Japanese educational system is still geared to passive learning. Western teachers in Japan are often dismayed by the lack of challenge and questioning from students. It is often attributed to language difficulty, or to a natural diffidence or reticence. But the Japanese student is accustomed to absorbing information from his teacher. Today, more and more criticism is being lodged against the system that puts discipline and group effort before creativity and individual expression. But older workers fear the breakdown of the old system that instilled discipline and toughness. One such person remembers how in middle school everyone had to comply with a dress code that forbade wearing more than one thin undershirt, even in the dead of winter and in normally underheated classrooms. The chattering teeth didn't detract from the mental effort, he insists, and in fact, bonded the group and gave them a sense of spiritual strength.

Imitation isn't for everyone, Kikuchi will admit. He is reminded of an American woman who joined his research work at the MITI laboratory:

> I tried to teach her how to use the spectrometer, but she was full of her own way; she never followed my instructions. Everything had to be her way; it was a difference in cultures. It took her a long time to get to the central core of what I was teaching, but once she arrived there it was good for her to know she had done it herself. Perhaps there should be a compromise between the two ways.

There is another aspect of the subject that Westerners such as Kikuchi's independent student fail to grasp: the nature of education and work in Japan is social. Kikuchi feels that the Japanese have a cultural advantage in their ability to achieve success through teamwork. He laments the move toward individualism introduced into Japan from the West: "Japan used to be a honeybee society before and during the war, but not so much now. I say we must be careful; otherwise Japan will never be the same, it will be changed, with too much individualism."

Kikuchi himself, while working in Sony Corporation laboratories in 1955, was instrumental in helping a team of researchers translate the Bell Laboratories invention of the transistor into a new type, one with a high-enough frequency to use in radios. It was no small feat; the job required knowledge, ingenuity, and inventiveness. In crucial experiments, one approach that the Sony team had not even bothered to try was one that had been tried at Bell Labs and discarded as unavailing.

The reasons for not following the old lead were obvious. "In those days," says Kikuchi, "the voice of Bell Labs was like the voice of God." If the geniuses at Bell Labs said it couldn't be done that way, then it couldn't be done. But a young scientist audaciously suggested that the American researchers hadn't pursued the process far enough. Kikuchi told him go ahead with the experiment even though it had been tried many times before; sure enough, the young man's team made the breakthrough.

When physicist Leo Esaki was awarded a Nobel Prize in 1973 for his work in miniature electronics, he was employed by IBM in the United States. But his pioneering work, the development of the tunnel diode, was done in the Sony labs more than a decade before. Today at Sony the work is presented not as the development of one man but as a group effort.

Although some progressive companies are attempting to instill a sense of creativity in their young research staffers, true Western-style individualism and eccentricity is not wanted. It is still the group effort that works in Japan. Foreigners given the still rare opportunity to work with Japanese in the university and the workplace often find this to be true.

They have trouble being accepted into the group and then adapting to the social side of the endeavor. Often they are not even invited in. Kenneth G. Pechter, now a University of California Ph.D. candidate, says he went to Japan with a fine technical background but was not adequately prepared for "how things work" in Japan.

An M.I.T. exchange intern at Tokyo Institute of Technology, Pechter experienced firsthand the group methods of Japanese scientific research first hand. Besides the expected work on the research project at hand, says Pechter:

> We studied a lot of things that I couldn't figure out why. We would go off on a weekend and have a seminar on some subject—the environment in the twenty-first century, for example—and everybody would make a formal presentation. I couldn't figure out where that went, how it fit with our joint project on computer systems and expert systems. But we'd go there and study the environment. We'd have whole seminars on the subject of infinity, the mind, or mathematical philosophy. It took a long time for me to realize these were group-building exercises.

Pechter stuck with the program and participated as best he could as a member of the team. As a result, he was accepted as part of the group, and his internship was regarded by the Japanese as a success. Another American researcher, who said he could not see the rationale for these sessions in subjects outside the field, skipped the weekend retreats. "He was considered a failure because he cut off the paths of communication," Pechter says.

Tea and Technology

Japanese social critics lament the passing of fine, old disciplines. Eager innovators have found ways to robotize and automate everything possible—even that most labor intensive of Japanese culinary arts, making sushi. But the old ways are still venerated, and much of what is new is mere novelty and fad. The Japanese willingness to accept and allow the old to coexist with the new does not do away with reverence for old ways. To many minds, some things can only be done traditionally—the building of a teahouse, for example, in which the aesthetic dictates the design.

When Joe D. Price, the premier American collector of Edo period Japanese art, and his wife Etsuko decided to have a Japanese-style teahouse built on their property overlooking the Pacific in Corona del Mar, California, they hired a renowned Japanese architect and a Japanese construction company. Eight workmen arrived from Japan together with almost all the materials, most of it precut so that it could be assembled by means of traditional Japanese joinery. American workmen were still putting the finishing touches on the main house when the Japanese workmen arrived. The Americans were amused to see the Japanese show up in immaculate uniforms and then unwrap their glistening hand tools—many odd-shaped saws, augers, and edges—and lay them out like so many samurai swords. There wasn't an electric drill, saw, or nailing gun to be seen. When one of the wooden beams turned out to be not quite right for the job, a workman flew back to Japan to select a replacement and bring it back.

Amusement among the California craftsmen gave way to awe as the Japanese created an exquisite hand-built structure of unpainted pine and cypress, with aromatic tatami matting. Out of sight were all the modern conveniences, a demonstration not only of craftsmanship but of adaptation, of which the Japanese are acknowledged masters. In Japan such human technology supports the link to the past. Shinto's grand shrine at Ise, for example, is rebuilt painstakingly and replaced every twenty years. When the new shrine is finished, the old building on an adjoining plot is dismantled and a new twenty-year construction program on its replacement is begun immediately.

Japan's reverence for the craftman's touch can border on obsession, one with commercial applications. The application of the name of a famous tea ceremony schoolmaster to assembly-line ceramic bowls can raise their price dramatically. And in a world where the work of human hands is less and less visible, the value of anything made by human hands must naturally rise.

At the other extreme, modern construction in Japan's cities is so efficient that small buildings seem to rise overnight. The sudden appearance of a new structure comes as a shock sometimes because construction sites are masked from view to keep down dust and to minimize the danger to pedestrians from falling objects. The canvas or plastic sheeting is only removed when the building is just about finished. Building foundations are designed to withstand the earthquakes that rattle Japanese windows somewhere almost every day. The gas lines for furnaces and hot water heaters are equipped with automatic shutoff valves, the result of lessons learned in the disastrous fires that swept through Tokyo and Yokohama in the 1923 earthquake. Today, after every tremor above a threshold intensity, janitors in office and apartment buildings and householders can be found trooping to their furnaces to reset gas valves.

Japanese managers searching for ideas around the world adopted Western robotics technology and automation while Westerners were still eying the technology only warily. At Nissan Motors the first robots were immediately given the names of movie stars—their pinups affixed to the robot arms—to try to make them seem less hostile. At the time, the United States already had the world's highest manufacturing productivity, labor peace, enough exports to satisfy most companies, and no serious disruption of local markets by imports of Japanese manufactured goods. I attended a robotic welding demonstration held for American automakers in Detroit, but they were not impressed. Perhaps for shipbuilding, one Detroit engineer suggested.

Things were different in Japan, which had a need to produce goods more efficiently. Cost has been central to Japan's export offensive, and new techniques were a godsend. Productivity is not a measure of how hard a human being can work, but how much work he is able to produce in a given period of time. The Japanese realized early on that new machinery could raise the output of every worker faster and more reliably than trying to force the worker to work harder. The Japanese industrial worker was already being pushed to work as hard as he could, and the pace was already appearing inhumane to some.

Adaptations had to be made. The old Western industrial system of making a batch of parts, inspecting them, and throwing out the bad ones, would not do in Japan. Every American auto assembly plant had a giant repair lot, where cars with defects that had been noticed were taken to be fixed after they came off the assembly line. In land-poor Japan, there was no space to park brand new cars that wouldn't run. The challenge, then, was to make them right the first time. Emphasis had to be placed on coordination, with engineers, designers, and factory experts working together in a team.

The parts were designed so that they could be made easily and quickly, and so that with the proper tools it would be difficult, if not impossible, for a tired worker to install them improperly. They also designed the process of assembly, making everybody on the moving assembly line inspect the operation that had gone before. If something was wrong, the line could be stopped so that the defect could be fixed. Of course, not every car comes off the line in a Japanese assembly plant without defects. But a recent analysis found sixty defects per one hundred cars made in Japan compared with eighty-two defects per one hundred cars made in American-owned factories in the United States and more than ninety defects in Europe.

The authority to stop the assembly line is the authority to shut down production—not something handed lightly to a single man or woman in coveralls. If everyone on the line is given this power, management needs to be certain every man is a loyal supporter of the team. It also helps to explain why, for the most part, foreign adaptations of Japanese industrial quality circles cannot be transferred whole into other societies. Besides discipline and a cultural bias toward group effort, the sense of loyalty exists both ways in Japan. Management is willing to divulge much more proprietary information to workers, such as the cost of parts and routine productivity statistics, than most American managements find prudent.

The Zero Defects program for military procurement, imposed on some Japanese companies during the Korean War, introduced them to modern quality control. In fact, much of what Japanese companies learned of quality control was learned from Americans, including the legendary W. Edwards Deming. Deming is an engineer who was a prophet unheralded in his own country until he taught the Japanese how to raise productivity and make consistently top quality products. The most prestigious award for quality in Japan today is named for him. Things Deming taught, such as efficiency in manufacturing and the lowest possible inventories, have been central to Japan's continued success.

The automobile industry is a prime example. The M.I.T. researchers who studied the worldwide industry in a major five-year project, have termed the Japanese automaking method "lean production." It is accomplished though "lean design" and sensible innovation. All engineers at Japan's Honda Motor Co.—electrical, mechanical, and material engineers—spend the first three months of their employment working on the assembly line to become familiar with the product and the process, and how a particular specialty relates to the car that will be delivered to a customer. This practice is common in many industries in Japan. In their study, the M.I.T. researchers calculate that the Japanese carmakers can produce a certain type of auto in 16.8 hours, whereas it takes American makers in North America, which includes plants in Canada, an average of 25.1 hours to make a similar car. In Europe the figure is 36.2 hours. How can this be?

There is a Japanese expression, *mottainai*, which is used to refer to the sacrilege of wasting the earth's bounty. In the United States one can sometimes still hear the expression, "There's plenty more where that came from." In Japan, if there is more where "that" came from, it is a long and expensive distance away. Japanese are schooled in this philosophy from an early age. The Japanese system is to make every piece perfect and useful, contrary to the large-scale Western manufacturing philosophy of build, inspect, use, or reject.

The need to conserve originally led Japanese makers to build new steel plants perched on tidewater, so that raw materials could be delivered directly to the mill by ocean-going ships; the finished product would then be shipped away on the same ships. Such thinking conspired to produce manufacturing systems that would keep production high and costly inventory low. "This pile of steel is costing me money just while it lies there not being used," a machine tool company proprietor told me during a tour of his plant in Nagoya. "We are going to have the steel delivered to us when we need it, and not before." This is the now famous Kamban system of Toyota Motor and other companies.

Examples of innovative approaches to making things economically and correctly are plentiful in today's Japan. In a small, nondescript factory in the outskirts of Nagoya, and in a sprawling modern production plant on the Kanto plain in the shadow of Mount Fuji, machine tools make machine tool parts without human intervention, three shifts a day. At night at the Yamazaki Company plant in Nagoya, there is no reason to turn on the lights. One watchman with a flashlight keeps an eye on things. None of the techniques being used is a technological secret. In fact, when the key was turned on at Yamazaki's first automated factory, the whole operation was made possible by an American DEC computer.

Buying and Spying

Innovation by adaptation, buying, borrowing, even steal-
ing proprietary secrets, are common practices in Japan. A
school for industrial espionage was once set up and even
advertised by an enterprising gentleman in Tokyo. But it got
so much notoriety in the domestic and foreign press that the
owner was forced out of business. The practice is not confined
to the homeland-workers who change companies, and spies
posing as industry "analysts" are still a constant source of
the loss of Silicon Valley secrets. An FBI sting operation
pounced on six Hitachi and Mitsubishi employees when
they tried to buy IBM data that would enable them to make
their computers IBM-compatible. Both companies paid fines
and later entered joint agreements to share technology
with IBM.

In Osaka, I once asked permission to take a photograph in
an assembly area while on a tour of a Matsushita Electric
Industrial semiconductor plant. The company officer who
accompanied me asked me to refrain from taking the picture.
Persisting, I pointed out to him that the plant seemed to have
no device in it that I hadn't seen in similar plants in Japan
and in other countries. "It isn't what is here," my courteous
guide confided conspiratorially, "but what is not here."

What was there, or not there, I assumed, was an innovation
in the technique of making semiconductors, a field in which
Japan has excelled, grabbing the major world markets not
only in the electronic devices themselves but also in the
machines that make them. The Japanese did not invent
the semiconductor, but adapted it and refined it to compete
with the best that the inventors could produce. Moreover,
they have excelled in the design and production of the equipment that makes the electronic devices, the fingernail-size
devices that are raw materials of the future. There is creativity in recognizing where the future lies and in preparing
for it.

Makoto Kikuchi has a name for what some might call
industrial espionage. He classifies creativity into two cate-

gories: independent creativity and associative or adaptive creativity. Associative creativity, he says, is very good for innovation, which to his mind is Japan's strength. Japan's history is rich with foreign borrowings and adaptations. In the sixth century, Prince Shotoku welcomed and nurtured Buddhism from far away India, via China and Korea, and the Japanese made it distinctly Japanese. In the eighth century, Japan was importing urban planning from China, agricultural engineering from China and Korea. By the beginning of the seventeenth century, the Japanese had learned shipbuilding from Spanish and Portuguese seafarers, and Japanese ships were visiting such far away places as the Philippines, Thailand, and even Mexico before the Japanese isolated themselves.

Today one in every five patents granted in the United States is to a Japanese firm, and the share is expected to increase by about 1 percent a year. A recent study by the American Association for the Advancement of Science noted that these patents are mostly in direct commercially translatable fields such as automobiles, computers, electronics, and pharmaceuticals. For the last few years, the three or four top companies getting United States patents have been Japanese. Economist Pat Choate, a Washington public policy specialist, charged in his disturbing work *Agents of Influence* that a large percentage of Japanese patent applications represent a kind of harrassment of other genuine inventions. He called it patent flooding. The scheme is to apply for nuisance patents for peripheral parts surrounding a foreign invention, making it difficult for the originator to market the product without making a deal with the holders of the nuisance patents. Choate maintains this course of conduct is practiced by some of the largest manufacturing companies in Japan.

Unscrupulous individuals have figured out such schemes before. For a long time it was not unusual for a foreign company to enter the Japanese market with a product only to discover that the foreign company's own trademark had been registered by a Japanese individual or company. This made it impossible to get into the Japanese market under one's own name without making an arrangement to buy it back.

This sort of reckless and malicious toying is still viewed by many Japanese officials as acceptable behavior. After a two-week tour of the United States a few years ago, a leading member of the ruling political party asked me, "What do they mean when they say 'fair trade?' " Some untraveled Japanese are at a loss to understand Western concepts and conventions. But many thousands of Japanese businessmen are well-traveled enough at home and abroad that they understand the meaning of fair competition. In the Japanese context, much depends on size, power, political influence, and membership in the right circles, which determine what you can get away with. Putting in the "fix" in Manila is very different from trying to do it in the United States. Japanese businessmen are often bewildered by the rules. Some Japanese executives still see themselves as very different, and in some way immune, from the rules of the game when dealing abroad, just as Japanese tourists once delighted acting out the proverb that anything goes when one is away from home.

When two motorcycle manufacturers, Honda and Yamaha, got into a vicious battle over the share of the motorcycle market in Japan, the battle ended in an apology and the resignation of one company president. (Yamaha lost.) Japanese companies compete tooth and nail for a share of the market, but they do not generally try to run each other out of business. Alarmed Western businessmen worry that the line at which cut-throat competition ceases doesn't extend to companies beyond the seas surrounding Japan.

A researcher for a large Japanese electronics company apparently felt no embarrassment a few years ago in telling how he made the major breakthrough in producing a tiny but powerful lithium battery whose charge could last as long as ten years. His problem was that the batteries kept exploding in the laboratory when he tried to recharge them. The researcher made a trip to the United States to attend an exhibition of the Institute of Electrical and Electronics Engineers, but in fact he wanted to find out how American companies were able to work safely with lithium. At the dedication of a new factory he met an American electrical engineer who had been working on lithium batteries. The engineer told him that the new building being dedicated was designed so that the humidity could be kept extremely low, no more than 5 percent. A light went on in the Japanese researcher's brain. He hurried back to humid Japan, had the lithium battery assembly line enclosed, and drew the humidity down to 5 percent. His batteries stopped exploding; he had solved the problem. The batteries powered Kodak's original disk cameras and found many other applications.

However, things are changing rapidly as Japan gains ascendency in many new technologies. A University of Tokyo professor, Takemochi Ishii, says it is no longer effective to send study groups abroad to look into certain new technologies. In such areas as high-definition television and large-scale integrated circuits, he maintains, "we have no place to go outside Japan to learn anything about it."

History Lessons and Death Rays

At the turn of the last century the Japanese ambassador to Britain, Baron Suyematsu, declared, "We have eaten Western apples and found them delicious, and we are not likely to give them up."

It was 1904, and the Baron was not talking about diet. He may have chosen a poor metaphor, but by tasting the long-forbidden fruit of Western industrialization, Japan had lost its innocence and banished itself from its peaceful, isolated Garden of Eden. "We have electric light in Japan; you will not doubt it when I tell you that we shall never return to oil or wax," he said. "We have railways; do you think we can ever go back to walking? Shall we destroy the telegraph wires and again employ messengers?"

No one expected the Japanese to give up what they learned from the West during their Meiji era quest for rapid industrialization. Many thought it amusing that the Japanese seemed so puzzled by the intricacies of Western machinery and assumed they would never master it. They were less amused when Britain's wooden weaving looms were redesigned as faster, automatic machines by Sakichi Toyoda, and when in 1929 a British company bought the patent from Toyoda for the stunning sum of £100,000. This profitable innovation behind him, Toyoda went on to create a new and giant company, building automobiles. (The change of the company name from Toyoda to Toyota was made for orthographic reasons having to do with the differing number of brush strokes used in writing it phonetically.)

Despite industrial successes in the early days of the Meiji era, and Japan's professional military performance at the seige of Peking during the Boxer Rebellion, few believed in 1900 that the Japanese were capable of being a modern industrial state. Eight thousand Japanese troops, the largest contingent in a seven-nation force, distinguished themselves by marching boldly into Peking and relieving the beleaguered Western diplomats who had been besieged by Chinese militants. When they scored their major naval victory against the Baltic fleet of Tsarist Russia in the Tsushima Strait in 1905—only a generation after two centuries of virtual isolation—foreigners insisted that the Japanese warships, some of them purchased abroad, must have been commanded by foreign tacticians and gunnery officers.

Hardly anyone realized that the Japanese Admiral, Heihachiro Togo, had something more potent than foreign advisers: he had a telegraph on each ship. Telegraphed position reports of the approaching Russian fleet were flashed to Togo by a series of Japanese patrol boats stationed south of the Sea of Japan. It gave the Japanese fleet enough warning to be hiding in a Korean habor, ready to pounce on the Russians. The stubborn and stolid Russian Admiral Zinoviy Petrovich Rozhestvenskij contributed mightily to his own defeat by making some bold and bad decisions, but the Japanese confused the Russians, outwitted them, and sent the Russian fleet to the bottom. By using the telegraph this way,

Japan became one of the first nations in the world to employ a form of electronic warfare.

In light of such tales, the so-called miracle of Japan's resurgence after defeat in World War II isn't all that much out of context. The progress of Japan since 1945 seems less miraculous to those who lived through it than to those who saw it from the outside. For if the miracle of the mid-twentieth century was remarkable, the miracle that preceded it—Japan's nineteenth-century modernization—was no less so. And it was in the spirit of the great nineteenth-century modernization that the revival after the Pacific War was built.

Most critical analysts have correctly pointed out that while the Occupation banished some of the trappings of the old prewar Zaibatsu industrial cartel system, many of the old leading individuals and institutions, such as banks and manufacturing companies—the heart of the old cartels—were able to reassert themselves in new dress. These old companies had been granted monopoly status by the government in the Meiji Restoration beginning in 1868 in order to create a modern industrial economy. This time the old core companies—Mitsui, Mitsuibishi, Sumitomo, Yasuda, and others—began to modernize their thinking and practices. The Occupation's purge of top officials of these giant companies was also, surprisingly, an aid to the companies. Many younger, second-echelon managers, men more technically oriented than their elders, now found themselves in charge. They invoked many of the management and labor practices assumed to be of ancient vintage, such as so-called lifetime employment, seniority-based wages, and company unions.

Today virtually identical groups of companies, now called *keiretsu*, serve much the same function as the old *zaibatsu*, but more or less within the framework of new antitrust laws. The *keiretsu* have less direct influence on government than their predecessors did, but then times have changed, perhaps for the subtler. The organizations centered around industrial firms, such as major automobile companies, are the largest in Japan. Loyalty within the industrial groupings is familial and strong. It is still customary for a Mitsubishi employee, for example, to drink only Kirin beer or use a Nikon camera, those products being made by sister companies.

The manufacturing giant will own portions of all the companies in its group, whose representatives belong to the parent company's board of directors. And although initially most of these smaller member companies devoted all or most of their production to the giant, today some small-parts makers in the automotive grouping sell as much as half their production to other manufacturers.

Near the end of the Pacific War, the Japanese were cut off from their captive sources of raw materials by the Allied navies. They had begun work on many new and exotic weapons, including the basic research necessary to produce an atomic bomb. They were far behind, and their technology was uneven. Oblivious of the top secret Manhattan Project in the United States, Japanese scientists thought it would be at least another decade before they, or anybody else, would create a manmade atomic reaction, let alone a bomb. When the Enola Gay dropped the first atomic weapon over Hiroshima, Japanese scientists still thought that separating enough U-235 for a first test bomb would take several more years' work.

A Japanese scientist, Hidetsugu Yagi, had created an ultrashortwave device, the Yagi antenna, that would further the development of radar. But Japan was not able to develop a suitable full-scale radar device. The value of the antenna wasn't realized in Japan until after the war when it was revealed that the U.S. Navy had used it against the Japanese. Toward the end of the war, United States bomber and fighter aircraft were able to fly bombing and reconnaissance missions over the home islands with virtual impunity because of Japan's lack of radar.

During World War II, before Japan was being harassed daily by American bombing raids, aircraft factories were turning out formidable opponents for Allied fliers, including the long-range Mitsubishi Zero fighter. The Zero dominated the skies of the Pacific for a long time with its high maneuverability, speed, rate of climb, and range, partially achieved by denying heavy armor plate protection to the pilot. When the first Zero fighters appeared over Manila in 1941, United States military intelligence officers surmised that the Zeros had flown from an aircraft carrier that had slipped into Philippine waters unnoticed. Actually, the planes flew from Japanese bases in Taiwan, a long distance for fighters of the era. Many Americans insisted during the 1941–1945 war that the Zero had been built from designs stolen from the United States, overlooking the fact that the Zero was more than a match for the best that American fliers had to fight with at the time.

The attempts to create new weapons with meager raw materials and no access to new Western technology continued. By the end of the war, Japanese engineers were testing radio controlled air-to-air and air-to-ground missiles. They also conceived a surface-to-air missile, which would use a pair of crude tracking radars and a simple computer to analyze the data and control the missile's flight. Specialists at Tokyo University designed a missile that was to home in on the shock waves of enemy naval guns as they fired. None of these guided missiles ever got past the experimental stage. A death ray, possible forerunner to today's directed energy weapons, was also undergoing testing. Occupation forces, rummaging through laboratories in an attempt to uncover the kind of research going on in the last stages of the war, found one such instrument, which could concentrate light into a potentially lethal beam. It could, reportedly, kill a chicken at twenty-five feet—but it took about a half-hour.

Technological Experimentation Today

Japanese peacetime technology is much more successful and is being recognized around the world for its quality. A National Science Foundation study shows that today certain Japanese patents in advanced technology are more often cited by researchers for non-Japanese companies working on new devices than are American patents. The situation has led some analysts to warn that American technology is falling behind. But it should be noted that some American companies refrain from patenting their new developments to keep them secret.

Meanwhile, computer makers such as NEC and Toshiba are vying with United States firms to produce the world's fastest parallel processors. Japan's machine tools dominate world markets. Japan's aerospace industry is dealing with the state of the art, including space applications and the challenges of hypersonic travel. Many components of the Boeing 747 jumbo jet and the Boeing 767 jetliner are built in Japan by an aerospace consortium of heavy industry companies. The Japanese aerospace consortium will help to design and build part of the new long-range Boeing 777 jet. A large contingent of United States-based Japanese engineers is now on the scene, participating in the design of the new 777 jet, and a smaller group is working with Boeing on the next generation supersonic transport, which is still being drawn on design terminals.

The Japanese H-II rocket will soon be able to launch a two-ton satellite into geostationary orbit 23,000 miles above the equator, or a nine-ton satellite into low earth orbit. It will be capable of sending a 1.5-ton space probe to Venus or Mars. The current rocket, the three-stage H-I, with its domestically developed second-stage and third-stage engines, can now orbit 1200 pound payloads into geostationary orbit. The H-I has been launching Japan's communications satellites since 1987. The guidance technology, however, for these rockets was designed from American models.

For a nation with chronic land problems and lack of raw materials, it seems fitting that space should represent a resource to be exploited. For the Japanese, getting there is not going to be enough. Japanese experiments on manufacturing in the vacuum of space have flown on the United States space shuttle, and Japan is a codeveloper, with the European Space Agency, of an experiment module for the United States space station *Freedom*. If the space station is ever built, the joint Japanese and European part of the craft will be a place where practical space-borne manufacturing can be tested.

Japanese firms build large amphibian flying boats for search and rescue at sea. Together with American, British, German and Italian companies, the Japanese aerospace consortium helped to design and now builds crucial parts of the V-2500 jet engine now competing for sales with General Electric, Pratt & Whitney, and Rolls Royce in the competition to power the world's newest jetliners. They build helicopters under license from American and German companies, and Japan's defense agency has been flying Japan-built American-designed fighters for many years, including the F-4 Phantom and more recently, America's frontline fighter, the F-15J.

The Wheel Reinvented

The question of Japanese as copiers may seem moot now that the world is flooded with well-made and innovative Japanese products, but the questions recurs constantly in patent infringement cases in the U.S. and Europe. Among the keys to Japan's kind of creativity is an openness to new ideas and a fondness for the novel. Some call it an innate love of fads. What can one say about a country that is constantly reinventing things the rest of the world has taken for granted?

It wasn't enough to make radios; the Japanese had to make them smaller, better, portable and powerful. When a Japanese automaker asked Detroit auto editor James Dunne to drive an early model of their line, he mentioned that he found it inconvenient to adjust the outside mirrors. Within months the Japanese had not only made the adjustment easier, they had added motors to drive the mirrors, a first in inexpensive cars at the time. The Japanese were the first to employ four-wheel steering on production cars, made the rotary engine practical, and pioneered the making of low emissions engines and ceramic engine parts.

Nothing seems to be beyond Japanese experimentation. For many years, Japanese-made Western-style toilets have had dual large and small flush cycles. And in some models the top serves as a basin where fresh water can be used to wash the hands before the water flows into the tank. A bathroom fixture maker has redesigned the toilet seat—though the Japanese traditionally use a squatting fixture—first heating it, then adding the advantages of a bidet. One company even tried, unsuccessfully, to design a urinal for women.

There is newfound hope for youthful creativity at the major Japanese auto companies, all of which have established design studios in the United States. For a variety of reasons, including the need for an innate understanding of the local market, these studios are staffed with American and Japanese designers and stylists. The Miata, Mazda Motors Company's sensation of 1988, was the brainchild of one of the Americans in Mazda's California design studio.

Trying something new or different as a way of making a breakthrough was in mind when the Ministry of International Trade and Industry announced that it would fund a project aimed at producing what it called the fifth generation computer. I went to visit the man in charge of the project, Kazuhiro Fuchi. Just what was the fifth generation computer?, I asked the engaging young research scientist. "I don't know," he replied, disarmingly. "That's why we have this project." It seemed quite logical to him. And it set off tremors among computer scientists around the world.

As the project was structured, major Japanese computer firms assigned bright young engineers to the headquarters in Tokyo, where these fresh minds were to probe the problem of the next giant step in computer design. (One company conspicuously not invited: IBM Japan.) Their first challenge was to build a computer with which they would design the next generation of computers. It was to be a machine that would design a machine whose dimensions and tasks were not yet known, except that the goal would be a machine that could think like a human.

No fifth generation computer was built. But the project is not considered a failure. Three years after its founding, and after scores of articles were written about the new threat from Japan, computer scientists from around the world gathered in Tokyo for the first International Conference on Fifth Generation Computer Systems, and to a man, the delegates thanked the Japanese for jolting their home governments into reviving their underfunded and practically moribund computer research projects. "The thought that the Japanese might make the breakthrough which could make obsolete everybody else's," said one European delegate, "certainly gave us a start." The research was valuable experience for all the young scientists who gathered in that nondescript skyscraper in Tokyo. Each of them went back to his own company well versed in what other colleagues on the project were doing and thinking.

The hardest part of the project, recalled the late Tohru Moto-oka of Tokyo University, was getting Japanese industrial leaders to assign the researchers to the project. "It's a fundamental problem of Japanese society that is not so easy to change," said Moto-oka, who conceived the fifth generation computer project. "Usually the president cannot understand the middle-level managers, who have a responsibility to realize a short-term goal, and these managers have to use the young people in short-term projects. We had to fight for each one." The project prospectus specified that it wanted young people new to their companies; the idea was that these young people would not be indoctrinated yet, like good Japanese salary workers, to do research in a specific and rigid corporate methodology.

Moto-Oka likened the seemingly quixotic project to the building of the space shuttle:

What I had in mind was, first, the fact that the space shuttle is not just launched into space for exploration. In this world

it seems that there are many who do their best only in an
environment of competition; and it may be that cooperation
through competition is the only way of eliciting vigorous activity from such persons.

The search for a new creativity is shaking Japan's educational institutions, not the official establishment, in particular the hidebound Ministry of Education, where, lament the
reformers, a resistance to change survives all onslaughts.
Creativity, which requires that people challenge the existing
order of things, is anathema to the continuing norm in Japanese education. Classroom behavior is passive and disciplined, rarely challenging, most likely because success in the
system is based on the ability to pass tests successfully. But
the system is so debilitating that once students make it to
college they are permitted to coast until graduation. In the
Japanese system it is very difficult to get into college, and
once in, it is virtually impossible to flunk out; quite the op-
posite to the situation in the United States, where it is easy
to get into college, but also easy to fail. Even eager Japanese
students sometimes find themselves frustrated by the indifference of professors. A visiting professor at Japan's University of Tokyo told me that he took several of his students to
a coffee shop for a chat and found the students animated and
eager for an exchange. "None of these students had ever had
the chance to talk one-on-one with any of their teachers,"
said the professor. "It blew my mind."

Not Created There

Even though Japanese companies are always searching for
new ideas, they also sometimes suffer the "not invented here"
syndrome. Professor Jun-ichi Nishizawa, who invented the
semiconductor laser, recently recalled how he took his invention to a Japanese company and explained the possibilities for developing commercial applications from it. He
could elicit no interest. But when the invention was com-
mercialized in the United States, he was chastised by the

same company because he had brought his device to the Japanese company before he could show them a practical application for it.

The relationship of academia and industry in Japan is prickly, and the lack of cooperation is now being recognized; hence the move by Japanese companies onto American campuses to exploit the creative energy found there. It is commonly realized in Japan that only five Japanese scientists have won the Nobel Prize, compared with 150 Americans.

Professor Nishizawa has said that to do basic research in Japan, "You need the scientific curiosity of an explorer of uncharted wilderness." You also need a lot of support. Until recently it was a common complaint among scientists that they couldn't get any research funds unless they were working on something that was being pioneered abroad; now the complaint is that research funds tend to be granted only in glamour fields such as superconductivity and biotechnology. Nishizawa likens it to a gold rush mentality. Most of the challenging research comes from companies, not from university laboratories, and there is little cooperation between industry and the universities.

Faddish displays of interest in creativity have encouraged most of Japan's major companies to establish centers of activity where young workers are permitted to range freely over new ideas for products and processes. Now recruiters who in their rounds of the universities once shunned individualistic seniors have their eyes open for that occasional brilliant loner.

Honda Motors, founded in 1946 by the imaginative maverick named Soichiro Honda, a motorcycle racer and builder, was not encumbered by traditional thinking. His company became the biggest Japanese automaker in the United States by dint of imaginative thinking. In 1989, 1990, and 1991 a Honda model, the Accord, was the highest selling car in the United States. Tadashi Kume, an engineer who came to head the company after the retirement of Honda himself, continued his former superior's belief in *zakkubaran*, "outspokenness" a rather rare commodity in communal Japanese companies, where consensus is the norm. "At board meetings I may say something and maybe somebody disagrees with me," Kume says, "and they would not hesitate to say 'I disagree with you.' " In these sessions, ingenuity and ideas are sought.

Despite the "not invented here" syndrome and old-fashioned lockstep management, some companies actively seek out new ideas from within. Japanese firms sometimes seem to make a fetish of employee suggestions. In fact, in some companies, workers are required to make suggestions on a regular basis. Material rewards for such suggestions tend to be minimal, usually a company pin or a small bonus. The object, explains a Japanese company chairman, is "to imbue the employee with the idea of the shared fate of everybody in the company. Every suggestion is taken seriously." Maybe. Many if not most employee suggestions under the forced system tend to be worthless in themselves, but they serve as a reminder of employee responsibility and perhaps as a reflection of corporate esteem. It helps give the worker a sense that he or she is contributing.

The facsimile machine and the copier, business tools that have swept the industrial world, were developed into consumer products by the Japanese from "invented elsewhere" technology because the Japanese electronics companies had a vision of the future and a solid grasp of what could be done with it. They could see that increasingly crowded cities and correspondingly slow delivery services were not likely to make life easier for businessmen or ordinary citizens who needed to communicate quickly. Furthermore, hampered by a written language not easily adaptable to keyboard use, the facsimile machine was particularly useful in the home. This technology has also proved useful abroad as urban congestion chokes more and more cities.

The idea of adapting the giant and costly videotape recording machine, then being used by American television stations, into a small home unit utilizing a handy cassette, came about as a way to "shift time" from the broadcaster's initiative to the viewer's. The first small units were built by

Ampex in the United States, which still holds the basic patents, but the project was abandoned by Ampex in 1972, and no other American company pursued the idea.

Yet even in Japan, convincing management to market new products is not always easy. The chairman of Sony threatened to quit if his board, which was cool to the idea, would not approve production of the personal portable audio tape player, Walkman. "I said, 'If we don't sell 100,000 units by the end of the year I will resign,'" recalls Akio Morita. He had no intention of resigning, and the product proved to be an immediate hit.

Sometimes ideas are opposed not only because they were not invented here, but because they were invented at all. The marketplace is littered with products that have not caught on. In electronics shops in Tokyo you can find a bewildering array of competing items, many of them destined to fail. But one of the hallmarks of the successful Japanese consumer goods company is a willingness to market—even to proliferate—new products to increase its market share.

Hajime Karatsu, director of the Institute of Research and Development at Tokai University, recently wrote in a Japanese daily, "We don't have to lose sleep over a supposed lack of creativity. No matter how superior a technology seems, challengers soon appear. Human ingenuity is limitless, and Japanese are inventive." As an example he cited Bulova Watch Company's invention of the electric watch movement, a breakthrough in the industry: "Bulova monopolized the patent and refused to grant manufacturing rights to Swiss or Japanese firms. One company, however, couldn't supply the world market. While the Americans were puttering around, Japanese developed quartz-crystal digital watches, and the game was over. Bulova ran out of time."

Professor Yoichiro Murakami of Tokyo University, who specializes in the history of science, reminds us that historically in Japan, refinement of tradition has been more heavily emphasized than new departures. Murakami argues that a change toward Western concepts of creativity conflicts with fundamental values, but that Japanese culture, which has no immutable set of beliefs and is less guided by codified religious principles, can make the change. He wrote: "We must try to persuade those who support the 'free-ride theory' that just as there are people who sow seeds, so should there be people who nurture the seeds and make them grow." The challenge facing that system, obviously, is to create more sowers and to ensure that they do not suffer at the hands of the nurturers.

CHAPTER ELEVEN

HARD WORK, HOLIDAYS, HEART ATTACKS

Proud of their nation's rapid rise to the economic strato-
sphere, and perhaps a bit dizzied by it as well, Japanese in
increasing numbers are growing bolder in their disdain for
foreign education, foreign work habits, and foreign society
in general. This newly unleashed arrogance finds its voice
not only in rabid nationalists and xenophobes, but in government officials and some prominent businessmen.

The United States can blame itself for the audaciousness
of new Japanese assertions that Americans have lost the work
ethic and that the society is fragmenting as its industry "hol-
lowed out." The arrest and conviction of America's junk bond
kings Michael Milken and Ivan Boesky, the failure of some
notable leveraged buyouts, and the virtual collapse of the
savings and loan industry were not ignored in Japan, where
financial conservatism is still the watchword. In a series of
formal trade talks between Japan and America, aimed at
identifying mutual structural impediments to trade, the Japanese responded bluntly when invited to comment. They
cited their view that Americans should abandon their concentration on leveraged buyouts, mergers and acquisitions,

213

and money trading, and turn to an era of productive industry, better education, improved services, harder work, and harder selling.

Though many of the comments were accepted by the Americans as valid criticisms of the United States economy at the time, Japan was, itself, just recovering from the so-called bubble economy of the late 1980s, when land values and stock prices soared, creating instant paper millionaires. Money scandals in business and politics continue to unfold, and tax-dodging schemes are highlighted, together with stunning revelations of vast sums of illegal profits laundered by the purchase of foreign art treasures.

Westerners have been fascinated, puzzled, and perhaps misled by notions of Japan as a nation of workaholics. The conventional wisdom is that the Japanese have a homogeneous society with cultural traits that enable them to work longer and harder and more efficiently and with less concern about fatigue and leisure. The theories of Japanese worklife are many, some of them ludicrous: "The answer is religion," a Japanese friend confided one day. "In Europe and America you have all these religious taboos, inflexible rules. In Japan we are not religious, we can work every day, we can eat anything, we can do what is necessary to act in the situation. I think we are the logical ones." This, in my friend's opinion, is what gives Japanese industry an advantage when the nation's unfettered, situationally ethical workaholics are pitted against the indulged, prone-to-strike, and religiously constrained Western worker.

This unflattering Japanese view of the Western worker is common, even if the bizarre idea of religion as industrial policy is not. But conventional assessments of what makes Japanese industry so efficient are often off the mark. Devoted, willing, educated, and competent workers are part of the story. Some analysts, many of them pessimistic Japanese academics and economists, argue that Japan's industrial edge will be blunted by a desire for easy living, and that Japan's high rate of competitiveness will sink, falling in line with the West. They point out that Japan's customary steep rise in the rate of productivity began to slow on the thresh-hold of the 1990s. Their view is that today's young Japanese are losing the work ethic even as the central government is trying to persuade companies to grant more vacation time, shorten work weeks, and force workers to learn to love leisure.

The critics have a point. Japanese are now freely changing jobs for the first time in the postwar era. Corporate head-hunters are beginning to find Japanese executives and profes-sionals who are willing to discuss job changes, and they are placing executives with rival Japanese companies outside the traditional seniority system. Companies that do not satisfy the more demanding professional needs of new, profession-ally trained employees are now facing the possibility of los-ing them. It is the beginning of what would be a remarkable change in the Japanese corporate world if it continues. Now, not all young Japanese feel the need for the sacrifices their parents made to aid the growing industrialization of Japan. Some are brash enough to buck the system.

This sea change comes at a time when Japanese industry is finding that it must better utilize available talent. Despite the success of major Japanese enterprises using the old sys-tem, one can only speculate on how much talent has been wasted by management failure to use the special strengths of employees. Managers argue that moving employees around through many jobs during a working life expands a worker's talent. Certainly it has given the companies a flex-ibility that most Western companies cannot match.

The pool of young Japanese is shrinking with the aging of the population and the arrival of less-than-zero-population growth, and the young graduate is more likely than his father to be the engineer he wanted to be. Fully a third of newly hired Japanese at major corporations change jobs within the first two years of their employment. Analysis shows that much of that shifting of jobs is within the same company or at affiliated or subsidiary companies. Rather than a sign of disaffection with the system, the job changes can be seen as a sign that these workers are trying to find their rightful place in it, a place where they can be more, not less, productive and more gratified.

Notwithstanding the anecdotal reports of a decline in the Japanese work ethic among the youth, prudence suggests that it is unwise to expect a significant slowing of Japanese productivity rates or individual job performance in the near future. Most assessments in the West predict Japanese productivity to be approaching a par with the United States around 1995 and surpassing it by 2000. True, others are nearing the Japanese standards for quality of work, especially in the highly technical electronics fields, in which highly complex machinery in clean rooms from Hong Kong, Taiwan, and Korea to Singapore and Malaysia are producing world-quality goods.

The Japanese by any world standard still work very hard, long, and effectively. Westerners often love their companies, as Japanese do, but they do not tend to identify their personal values with those of their company, as is often the case in Japan. With the changes taking place, Japanese industry may become even more effective. And in any case, productivity is primarily a function of capital, not labor. Even Detroit has learned that the way to get more production and better-quality work from an employee is not to try to make him or her work harder, but to provide better, more efficient tools and place more emphasis on the design of the product and the way it is manufactured.

Japan keeps raising its productivity—48 percent in the manufacturing industry as a whole from 1980 to 1987. American productivity in manufacturing rose only 33 percent in the same period. But United States productivity in 1992 is still higher than Japan's in the making of automobiles, steel, leather products, in printing and publishing, and in the pulp, paper, lumber and wood industries. It also leads Japan in some kinds of apparel, textiles, foods, and, of course, farm products. The only major sector where the Japanese outperform the United States on a man-hour basis is in the electrical machinery and chemicals industries.

Although United States auto assembly lines spew out more

cars per hour than do Japanese lines, it doesn't mean those cars are better than Japanese cars or cost less to produce. The yen has doubled in value since 1985, and yet the Japanese can still build a car for less money than Detroit can, even in America. Labor costs on Japanese cars built in North America are lower than American costs because their work force is newer and younger. Therefore, pay and benefits for these workers cost the Japanese companies less than does Detroit's older and more pampered work force. Also, Japanese affiliated companies supply parts help to keep costs down.

Quest for Quality

The president of Japan's Mitsubishi Motors once remarked at a year-end cocktail party that he was surprised by the early success of his cars in America. In the 1970s, these cars were of conventional design and not particularly stylish. Still in awe of Detroit's engineering manpower and talent, Teruo Tojo, an engineer himself, felt that when Detroit got serious about making small cars, Japanese companies would find only a small market in the United States. But Detroit didn't get the wake up call. Buyers' reports to the Japanese companies indicated the owners liked the quality. The key to good quality, Tojo said, is teamwork and constant feedback among the original designers, the men who figure out how the design will be put together, and the workers, who will actually produce it.

The president of Toyota, Shoichiro Toyoda, once pondered my question as to why Toyota Motor Company was so late in setting up its own auto plant in the United States, well after Honda and Nissan had done so. Toyoda said it was not quality he worried about; he felt he could get good quality from American workers. "I just don't think we can make a profit in America," he said. He has changed his mind.

In 1990 Japanese carmakers in the United States began shipping American-made Japanese cars back to Japan. American labor was not only good, it was relatively cheap with the revaluation of the dollar downwards. It required a lot of persuasion to convince Japanese buyers of autos to buy Japanese cars built in North America. These cars were built without union labor; the Japanese makers, afraid of foreign labor unions, have done all they could, legally and sometimes not so ethically, to avoid unions. Setting up their plants in rural areas, far from major centers of union activity, they have attempted to head off unionization by offering good wages to people in areas where jobs are desperately needed. Employees are screened in an attempt to identify people who may be potential malcontents or union organizers.

To get these jobs, states such as Tennessee, Ohio, Kentucky, and Georgia have offered long-term tax write-offs and have poured their own tax money into building facilities such as railroad spurs and highway off-ramps to suit the needs of potential Japanese investors. Attempts to unionize Honda and Nissan auto plants in Ohio and Tennessee have been unavailing despite United Automobile Workers campaigns and representational elections. Japanese management techniques include leveling mechanisms such as no reserved parking places, no special visible perks for management, a single dining hall, good pay, and appeals to the need for shared effort.

Back home in Japan, the lights still burn late almost every night in high-rise office buildings. A lot of that glow represents wasted energy on the part of diligent employees who are trying to show how loyal they are. In offices all across Japan, white collar workers eye the clock, the boss, and their coworkers before deciding when to leave work. "It is like you are doing something disloyal if you are the first to leave," a retired executive says.

A Japanese section chief once grunted to me, "Sometimes the hardest work anybody does around here is try to look busy." A Western advertising executive based in Japan says, "Nobody seems to do any work until five o'clock, and then they stay until nine and act overworked." And the chairman of a major trading company said with exasperation, "Young people today just don't want to work."

Long days and nights are required in companies' overseas offices: a New York-based representative of the giant corporation C. Itoh says, "We work all day with our American clients and then spend most of the night on the phone or sending faxes back to Japan." The grueling work makes Japanese yearn for home, where the hours are long but much of the night work is devoted to worker camaraderie over drinks. Being far from the home office—where the major decisions are made, promotions are earned, and solidarity with superiors is cemented—is seen as something of a duty and a gamble rather than a chance to make a name for oneself. There is also the danger in being away too long or liking the assignment too much. Foreign experience is being regarded with more favor today, but there is still an edge of suspicion for the executive who returns with a patina of sophistication.

The story, perhaps apocryphal, is told of the Japanese executive who was the soul of Western politeness in the United States. He opened car doors for his wife, allowed her to precede him through revolving doors, held her coat, and lit her cigarettes at cocktail parties. But each time he performed one of these Western rituals he muttered to her quietly, "Only while we are here." And true to his word, as soon as the couple returned to Japan his demeanor changed at home, as such behavior would seem a bit strange for an important Japanese executive who did not wish to be thought of as having adopted Western customs.

Wooing Workers

Finding young people to fit into Japan's new industrial and economic suit is difficult for many small companies, which are unable to offer prestige and advantages of the giant industrial firms. The normal rules of recruiting graduates by the big companies, which limits when and how recruiters can approach students, are constantly being violated. Some companies are sending new recruits on vacations to Hawaii as an inducement to sign on. A small producer of synthetic fiber fabrics in western Japan offered a new automobile to recruits. Pay has gone up, commuting allowances and better housing facilities are all being tried to attract the best of the shrinking pool of Japanese recruits. For the first time, selected workers are being offered contracts instead of lifetime employment, and one company has established a nine-month work year with a five-day week for certain engineers, in an attempt to give them a chance to continue their studies and keep up with the advances in their field.

Today's Japanese on overseas assignment brings with him a confidence his father never had. Among Japan's elite, there are now second- and third-generation Yale, Harvard, Princeton, and Oxford graduates. These men form a new wave of Japanese who understand the West, and they represent Japanese business, some of them in joint ventures with foreign companies. Unfortunately, few bureaucrats or politicians have had such exposure; on the contrary, a Japanese education is an essential for success in government or politics. Unofficially advising government is the extent to which these people can go in helping Japan understand how to live with the Western world. In Japan, politics is a profession, and those who attempt to enter from outside the normal route are never admitted to the inner circle of power.

In the early postwar years, Japanese knew that the only way to economic success was to build products for export. But before the war Japanese trading companies had only a handful of offices around the world and a cadre of employees insufficient to meet the needs of all the companies wishing to export. With the aid of Japanese ministries, principally MITI, Japanese manufacturers targeted markets based on information gathered in many ways, including during official government missions. The ministries make all of the information available to anybody who might want help in planning an export program.

When the Nissan Motor Company sent Tsuyoshi Sogo to the United States to try to sell cars in the 1950s, Sogo already had a bit of a feel for the country, having worked in New

York for a Japanese trading company before the war. But typical of many of the Japanese who first went abroad to sell Japanese products, he knew little about the line of business he was now engaged in. The first Nissan cars, brand named Datsun, were a flop. Underpowered, they overheated in city traffic and on the highway, and the engine bearings failed. Replacement was costly. Nobody wanted these odd little cars when the word got out.

Sogo recalls with a grin a transport ship that arrived from Japan in 1959 with 70 percent of its cargo of 550 Datsuns severely damaged during the rough Pacific Ocean crossing. Stevedores who knew how to ship cars were scarce in Japan. Sogo and his colleagues in California were delighted to see those 385 battered cars "because it was easier to get the insurance company to pay for them than to try to sell them. It took us a year to get rid of the undamaged ones." But persistence paid off; Japanese automobiles account for more than 30 percent of the market in America, and the market share in Europe continued to increase until percentage limits were imposed.

Japan's drive into foreign markets has become the stuff of commercial legend, and it was brought about by indefatigable young people who rarely slept. If Japan's companies were to mount an export offensive that would pay for the foreign raw materials, machinery, foodstuffs, and luxuries the nation needed, it was obvious that the companies would need a production system and a pool of labor that was up to the task. Capital was short, but Japanese industrialists had something just as valuable: an educated work force that was the inheritor of centuries of sacrifice and adversity, a people who believed in the enobling quality of all work. Besides, there was, and still is, only a meager form of social security waiting when retirement comes or the work stops. When the Occupation tried to purge top executives and managers because of their connection with the Japanese war machine, many top industrial jobs fell to the second echelon of leadership in the company. These men, hands-on engineers and managers, may have lacked formal managerial skills but

knew how the pieces ought to be put together. Much of what
the management would normally have done, such as the
setting of strategic goals, interim targets, quotas, standards,
and relations with other companies, was still accomplished
by the same managers who had always run the companies;
the purge was a failure in that regard. And other public
chores were taken care of by government ministries, most of
them run by the same bureaucrats and politicians who had
manned them during the war years. The links between conservative politicians and the *zaibatsu* interests remained
strong, as they do today.

A Tradition of Work

Long before the dark satanic mills of the Industrial Revolution found their counterpart in modernizing Japan, the
nation's mostly agrarian people knew hard work, deprivation, and exploitation. Taxed beyond reason to support landlords and warlords, peasant families were urged during the
feudal period to eat tasteless millet so that they could pay
their tribute with the fine rice they produced. Although
school enrollment was high, the demands for labor in the
fields, and later in the silk factories and in the textile mills,
prevented rural school children from attending regularly.
Even so, before the first compulsory education law was en-
acted, school enrollment was as high as 50 percent. Education was seen as one way out of the dead-end pigeonholing
of people by class.

Certainly a life of brute labor was nothing to aspire to,
and labor activists say laboring conditions are not yet what
they should be. Some of the worst working conditions today
persist in the few remaining mines of the nation, where the
lives of the underground workers are unavoidably in jeopardy. There is a tradition behind the danger: the thinly endowed mines of Japan were worked under most primitive

conditions as early as the fifteenth century, as one official report at the time noted:

> So narrow and winding were the mine roads that workmen going single file walked with difficulty. Small timber supports were used to sustain the roof and sides, while in lieu of the ladders were upright timbers serrated to facilitate climbing. Under such conditions, the ventilation and drainage were so bad as frequently to extinguish the lights, but so little did the miners appreciate the danger, that they were accustomed to continue work in perfect darkness. These men rarely lived to reach five and twenty years of age.

In the Japanese mines it was not only the workmen who suffered. Again, a report, written in 1904, states: "Because of the difficulties of transportation through these narrow passages little children were employed in carrying ore from mines in small baskets. Milling was carried on by women and old men who broke the ore and picked by hand."

Children, especially girls, sent away from home in the countryside to work in the mills and factories, not to mention the restaurants, teahouses, shops, and brothels of the cities, were usually paid little or nothing. Some were sold outright, and others became, in effect, indentured servants. The victims of the system were usually pleased to be eating; they sometimes even got rice, which they rarely ate at home. But of course countless numbers were terribly exploited.

About the time the American Civil War ended, more than 80 percent of Japanese lived on farms. But the Meiji era industrialization moved ahead rapidly, and as the trek toward the cities began, some of Japan's major industries were established and new skills learned. Japan's first modern shipyard was opened in 1861. Known as the Mitsu Bishi ("three diamonds") Dockyard and Engine Works, it began building vessels based on new skills and technology acquired in 1854 after a Russian warship was beached by a tidal wave at the port of Shimoda. The government-financed shipyard was turned over to Yotaro Iwasaki, a countryside samurai who went on to establish the commercial combine now known as Mitsubishi. Together with other industrial groups—Yasuda, Sumitomo, and Mitsui—the *zaibatsu* have controlled trade, made and broke politicians, and guided governments ever since.

In the late 1980s, when Japan's labor shortage was beginning to make itself felt, a much larger number of women began to find their way into the workplace. Japanese women in later postwar history were an underused labor resource. Even as more and more women graduated from university with intellectual skills, the upper-scale workplace remained largely closed to them. For example, until the 1980s, major international financial transactions could routinely be completed by telex, and the preferred male worker, with a written knowledge of foreign languages, could succeed by pecking out the words laboriously on telex keyboards. Today the financial markets of the world function around the clock, and instantaneous voice communication is key. Younger Japanese university graduates with foreign language fluency, many of them women, are taking jobs as highly paid money traders and dealers for Japanese and foreign companies in Japan. Although they still face a glass ceiling if they aspire to the boardroom of Japanese companies, they are gaining respect and responsibility.

Young educated women and housewives reentering the marketplace, full-time and part-time, are adding new ideas to the Japanese world of work. Until now women were expected to work until marriage, then perhaps return to the work force as part-time employees in factories and shops after their children were grown. Young Japanese women were expected to get married in their early twenties. The social goal was to avoid becoming a *kurishimasu keiki*, literally, a Christmas cake, stale and leftover, unmarried. The jobs available to young women were mainly in factories, where they lived in dormitories, or in service as clerks in shops, department stores, and banks and other offices. Some jobs were merely decorative, such as the stylishly uniformed, white-gloved greeters who bow to customers at the store entrances, or the elevator starters and escalator monitors who invite shoppers onto the automatic conveyances. The sheer number of female clerical help behind the counters of Japanese department stores is still a wonder to behold, and the service is often cloying; it is impossible to buy something in a Japanese department store and take it away before it is elaborately wrapped. Japanese managers see such service as indispensible to the store's image, and while new discount stores can dispense with much of the service, the fine old traditional stores of Japan cannot. Their executives say it would be a sign of the deterioration of their sincerity.

Few blandishments or distractions seem to seriously deter the Japanese employee from fulfilling his obligation to his company. Personal vacation time is the hardest thing for many Japanese to cope with. It is so alien to some that they don't seem to know what to do with it. Japanese workers questioned by pollsters say they enjoy the many long weekend holidays that everyone else enjoys throughout the year, such as Sports Day, Respect for the Aged Day, Boy's Day, Golden Week, the first week of the new year, even the Vernal and Autumnal Equinoxes. But many workers still feel uncomfortable being off while others in their group are still working. And although many young married workers claim they want to spend more leisure time with their families, the last champions of leisure time for middle-aged workers happen to be their wives, unaccustomed to having their husbands around the house all day long. In a 1991 survey of married women who do not work, many commonly refer to a husband who is home too much as a *gokiburi teishu*, a "cockroach husband."

Can't Stop Working

When a company is in trouble, workers will often rally around to offer help. During one deep recession, the giant Matsushita Electric company was forced to shut down some production lines and lay off several thousand employees. Many of them confessed that they felt ashamed to be at home and not at work. Some workers were taunted by their wives: How could they sit at home when their company was in trouble? Hundreds began to show up voluntarily at their plants looking for chores to do and busied themselves mowing the lawns, cleaning, and painting. Some workers became unpaid salesmen for Matsushita at exclusive retail outlets, visiting homes and explaining the virtues of Matsushita products.

Full-time Japanese workers have little in the way of a safety net in the rare cases of layoff. (In extreme cases, where industries have gone into decline, such as shipbuilding, the government pitches in to help pay for retraining and relocation of workers.) Until foreign competition forced a restructure of the industry, American auto workers, for example, had generous state unemployment compensation and supplemental unemployment benefits to tide them over the rough times. These generous funds are not matched in Japan, which is one reason for the development of so-called lifetime employment, in which a company commits to employ a worker until he or she reaches retirement age, and the high prices of domestic goods. Company profits, or high cash flow, help make it possible for the companies to keep employees on the payroll in times of economic stress—at least that is the theoretical rationale of the unwritten social compact. It would be most unlikely for an American worker to show up at the plant to cut the grass for free.

Nevertheless, under pressure from Western countries to moderate the onslaught of the expanding economic juggernaut, Japanese administrations have staged periodic campaigns to cut down the number of working hours of the diligent toilers of Japan. A few larger corporations set a new tone by shutting down for a week at a time in the summer, forcing all employees to take time off. But many companies mask actual working hours with hidden overtime. And when not hidden, the amount of overtime in some companies has been embarrassing: companies with 500 or more employees

worked their average employee as many as 242 hours of overtime in 1988. The Labor Standards Law continues to be subjected to complicated analysis and proposed revisions, but
so far these have had little effect. One suggestion now making
the rounds is to raise overtime pay from 1.25 times the regular hourly wage to 1.5 times or more, to discourage company managements from overscheduling overtime.

Even though the official six-day week has given way to
the five-and-a-half-day week, so far the plan has been a flop.
It was not until the early 1980s that Japan's banks began
to let employees have one Saturday a month off the job,
but some banks that reluctantly responded to the call of a
shorter workweek scheduled longer hours during the week
to make up for those lost on Saturdays. In 1990 the Ministry of Labor set the number of paid workdays off at twenty,
and made a point of calling on all employers to let their
workers take all of the time that is due them. The idea was
to decrease to 1800 the number of hours the average Japanese
works each year and to do it by March 1993. But the target
appears elusive.

By various imprecise reckonings, Japanese still are at their
jobs more hours a year than Europeans and Americans, an
average of 2150 hours. In the United States workers are on
the job for 1950 hours each year; in Britain, 1935 hours; and
in West Germany, 1600 hours. But these figures are deceptive, for Western figures represent all days for which the
employees are paid, including paid vacation, whereas the
Japanese figures represent only hours actually worked,
which means that tea breaks and paid holidays are not included. Obviously, the gap is decidedly wider than the available statistics show.

Despite the gleeful anticipation of travel agencies and resort proprietors, the nation's workers could whittle only
twenty-two hours off the annual clock in the first year of the
government's program of persuasion. Japanese workers are
officially entitled to an average of sixteen days of vacation
but typically take only nine, according to U.S. Bureau of
Labor Statistics. Very few Japanese ever take three weeks or

a month off work, even if they are entitled to it. "We consider it a kind of disloyalty," says a government employee.

Japanese politicians, businessmen, and bureaucrats do not like to make drastic changes rapidly. When a forty-six-hour work week was declared, it was not to go into effect until three years later and did not apply to workshops that employed less than 300 employees—which means by far the majority of workshops in the country. In fact, less than 10 percent of Japanese companies that have more than 300 employees are on a five-day workweek today, despite all the government urging, including television advertising and direct pleas to employees and employers. Not only have the number of hours *not* come down measurably, the rate of productivity keeps going up, albeit at a less steep rate than before.

Working Themselves to Death

Enter *karoshi*, or death by overwork, a faddish way to go in the 1980s and becoming more so in the 1990s. Local and foreign press detailed the high-pressure working life of diligent Japanese laborers and its morbid consequences. National interest in the subject soared with the publication of a book simply titled *Karoshi*, which consisted of entries from the diary of a young executive who died of heart trouble. His wife insisted it was because of overwork. Reflecting on his many nights away from home entertaining clients and establishing alcoholic rapport with his colleagues, the exhausted worker wrote despairingly of the demands of his job and its destruction of his personal life. Ruefully he wrote, "Even the slaves of the past probably had time to eat with their own families," a luxury he rarely enjoyed. In a poll of 500 long-term employees of companies in the Tokyo area in 1990, the Fukoku Life Insurance Company discovered that some 70 percent said they felt stressed, nearly half said they had constant fatigue; some 28 percent said they had no creativity or motivation; and 23 percent said they frequently called in sick. The most common self-prescription by the tired employees for their malady was simple: more sleep.

As the death by overwork syndrome rose in the late 1980s, dozens of Japanese families sued employers for the wrongful death of loved ones. In one case, a post office worker from Nagoya died of a stroke after being forced to work every day for four months. A court ordered the labor ministry to pay the family's claim for compensation, setting a new precedent. It should be noted, however, that the precedent doesn't have the force in Japanese law that it does in the United States or Great Britain. Nevertheless, the rash of cases forced the government to undertake some studies to assess the potential problem. A national lawyers organization offering to represent the families of victims of *karoshi* has helped to stimulate recognition of the problem and has led to even more complaints. But at most, only a few dozen such cases have made it into the legal system, and many social critics think the cases will drag on interminably in the courts and will discourage, rather than encourage, significantly more filings. With only about 15,000 private lawyers to handle all the nation's litigation, it seems likely such cases may find resolution quietly with arbitrated and negotiated settlements far from the public eye. By 1992, the government recognized that about thirty deaths per year could be attributed to overwork. An association of alleged victims of overwork claim the true number is as high as 10,000 deaths per year.

Overwork is a kind of motto among youngsters. Ambitious ones fight their way through a rigid career track of school, after-school school, and entrance examinations to get to college. They drill and memorize their way up the academic ladder, scheduling little time for sleep. However, once in college, they are rewarded with four years of relative rest. It is a small plateau on the climb into the world of business and the possibility of *karoshi*.

The sight of weary Japanese men and women on their way to work on the monumentally overcrowded public transportation system is sobering. Many men, suffering the aftereffects of a night on the town with business colleagues or clients, nod off at the first motion of the jammed subway car—sometimes while standing up, hanging onto a strap, and wedged against other bodies in a surprisingly unconscious, numbed intimacy. At the ubiquitous neighborhood sidewalk shops and station kiosks, hung-over workers swig the contents of tiny brown bottles of tonic to restore their drained vitality for yet another long day and hard-drinking night.

But to some the idea of massive overwork, particularly in the white collar field, is an example of the human capacity for self-delusion. In the contrary view, many of those extra 200 to 500 hours a year the average Japanese works are merely hours put in as a show of loyalty. "Nobody wants to leave the office on his own," says an advertising executive now working out of the country. "It is regarded as disloyal to get up and leave at the end of the day right on the dot, so everybody keeps an eye on everybody else until the consensus is that it is okay to leave. I don't think it means that a lot of work really gets done." One factor that contributes to a high degree of tension in Japanese offices is the seating arrangement of workers: at facing desks, constantly under the gaze of colleagues and superiors. Although this arrangement encourages solidarity, it also makes individual work habits— good or bad—public, and being under the constant gaze of a worker's superior can add to tension. On the other hand, a recent arrival in the United States confided that the American system of giving each worker a desk facing away from coworkers, and the separation of work stations by partitions, made him feel isolated.

Blue collar workers are much less visible to the casual or even the interested foreign observer; however, overwork is a constant concern as small- and medium-size companies, which comprise the vast majority of enterprises in Japan, struggle to meet production schedules forced on them by the giant companies they supply. This is not to say the large manufacturing concerns, particularly in heavy industry, are not without their critics—quite the contrary.

The seldom seen underside of the highly vaunted "just-in-time" production system, in which outside suppliers deliver parts and components to the production line just before they are needed, is what it does to the small suppliers who must deliver the parts. For the big company depending on the suppliers there is a great savings in inventory costs. Whereas Western companies have long been accustomed to having large and hugely expensive inventories of parts against the possibility of strikes and transportation disruptions, Japanese companies typically load those inventory costs onto the suppliers, who must deliver the goods just when needed. The suppliers tend to be close to the major factories they supply, and Western companies often rely on companies far away.

But to provide the materials for a just-in-time production system, many small companies, whether near or far, are continually strapped for funds. The big companies make them wait for payment when money is tight. Workers are often forced to work unremittingly to fulfill company commitments as production demands fluctuate. Many supplier companies are also members of a major company's *keiretsu*, or "family of companies," and are almost totally dependent on one company for their existence. These circumstances naturally render them vulnerable to whatever treatment their major customer metes out.

Unlike the pristine and well-ordered environments pictured at Japan's giant corporations—with their clean rooms and spotless assembly and manufacturing plants—most Japanese production comes from small shops and factories, staffed by diligent high school graduates pushed to the limit. Because the population is aging rapidly, the labor shortage in Japan is of great concern in government circles, particularly as the birth rate has declined. But the new affluence—which may mean satisfaction with compensation levels and acceptance of working conditions—has helped to shrink union membership from about 35 percent of the employed population in 1970 to approximately 25.2 percent by the end of 1990. (This figure, however, is still markedly higher than the 16.8 percent in the United States.)

Organizing the Labor

Japan's labor unions are organized around a single enterprise or company rather than the workers in a particular industry or group of industries. But some of these units are huge, even if not aligned along craft lines. In Japan most company units are affiliated with a nationwide organization, which tries to set overall wage and other contract demands. Each year agreements between individual unions in companies making steel or automobiles tend to set the scale of wages or other benefits. But they are not bound by a basic nationwide agreement, and there is no way a union can shut down a nationwide industry.

A new alliance of private sector workers, called *Rengo*, has replaced the old conventionally militant federation, *Sohyo*. One of its first moves was to change the colors of the flag from red, which hinted of communist menace, to green and blue, the new colors of the ecological movement. Their challenge is to reinvigorate the labor movement at a time when interest is flagging and members say they feel alienated. The new confederation has started a new round of social activities and mailings, including family publications, a mail-order service, and vacation bargains. An *Asahi* newspaper writer recently commented that one of the goals of the new organization is "to promote industrial peace." President Ryoji Menjo told him, "We don't wear red headbands anymore. The union offers workers more than just higher wages. It also provides an opportunity for personal growth." This change from pocketbook and workplace issues is seen by many social critics as a betrayal of the best interests of the unions' overworked members.

Pillars of Success

Labor peace is certainly one of the pillars of continued Japanese industrial success. The so-called enterprise unions of Japan have a distaste for work stoppages, and the figures show it dramatically. Japan lost 163,000 worker days due to strikes in 1988; the United States lost 4,363,000 days. Japanese company unions, organized by company and not by a nationwide industry, do not have the power to shut down the nation's vital functions; but they can certainly disrupt life when they choose to. Some unions, such as those in public service, can disrupt and inconvenience millions in short strikes. It is common for rail company unions to announce their intention to call a rush hour strike so that commuters can make other arrangements to get to or from work. The lunch hour strike is also a favorite of Japan's organized labor. It is designed to send a message to management but not to disrupt the flow of work and, presumably, company profits. This is the very antithesis of Western labor's notion of the strike as its only weapon, designed to damage or shut down a company that does not cooperate.

It would be a surprise in the West, but surprises no one in Japan, that the longtime head of the metal workers federation, which represents company auto unions, was a man whose hobby was sailing his own yacht. And the president of the union at Mazda Motors, then called Toyo Kogyo, rose to head the company. He signed the first Japanese labor contract with the United Auto Workers when Mazda set up an assembly plant in Flat Rock, Michigan.

The annual *shunto*, or "labor offensive," led for many years by the old labor federation, managed to set a pattern wage, which then was generally followed by companies in their own union negotiations. Outsiders called it collusion between the federation and the industries, but the system brought modest wage increases and labor peace. Although this system has not prevented dissatisfaction with working conditions, violent labor protest has not been seen in Japan for thirty years.

When the Japanese export offensive took hold in the 1970s, Western analysts were quick to attribute the Japanese industrial success to government protectionist policy and a work force culturally different from its counterparts abroad. There is no question that government policies kept competing foreign goods out of Japan so that its nascent industries could gain strength and dominate home and later, foreign markets. Those controls are to a great extent gone, though some still linger; and all nations have protection of some industries, particularly agriculture.

But the work force of Japan and the techniques that make Japanese enterprises so successful are still not clearly understood. Though much has been made of the theory of Japanese uniqueness, Westerners who have worked blue collar jobs alongside Japanese find that the Japanese attitudes toward work, their foremen, the company, and their fellow workers are pretty much the same as attitudes of Western workers. A Japanese worker can get just as angry with a fellow worker, or a foreman, but he is better at masking it.

Japanese workers see their labor carrying with it the dignity and reputation of their group, their company, their family, their nation. There are few Japanese who make a living without working. Inherited wealth is heavily taxed, and while gigantic fortunes have been made by people who were fortunate enough to have expensive land, a life of market speculation is not for many Japanese individuals. Older Japanese workers still have memories of wartime or postwar deprivation, and there is hardly a Japanese teenager who has not heard the hardship stories from parents and other relatives.

The Japanese worker is still trained to be more punctual, more loyal, more careful, more flexible, and less willing to express discontent than his Western blue collar counterpart. The small- and medium-size enterprises that are the sinew of Japanese industry have obligations to banks, suppliers, and the companies they supply. As workers identify with their company and its values and tie their future to that of the company, they are more likely to be cooperative than antagonistic. Moreover, the industrial scene believes that the Japanese are unlike anybody else, that they share their island fate in a hostile world, and that all have some role to play in the healthy development of their nation. No matter where one goes, the giant companies dominate, and the small companies work for them. Despite the attempt to shorten work hours, it is common agreement that leisure is not the goal of life and that all work has dignity. Moreover, despite plenty of concrete examples to the contrary, there is a pervasive sense that a company cares about its employees.

When the initial shock of Japanese competition hit the West, manufacturers, economists, and newspaper pundits began searching for clues to Japan's ability to excel. Many sought the magic bullet that would explain the phenomenon. Aided by Japanese eager to help, they immediately seized on what became in common analysis the three pillars of Japanese success: lifetime employment, seniority-based wages, and a system of benign company unions. These mainstays were supported by national councils of advisors to government ministries, particularly MITI, which set priorities. With support from government, companies could keep wages low and production high. The free trading nations, particularly America, would provide the busy workers of Japan with a wide-open market. But the scenario was never that simple.

Most Japanese workers do not have true lifetime employment, and less than 20 percent have it today. From a practical standpoint the companies that still use the old system, or some modification of it (under which an employee expects to spend his entire career until age fifty-five or sixty at one company), tend to be the large companies in direct competition with other worldwide industries. This *nenko* system creates an expensive bulge in the wage profile of the companies, as fewer low-wage employees are added each year.

The seniority-based wage system, long under attack, still remains the norm. In this system, worker pay is keyed mainly to seniority rather than to job description. The arrangement enables employers to shift workers around at will and train them for a large number of jobs if necessary, without having to pay attention to the differing wage rates, scores of job classifications, and shop rules that exist in the typical American industrial plant.

American unions plainly frightened Japanese automakers. When they came to the United States, all but one picked rural sites, away from areas with a history of labor unions. They also screened their employees most carefully, and still do, for the kind of workers from whom they can reasonably expect dedication, loyalty, and gratitude for the work, in addition to whatever mechanical or intellectual skills are required. Attempts to unionize these companies have failed, but that does not mean workers are happy. "They just don't understand the American worker," says management consultant Peter Drucker. "And they don't understand how things work in this country. They are not good managers overseas." Hence the need for local managers. One Japanese manager, bewildered after reading about American equal employment opportunity regulations, asked his American advisor, in all seriousness, whether it was legal to have separate rest rooms for men and women in his plant. In several U.S. cities, Americans with work experience in Japan now routinely conduct classes for Japanese executives in how to survive overseas as managers.

Quest for Quality Workers

In its purest sense the Japanese wage system is more or less irrational, at least in economic terms. To pay a machine operator more than an engineer because he has been on the payroll longer, or to hire an engineer to operate a machine, is not an obvious formula for economic success. In actuality, Japanese companies put engineers out on the plant floor to see how their own work relates to the actual products and to the ability of workers to produce them. Japanese experts say the hands-on experience is invaluable for the engineer, who is often far removed from the making of the product. (In response to their work experience, one thing Japanese engineers learned to do is design the parts and pieces so that they cannot be put together incorrectly, a great productivity enhancer.)

Another factor is the concept of the quality circle, based on employee suggestions. The quality circle, integral to the

Japanese company, simply has not worked well in all but a few American firms. Japanese companies have learned that employees must be made to feel that they are valued and that their ideas are wanted. A candid company president has remarked that when you require suggestions, you get a lot that are useless, and certainly some employees are not enthusiastic about the constant demand for proposals. To keep the program going in hopes of getting the stray valuable one, all suggestions must be considered. Even so, there is no joking in management about the "QC" system and its form of worker participation in decision making. "Who knows better how to make our products than the people who work with them in their hands every day?" says one manager.

Company commitment to employees is further demonstrated by the amount of information the company divulges to the members of the quality circle. In the United States, where a union routinely sees itself as an adversary of a company—and where the disparity of wages between top management and worker is vast—divulging cost and other inside company data to workers is considered out of the question. A Japanese company will tell its employees how much it costs to buy a widget; Western firms will not. The constant in Japan's economic success is the Japanese worker, who has been brought up in an educational system derived from Confucianism that prepares citizens for service while emphasizing loyalty, discipline, and work.

CHAPTER TWELVE

POLITICS, COLD CASH, AND CORRUPTION

A practiced American politician, the late California Democratic Party leader Jesse Unruh, said money is the mother's milk of politics. In Japan, the same proposition holds true. Large quantities of money continuously pour into the Japanese political system, and often the result is scandal.

Political bribery scandals have directly or indirectly touched virtually every important political figure in postwar Japan. These scandals are the delight of the press, which is perpetually outraged by the corruption. The public, swerving from outrage to bemusement and indifference, very often returns the tainted to office. All Japanese politicians face the same nagging problem in their quest for power: the need for money, and lots of it—in cash. So despite scandal after scandal, the same political figures surface again and again within succeeding governments, as the spoils of office are passed around.

There have been more than a dozen major political bribery scandals since World War II, and they are being revealed at an increasing rate. As the fortunes of Japan's ruling Liberal Democratic Party fluctuated in elections over a spate of scandals in and out of politics, party leaders pledged reform. A panel of upright citizens and public officials produced a high-sounding outline for reform in 1989. In the words of the prime minister who ordered the plan, Noboru Takeshita, that year was to be "Year One of political reform." The outline recommended a new reform of the way politics is financed. It declared flatly that the electorate's loss of confidence in politics was due to the colossal amount of money it consumed.

Ironically, Prime Minister Takeshita resigned because of a bribery scandal involving sixteen top politicians of his own party.

Political scientist Rei Shiratori has written that the corruption that characterizes Japanese politics is "woven into the political and social system." It is probably true that corruption could be found in the political life of any nation, but the Japanese political system has never moved concertedly to engage it and end it. Old-fashioned wheeling and dealing is still the order of the day.

The custom of collecting vast sums of money and distributing it as political largesse is so ingrained among the power brokers that three years, three major scandals, and three interim prime ministers after Takeshita, the reform plan was still being studied. Complicating the proposed reforms are electoral features that have nothing to do with money and ethics but are seen as handicaps by opposition political parties, which are therefore opposed to the plan.

In the Japanese system the need for money does not stop when the last election campaign debt has been paid off. The need is likely to become even greater. Staying in the good graces of the electorate requires constant replenishment of the coffers of every politician. This populace includes not only members of the national diet but also members of the prefectural (state) and city assemblies as well. The bill total soars because there are so many people trying to get the attention of the voters. In fact, Japan has more political offices and politicians running for office than most countries. Although Japan has only half the population of the United States, it has 765 members in its diet (the United States

Congress has only 535). The overpopulation of politicians continues down to the city level. For example, the sister city of Los Angeles, Nagoya, a sprawling manufacturing city between Tokyo and Osaka, has a city assembly of seventy-seven people; Los Angeles has a city council of fifteen members.

An amusing Japanese adage, often attributed to a former prime minister whose career is studded with scandal, declares that when a monkey falls from a tree he is still a monkey, but when a politician loses office he loses his identity. That notion would explain why politicians everywhere fight hard to keep from falling out of their tree, especially if politics is a way of life, or, as in Japan, the family business. (Fully 40 percent of the candidates for a recent lower house election were children of current or former diet members.) But merely staying in the tree is not the whole story; being there is bliss. Anybody who has held a ministerial post, even for a short time, assumes an elite status. Diet members always wear their plush velvet and gold chrysanthemum lapel pins that identify them. Wherever they go, they are routinely deferred to and accorded special treatment. Reaching cabinet rank is even headier stuff. It also makes it easier to raise money, especially if they happen to be members of the ruling party.

Japan's Liberal Democratic Party was created by an uneasy merger of conservative parties, and has been in control of the government since 1955. Critics of the LDP argue that it is neither liberal, democratic, or a political party, as political parties are usually structured. The party is in actuality a coalition of factions, each faction centered on an individual political leader. These leaders have differences in style, but all subscribe to the basic tenets of Japanese conservatism. The LDP is the ideological home of the nation's business establishment, which contributes heavily to the party and to the faction leaders.

To become prime minister, a faction leader must be elected president of the party. To do this he must flex his political muscles before the leaders, to show that he has solid support from the factions. Coalitions are formed in order to build that kind of strength, and the making of deals is crucial to success. Veteran political reporters say $2,800,000 in cash was the price a faction leader exacted from another for support in a crucial election of the 1980s. The diet, not the ruling party, technically elects the prime minister, but the vote is a foregone conclusion by the time it reaches the floor.

The proverbial smoke-filled room more often than not dictates the choice, and often a compromise candidate is chosen. These interim choices last only as long as the faction leaders wish, or until something such as a scandal topples them. Sometimes that takes only a few months.

Occasionally, in a deadlock, the choice for an LDP party president has been left to a nationwide vote of all party members, a rarely employed demonstration of democratic practice. This was the case when the veteran politician and former cabinet minister, Yasuhiro Nakasone, the leader of one of the smaller LDP factions—but highly unpopular among other party leaders—forced himself into the office. Three faction leaders squabbled for months over whom should have the post of party president, but neither one had the strength to prevail. Nakasone forced the vote and won, with support from two other factions. He took advantage of a party rule that calls for a nationwide referendum of party members if there are more than three candidates for the job and the decision cannot be made by other means.

The back scratching in the system is crucial, and it includes deals for the important cabinet portfolios. No prime minister can hope to form a functioning government without parceling out important posts to members of what are in effect his internal opposition, and so most governments are full of political tension and frequent shuffling of cabinet members to satisfy other factions.

Faction leaders are supported in their quest for power by people and organizations of means, such as corporations, wealthy individuals, and unions and federations. Separately, the party itself raises its own funds. For any faction leader, control of the party means control of its money. With this comes the power to support other factions and candidates,

or to punish them by withholding money, facilities and appointments, or party endorsement to run for office. To guard
against a possible shortfall of funds when a rival controls the
party machinery, faction leaders must build their own private war chests.

They must have ready cash because of one of the prime
corrupting influences in Japanese elections: the need to buy
votes, virtually one by one. Japanese politicians are not
forced to pay for expensive television time as their counterparts do in the United States. They are given brief, equal-
time segments on the government-owned radio and television network, NHK, where they appear, in turn, in a similar,
no nonsense "talking head" appearance. To politicians, such
a level playing field, without debate or dramatic commer-
cials, is inadequate, especially in electoral districts with
many candidates.

Neither is there need to publish full-page political procla-
mations in newspapers or on billboards. The newspapers
rarely accept such advertising, and the election law provides
every candidate a spot on an election bulletin board in each
neighborhood. Consequently, the electoral process is much
simpler, much more direct, and in many ways closer to the
people than in almost any other country. The campaign is
short but intense. The candidates—often wearing white
gloves and sometimes pristine white sashes to declare symbolically their sincerity and political purity—travel throughout their territory with loudspeakers calling for votes. Weary
citizens often complain of the noise pollution, but no one can
stifle the cries of the politicians. Some poorer candidates
travel by car or van, whereas others, better financed, travel
in style, in motorbuses with built-in sound systems. Some
candidates find a bicycle and hand-held bullhorn sufficient.

Of course no incumbent politician can expect to get elected
or stay in office on the strength of a whirlwind campaign, a
few small posters, and a gloved-hand plea. If he is an incumbent, he must be known to be generously responsive to his
constituents' needs. Just as Japanese companies purport to

pamper their consumers—catering to their every whim of quality, service, and style—so does the politician respectfully acknowledge the voter at the proper time. Every wedding, birth, and funeral in the diet member's district elicits an envelope of cash as a token of felicitation or condolence from incumbent diet members. Festival organizers need financial help with the decorations, and somebody must buy the sake. Widows and orphans expect aid, or a job for the child, during difficult times. The opening of a new store is not complete without a giant wreath of congratulations and good wishes from the local diet member. Traditional gift giving at the new year and again at midsummer puts a further burden on the office holder, for he must hand out bonuses to his staff and make special gifts to valued and loyal constituents. He will often pay for their trips to visit the capital. He sometimes pays the party dues of some of his constituents, a burden that costs each faction several million dollars a year.

Members from large districts can spend many thousands of dollars a month on this kind of constituent service, and some members have multiple offices, each staffed with several secretaries who do nothing but tend to constituent service. The money for this operation comes from political contributions from companies and their executives, from labor unions, businessmen, local federations, and sometimes from shady and obscure sources. For candidates endorsed by the party, there is a small stipend from the party treasury for campaign expenses. With some special exceptions, it is never enough.

The Ministry of Home Affairs sets the legal limit on what a big city candidate may spend on an election at about $150,000. Insiders say that the legal limit is laughably low and that candidates routinely spend well over their legal limit. The system, in the words of Meiji University professor Kaoru Okana, "shortchanges the public and debases democratic ideals."

The process of collecting contributions is easier for politicians if they have been appointed to a plum cabinet post.

Over the years, diet members and cabinet ministers have prospered with the home folks by promising Bullet Train stops on planned new lines, new stops on existing railroad lines, and new government building projects, such as highways for remote areas. The posts of transportation minister and construction minister are highly coveted for the influence they command in this regard. They have also, historically, been the seat of many money scandals. With the exception of the Communist Party of Japan, which publishes a lucrative newspaper, and the Clean Government Party, which relies on a Buddhist lay organization, *Soka Gakkai*, the other opposition political parties find it more difficult to raise large amounts of money. Fortunately for them, major Japanese political donors traditionally spread some of their money among the opposition parties (and so do the bribers) against the possibility they may, someday, have power.

Besides hitting up businessmen for financial help—corporations may legally only donate small sums, but there are many loopholes—a politician in need of cash will often throw a cocktail reception to raise more. There is usually a rash of such parties before every election. Important friends send out an invitation in the name of a committee "to encourage" the politician. The tickets are often as high as $250. A wealthy person eager to make an impression with the candidate will buy many tickets as a way of making a legal, unlimited contribution. The sums collected in these short soirees can be astounding. Former prime minister Takeshita was widely reported to have raised $14 million in one party when he was building a war chest to succeed Yasuhiro Nakasone. Thirteen thousand well-wishers showed up, although it was reported that 70,000 tickets at $200 each were sold. Takeshita was well known to the banking community, having served five terms as finance minister, and sixteen banks were said to have each bought 500 tickets to the affair.

The ruling Liberal Democratic Party, fearful of losing a majority in the Upper House in 1974 after a debacle in 1972, became notorious for the amount of money candidates spent to win. In the internal fight for control of the party, it was said, more than $6 million changed hands. Because so many candidates were running, donors were confused about how they should allocate their money. So business supporters and party leaders convened and devised a new and more efficient support plan. Under the plan, an industry group was assigned to each candidate. Businesses large and small in that industry not only donated money, but also ordered employees to campaign and get out the vote for the candidate. The expression "five you win and three you lose" came into use in that election. It was a play on the phrase used by students preparing for examinations: if you study most of the night and get only three hours of sleep, you will pass, but if you waste your time by sleeping five hours every night, you will surely fail. In the political context it meant that Yen 500,000,000 will win a seat but Yen 300,000,000 won't.

Despite all the money poured into a campaign, even candidates of the powerful ruling party sometimes lose to socialist, liberal, communist, independent, or other opposition. The LDP vote margins, though never below 44 percent, have dwindled from early highs of nearly 60 percent, forcing the party to seek like-minded smaller parties and independents who cooperate with them. Some analysts say the ruling party would do better if it were not so greedy. What complicates the electoral picture is the way Japan has sliced its giant electoral pie. Japan's constituencies, with one exception, are represented by more than one diet member. Most districts have three to five seats. The big districts attract candidates from all parties, but the LDP frequently floods the roster with many candidates, aiming to sweep the constituency. When this happens, the total LDP vote is split between so many candidates that it allows other candidates to win on relatively low vote totals. Reformers argue that the LDP should put up fewer candidates to avoid the problem, and in some constituencies the party carefully limits the number of approved candidates.

After the noise and hoopla of the election, the need for

money continues. A diet member earns a stipend of well over $200,000 a year, which includes correspondence and transportation allowances. Each member may hire two secretaries at government expense, is given a modest office in the diet building complex, and a rented apartment in Tokyo. He receives a railway pass and money for other "miscellaneous expenses." A diet member who has served twenty-five years also is provided with a chauffeured limousine.

It is obvious that the official income of a diet member is simply not sufficient to finance elections and the kind of constituent services that are required. "Yes," said a rising young LDP politician over lunch one day. "A diet man worth his salt will easily spend many times that much if he is doing his job right."

A Culture of Corruption

News of political bribery and corruption has been a mainstay of Japan's press. Nationwide television and radio seem transfixed by the subject and never tire of the political personalities involved. During each election, thousands of people are charged with election law violations, but functionaries, spouses, and supporters of individual candidates consider the problem more a game than a serious ethical issue. The law makes it illegal for a politician to give a voter any drink stronger than green tea on election day, but others make the sake flow freely. Household solicitations, rides to the polls, and money are also used as incentives for voters to write the correct name on the ballot. All these illegal acts are not taken seriously. And nobody regards the behavior as scandalous if zeal causes a candidate to cross the line. True scandal involves bigger names and bigger stakes.

The first great postwar scandal broke only a few years after the war, in 1948. The government of Hitoshi Ashida came crashing down after only seven months in power. One of the founders of the Democratic Party, Ashida parceled out cabinet offices to rival party members in such an evenhanded way that it angered his party colleagues. Although he was an anticommunist and a moderate, his cooperation with the socialists was unacceptable to his fellow conservatives. Six months after taking office, scores of high officials, including Ashida's deputy prime minister, were arrested for corruption in allocating government money to Showa Electrical Company. Takeo Fukuda, destined to become a major conservative faction leader and a prime minister, was one of the officials implicated. Ashida was arrested after all the others and was charged with corruption. Some ten years later, Ashida was acquitted. By then, all sixty-two of the political figures eventually charged in the case had been acquitted. In 1962, the former finance minister and the former president of Showa Electrical were found guilty. Ashida stayed in politics for many years, his reputation seemingly undamaged by the scandal.

By 1954 Japan was working overtime to replace the wartime merchant marine fleet that now lay on the bottom of the Pacific. Government subsidies were voted to reduce interest rates on money borrowed to finance the construction of merchant ships. Eisaku Sato, the secretary of the Liberal Party (a precursor of the merged Liberal Democratic Party), was accused of accepting a large payoff from a company that was getting government shipbuilding subsidies. Also implicated was another prominent figure in the party, Hayato Ikeda. The scandal threatened the government of Shigeru Yoshida, a key figure in rebuilding Japan and in cementing postwar relations with the West. Opposition parties were poised to capitalize on the publicity. Before the scandal investigation got out of hand, Yoshida set the pattern for the future in handling embarrassing cases such as this. He simply ordered his justice minister to postpone the arrest of Sato and Ikeda until the end of the current session of the diet, ten days away. When the diet session ended, neither man was arrested and the case was dropped. The prosecutor's office had refrained "for their own inscrutable reasons," as Yoshida described it in his memoirs. The rationale was that the money was not accepted for personal gain, but for the party.

The blemish did not retard either man's political career. Ikeda became prime minister in 1960 and led a popular and successful movement to double the income of Japanese wage earners. He left office in 1964 to make way for Sato. Sato held the post of prime minister for a record eight years, and he was awarded the 1974 Nobel Peace Prize for his anti-nuclear diplomacy. Ironically, the justice minister who quashed the prosecution of Sato later found himself appointed to another cabinet, and in due course, he was arrested with seventeen of his colleagues for receiving bribes to change the routing of new railroad lines. No one intervened to prevent his prosecution. Although he was let off with a suspended sentence and a small fine, his political train, unlike Sato's, was derailed.

Unpopular people within the party do not get treated as well as popular ones, and sometimes the actors don't play their expected parts. Prime Minister Takeo Miki, a man of rectitude, did not stay his justice minister's hand from prosecuting a former prime minister and leader of the LDP's biggest political faction, Kakuei Tanaka, the man Miki succeeded. Tanaka was indicted for taking $2 million in bribes from the Lockheed Corporation; the case reflected shame on Japan, and Miki was outraged. "Factions," Miki told me in an interview, "are a kind of cancer in Japanese society."

The Tanaka case is the most visible bribery case of the postwar era: a prime minister was charged, eventually convicted, and sentenced to jail. But he never served a day behind bars. He kept his seat in the diet until he suffered a stroke. Through the long ordeal, Tanaka remained, arguably, the single most popular, and certainly the most powerful, political figure in Japan. The nation's mainstream press saw him as corrupt, and the conservative political establishment had always viewed him as a crude, ward-heeling outsider. But to the rank and file he was something of a populist folk hero. He confronted and bested the bureaucrats and reveled at being called the "computerized bulldozer." His plans to create jobs and rebuild Japan through the pork barrel were applauded widely.

Tanaka was also so good at fund raising that he doubled the amount of money donated to the LDP during his two years in power. It was surprising, then, to Takeo Miki, who became head of the party and prime minister after Tanaka was deposed, to discover that the treasury was not only empty, but that the party was Yen 10,000,000,000 in debt.

Tanaka's known Lockheed bribe was $2 million, but that was only part of the $11.9 million that Lockheed admitted paying in "commissions" to Japanese businesses and individuals to persuade All Nippon Airways to buy its L-1011 Tristar passenger jets. Tanaka's bribe came to him via Lockheed's legal Japanese agent, Marubeni Corporation, which itself got a fee of $2,800,000. Marubeni's money was a legitimate commission on ANA orders of fourteen jetliners and options to buy eight more. The court discovered that Marubeni kicked back $700,000 to ANA, and also paid $100,000 to seven high-ranking politicians, including the transportation minister and his deputy and one of the LDP's godfathers, Susumu Nikaido.

The former managing director of Marubeni testified that he once met Tanaka's private secretary in a back street of Tokyo's Sanbancho district, behind the British Embassy and a stone's throw from the Imperial Palace. There he handed over two cardboard boxes neatly filled to the brim with Yen 10,000 notes. The next time the executive made a delivery he cut out the middleman and took the cash directly to the prime minister's home. In formal fashion, the transactions were recorded on the books, each million yen referred to as a "peanut," a "piece," or a "unit." After a trial that dragged on for seven years, Tanaka was convicted. Immediate appeals were lodged, and they dragged on for another six years. All through the trial and its appeals, there was a constant stream of visitors, benefactors, and supplicants to Tanaka's home, where he continued to pull political strings.

Tanaka was an outsider to the cozy and inbred coterie of Liberal Democratic Party politicians, a man who had no illusions about what motivated men. His father was a horse trader from Niigata in the snow country on the northwestern coast of the main island, Honshu. Kakuei entered politics with a will, after a successful career as a contractor in the rough-and-tumble of the gangster-infested building trades. Elected to the national diet, he was arrested in 1948 during his first term for taking a bribe from a mining company to vote against nationalization. The inconvenience didn't discourage him. He ran his first reelection campaign from jail. He beat that charge of bribery and was freed in time to accept the voters' mandate. He was known as a man who was always ready to make a deal that would obligate someone to him.

When he became prime minister, his home district ranked low on the list of prefectures receiving government public works projects and subsidies. The district soon rose to a ranking of third. Generous to a fault, Tanaka thought nothing was too good for his home prefecture of Niigata, and the voters of Niigata's Third District returned the compliment with their votes. He built a $5 million tunnel and a road to service a hamlet of only sixty households. He even managed to allocate federal funds for snow removal.

Tanaka could demand favors and money and support simply because he handed out favors and money and gave support. When he took over as minister of finance on his way to the top, he scandalized the stiff old bureaucrats at the tradition-bound institution by passing envelopes of money to favored employees on special occasions and as seasonal gifts. The recipients called them special bonuses. Others called them bribes. One year while prime minister he extended his generous cash bonuses to members of the diet.

The bureaucracy is said to be incorruptible. It can stymie any politician in command by interpreting the regulations strictly or in a special way. Tanaka explained to colleagues that the main challenge to a politician in office was to learn how to deal with these functionaries. He applied his coarse charm to the ministries of posts and telecommunications, transportation, and construction before taking the portfolio at finance. He boasted to commentator Hirotatsu Fujiwara about such prowess:

> The bureaucrat is an animal, all things considered, [and] wants only to obtain higher rank . . . . I give them a little pocket money, a promotion, or perhaps take them out someplace nice. If they want to stand for election, I help them out. And if I take care of things for them in this way, they will keep in line.

When he took over as minister of finance, he told his assembled bureaucrats, "You are the elite of the elite. You have the best brains in Japan, so I'll leave all the thinking to you. This unworthy Kakuei will bear complete responsibility for the consequences."

The nation's businessmen appeal to the politicians to help them with the bureaucrats who have power over them. Fortunately for the businessmen, many of Japan's political figures are graduates of the bureaucracy and still have influence there. Tanaka was not a graduate of the bureaucracy, but he was practiced in buying influence. Many bureaucrats enter politics, and many more retire to go to work for companies in the industries they have regulated. Japanese who are wise in the ways of these men suggest that no bureaucrat in the ministry of transport who expects to go to work for, say, Japan Railways is likely to rule against the best interests of the railroad while he is in office. But Tanaka used the system beyond its limits.

When an election campaign required money and favors, Tanaka had no qualms about putting the arm on potential contributors or demanding favors. He chose to make important calls before dawn, preferably at five o'clock in the morning, so that none of his potential contributors could say they weren't at home when he called.

Of the long list of politicians involved in money-tainted scandals, including a half dozen prime ministers, only Tanaka suffered the ignominy of being expelled from the party whose president he had been and brought to trial. The old boy network didn't come to Tanaka's aid. He wasn't one of them, never having graduated from a prestigious university—or any university at all, for that matter—and the next prime minister was Takeo Miki, a man who professed high ethical standards. The justice minister, Osamu Inaba, though a member of another LDP faction, was, ironically, from Niigata, and it was assumed that Tanaka would be given a reprieve. Miki shocked Tanaka and the nation when he refused to order the justice minister to quash the indictments.

Nevertheless, even while standing trial, Tanaka was reelected repeatedly to his diet seat as an independent. Three other diet members who were accused but never indicted in the Lockheed scandal were also reelected to their seats. One was accused of running up gigantic gambling debts in Las Vegas, which were paid off with Lockheed money. Kicked out of the diet, he had only to wait a few years to be reelected to his old seat by constituents, who evidently felt he had been punished enough.

From Tanaka's Lockheed bribery scandal of the 1972, to the Recruit, Kyowa, and Sagawa Kyubin scandals at the opening of the 1990s, Japanese have frequently been treated to the spectacle of their major political figures attempting to evade embarrassing questions with artful dodging, shading of the truth, and outright lying. It is customary for them to admit taking the money but insist they have broken no laws or done anything that would make the contribution a bribe. One politician recently declared his innocence by blaming his wife for accepting bribes. More often, it is some party functionary or one of a top politician's secretaries who takes the blame.

In 1992 the head of Prime Minister Kiichi Miyazawa's political faction, Fumio Abe, sixty-nine years old, stood accused of accepting $640,000 for helping the Kyowa Construction Company secure government contracts and supplying the company with information about government road-building plans. The police reported that Abe admitted taking the money but denied it was a bribe. He resigned from the party and from Miyazawa's faction, but clung to his seat in the diet. The prime minister apologized for the scandal. "I take this situation seriously," said Miyazawa. "To regain the trust of the people in politics, I will exert all my efforts to establish political ethics and undertake political reforms." But rumors swirled through Tokyo that there were others involved, including one former prime minister. Several weeks later, former prime minister Zenko Suzuki confessed before the diet, in a nationally televised session, that he had accepted an envelope stuffed with $77,000 worth of Japanese yen from Kyowa. It was a campaign contribution, said Suzuki, and did not use the money. Suzuki embarrassedly told his peers that when the Abe case broke he immediately returned the money to Kyowa.

Almost before the ink was dry, a new series of allegations surfaced. As many as 125 members of the diet, and some very prominent officials, had allegedly accepted payments totaling over $80 million from a parcel delivery service seeking new routes and other favors from public officials. The company, Tokyo Sagawa Kyubin, was also allegedly involved in a loan scheme in which it funneled money to companies controlled by the underworld *yakuza*. These allegations came on the heels of earlier revelations, readily admitted, that two of Japan's biggest securities houses, Nomura (the world's largest) and Nikko, had financed some underworld figures and persuaded customers to buy stock being manipulated by a well-known *yakuza* don who had connections with Tokyo Sagawa Kyubin. If the prosecutors are able to untangle the web and prove their case, it could be the biggest such scandal in Japan's history of scandals.

Recruiting Influence

The Recruit company scandal that broke in 1989 was a prototype for bribery in the new technological age. Bribery scandals of earlier post war decades involved heavy industry, such as shipbuilding, construction, and transportation. Recruit was an information, computer and real estate company, a fast-growing upstart firm led by a self-made man eager to have influential friends in high places. Started by publishing a jobs-wanted newsletter, Recruit grew to become a $4 billion company. The target figures in the scandal were offered shares of the company, which was seeking "better relationships" with the establishment. Some shares were offered at Yen 1200 each, about $9.25. Police said Recruit even lent some recipients the money to participate in the deal. When the stock issue was offered to the public, its price immediately rose to Yen 5000 a share, or $38.45. The insiders sold their shares and made tidy profits. (Under Japanese law there is nothing illegal about the straight financial deal. If bribery was intended and accomplished, the complexion of the case changes.)

Denying any bribery allegations, Prime Minister Takeshita, only eighteen months in office, resigned "to take responsibility" for the seventeen politicians of his group who made profits on the Recruit stock. One former Takeshita aide made $192,000. Takeshita himself admitted that his aides received more than $1.1 million in "legal contributions" from the company, and that one of his secretaries had received large loans from Recruit. He also conceded that a couple of years earlier, Recruit had donated $250,000 to his political support groups and had bought $350,000 worth of tickets to the Takeshita fund raiser that grossed $14 million. None of his actions, he declared, was illegal, but he apologized to the nation for causing the people to have a "severe distrust in politics."

Takeshita's predecessor, former prime minister Yasuhiro Nakasone, under whose regime the bribing took place, admitted taking a large amount in campaign contributions from the Recruit company. Nakasone resigned from the party for a time as a means of apologizing.

Hiromasa Ezoe, founder of the fast-growing Recruit group of companies, was trying to elevate himself and his company to the ranks of influential business advisers to politicians. He also wanted his company to become beneficiary of the ruling party's good offices. He and his company operatives made loans and contributions to many officials in a position to help Recruit in its business ventures. One of his mistakes may have been to spread his net too wide. More than 150 influential people, including members of other political parties, were offered similar, if smaller, stock bonanzas. Ezoe's deal went not only to sitting government officials but also to important businessmen, including Hisashi Shinto, chairman of the Japan's major communications company NTT, and several newspaper executives.

After nearly a year of investigation, sixteen people were indicted for various offenses. Even though Nakasone, Takeshita, and three other ruling party leaders were recipients of Ezoe's largesse, none was found to have violated the law. Two marginally prominent politicians and three bureaucrats were indicted for bribery, together with Ezoe and three of his executives. Four secretaries to three leaders of the ruling party, including a secretary to Kiichi Miyazawa, were fined $1400 for violating the Political Fund Control law. There were fifty resignations in business and politics, including three Takeshita cabinet members.

The ruling party announced that it was chastened by the Recruit case, but with the resignation of Takeshita, it was back to business as usual. No one in Japan expects any lesson to have been learned. Other political money scandals will inevitably break the surface, though no one knows what ingenious method will be employed and who will do the bribing. Tokyo newspapermen on the scandal beat say they know the takers will be prominent names; they always are. They see the political money game as a structural flaw, despite all the talk of reform.

Fund-raising through manipulation of stock prices is another technique coming under scrutiny since the Recruit scandal. Political figures become associated in the public mind with specific companies—in Tanaka's case, it was an oil company that was drilling in the Sea of Japan off the coast of Niigata prefecture. Conservative party politicians are close to Japan's captains of industry and commerce. To raise money, politicians often connive with brokers to buy a stock whose price is low, then circulate rumors that the politician is interested in the company. This strategem brings a flurry of activity to the stock, raising its price, after which the politician quietly sells his shares. One Tokyo financial reporter charted the movement of some of these "political" stocks on the Tokyo exchange. He found that in eight of ten recent elections, the stocks more than doubled in value in the few months just before the elections.

A Tokyo political commentator wrote recently that buying access to bureaucrats "is as Japanese as cherry blossoms and kabuki." In Japan "a career shouldn't be ruined over penny-ante expense account juggling." The case in question involved an official of MITI and a federation of textile companies. The Tokyo prosecutor's office alleged that the federation not only wined and dined the bureaucrat, but picked up his personal bar bill, which had mounted to a not inconsiderable $50,000 over thirteen years. A conservative commentator, Hideaki Kase, pointed out, in defense of the man, that Japanese have a permissive attitude toward drinking. He wrote in the business magazine *Zaikai*:

> We recognize that alcoholic beverages—sake, whiskey—have a mystical power to turn disagreement into a sense of unity. It's an ancient Shinto practice to offer sacred sake to the gods to gain their blessing. In the West, drinking together has none of this miraculous force. Sharing a drink with someone in New York or Paris is at most a way of getting to know that person better.

Business relations are often a life and death matter. A top official of a Japanese trading company leaped to his death from the eleventh floor of his company's building in Tokyo to avoid testifying in court in a bribery case. He left behind a suicide note with a kamikaze-like philosophy, which said that a man's life is short but "the company is eternal."

Such sentiments are proved again and again in the long history of Japanese bribery and dirty dealing. Time and again men found to have committed illegal acts for their companies are eventually promoted after the heat dies down. In the Lockheed case, one of those on trial was an official of the Marubeni Iida trading company, the formal agent for Lockheed and the go-between for Tanaka and All Nippon Airways, the purchaser of the planes. He was held by the police for two days and released; the prosecutor had decided that the official "had no positive intent to commit a crime."

Following orders is a common defense in business and also in political bribery cases, but in many political cases it is rarely the politician who is sacrificed. In his final argument to the jury in one of the Lockheed cases, Norio Hioki, the defense counsel, put it succinctly: "The people who caused the present case did not do so for their selfish interests. They did it all for the sake of their company. Their devotion to their company's work was at the very root of the affair."

The Lure of Money

If the problems of political bribery and inside trading are due to a structural flaw, as some insist, another symptom of its persistence may be the refusal of the system to give up the use of untraceable cash. The tax authorities lament that proper taxes are not being paid in the overheated cash economy. Cash passes from hand to hand, and bank clerks and company controllers flick through notes with practiced dexterity. The use of personal checks is still a rarity in the world's second largest economy. Shops and restaurants that deal in cash are prime suspects of the tax investigators, and so are farmers who bring goods to market outside the co-op system. One tax check showed that some farm households were reporting only a quarter of their true income.

Another tax target is the medical profession. Every year the biggest tax cheats are named just before the tax deadline, and doctors either head the list or are very near the top. It is customary for patients to give doctors, particularly before surgery, a major gift of under-the-table cash. Although credit card use, and debt, is climbing steeply, cash remains king. Today's affluent Japanese ordinarily carry large amounts of the stuff, a habit that has made Japanese tourists potential targets for muggers overseas.

It is not surprising to see someone check out of a hotel and pay a bill equivalent to several thousand dollars with cash. Nor is it unusual to see people buying big ticket items for cash. The postal system in Japan provides tax-free interest on postal savings accounts up to a certain amount, and at one point there were more accounts than people; families registered tax-free accounts in the name of their children and their pets. The Ministry of Posts also provides special envelopes for sending cash through the mails—clearly labeled that they contain cash so that, incredibly, nobody will steal them.

Most working wages are paid in cash, in stacks of crisp Yen 10,000 notes. Even large bonus payments of several months' salary are routinely paid this way at midyear and the new year. Japanese like to settle up their debts for the new year, and the balloon bonus payments make it easier to do so. Stores that extend installment credit usually include balloon payments in the repayment schedule to take into account the windfall system. The custom tends to inject the cash right back into the economy. Paying bonuses, even five or six months extra pay a year, also serves to keep company costs down. Salaries can be kept relatively low because bonuses aren't counted as salary when benefits are calculated. The bonuses save employers money because they do not have an impact on pension programs and other benefits keyed to salary.

The arrival of the credit card has had a clear impact on Japan's love affair with cash. The Japanese experience with credit cards is virtually no different from the West's; the percentage of deadbeats is as high in Japan as elsewhere. Unfortunately, there are still a lot of people who cannot establish credit and are driven to the loan sharks; in Japan that means the *yakuza*. The nation is shocked from time to time by tales of people deeply in debt who commit suicide, sometimes taking the rest of the family with them. Mothers despair that no one will take care of the children after the act and frequently kill the children first. Loan sharking appears to be on the increase as affluence grows. During Japan's feudal period it was the money lenders who often went bankrupt providing money to the local lords. Under the laws of the era, the lords could not be sued, and if an appeal did not result in repayment, there was no other recourse but bankruptcy.

It is customary for Japanese women to handle the finances of the household; the men are presumably too busy. It is also customary for men to bring their pay envelopes home to their wives, who then dole out an allowance to the breadwinner. A Japanese friend confided one night that in order to get mad money, he had convinced his wife that his company paid a very low bonus. He turned over to her one extra month's pay twice a year, when in fact, the company gave each employee an envelope with three months pay in cash in the summer, and another containing two months pay in the winter. He pocketed the rest and carefully budgeted it himself out of a box in his desk at work. All the while he continued to collect his weekly allowance from his wife. "What will you do if your wife ever meets the wife of one of your colleagues," I asked, a bit alarmed by the prospect. "What if this question comes up?"

"No problem," he said. "We all do it. Our wives think we work for a cheapskate company."

In addition to cash, the giving of gifts knows no better refinement than in Japan, where the proper gift is important. It is considered rude one-upmanship to give someone a gift that is more expensive than the recipient can afford to reciprocate. There is a thriving gift business at railway stations and airports, where traveling Japanese seem to spend more time buying gifts for friends and family back home than enjoying their vacation. Of course overseas travelers also look for items representative of the country they are visiting. Armed with Japan's strong currency, they now line up at Hermes in Paris, Tiffany's in New York.

An American sales executive based in Japan learned a costly lesson in dealing with cash. He braked his car too slowly at an intersection and bumped the car ahead. Both drivers got out of their cars and examined the point of impact. The American said he could see no damage; the Japanese was angry. He demanded Yen 10,000 for the inconvenience. Outraged by what he felt was an unfair demand, the foreigner refused to pay. His wife, sensing the true nature of the situation, cautioned him that he should be apologetic. He ignored her. "John, give him the money," she counseled. "Give him the money." But John was adamant. The discussion came to a halt when the Japanese driver developed a sudden case of whiplash. At that point John's ordeal began in earnest. Before it was over John and his wife had to visit the hospital, bearing flowers for the whiplash victim. John's Japanese lawyer advised him to make sure he and his wife stopped at the police station on the way to the hospital, to let the authorities know that they were doing the right thing, showing the proper remorse and sincerity. In the victim's hospital room were relatives and friends, all staring accusingly at John and his wife, who were desperately trying to show *them* their remorse and sincerity. There were flowers from well-wishers everywhere, and gift boxes were piled high in the cluttered little room, attesting to the popularity of the victim.

When it was all over, John's insurance company was presented with the hospital bill, and also with another bill of miscellaneous charges, including about $2000 worth of gifts the whiplash victim bought for others. When John protested paying for the gifts, he learned the facts of gift giving in Japan. John's whiplash victim was forced to reciprocate the kindness of people who brought gifts to him in the hospital during his convalescence. As John was the cause of the victim's obligation, John was obligated to reimburse the victim.

Cash solves many problems. The newlyweds of Japan, for example, don't have to fear the arrival of duplicate toasters and blenders, nor dread the ordeal of exchanging things; they get cash. At the white-draped reception table at the wedding luncheon or dinner, a polite young woman accepts the special cash-laden envelopes from the guests as they arrive. Similarly, the mourners of a deceased family member will get cash as well.

The wedding gift in cash sometimes barely covers the cost of the invariably lavish affairs, in which the bride makes her entrance twice, in kimono and western dress. Guests usually show up in black, or other somber colors, in order not to detract from the brilliance of the bride. The reason the newlyweds and their families need cash is the high cost of the wedding enterprise. A wedding hall ceremony with a banquet for one hundred guests can easily cost the equivalent of $25,000. Nowadays, guests are expected to bring from $150 to $200 per person to these affairs, and more if they are close friends of the bride and groom and their families. But a couple of hundred dollars is modest, compared with what is expected when a famous entertainer or sports star is married. Not only friends of the couple, but others in a long chain of family and business relationships and obligation chip in contributions.

When Princess Masako, a niece of the late Emperor Hirohito, was married in 1983 to a descendant of the great tea master, Sen no Rikyu, it was said that as much as $140 million in cash and gifts was showered on the couple. Politicians, bankers and other business associates of the families, even the many thousands of tea ceremony teachers of his school were expected to put a sizable sum into their wedding gift envelopes, and their students a lesser sum. A Japanese magazine came up with its estimate after analyzing the gifts given by guests at the wedding of a scion of a rival tea ceremony school. No royal personage was involved, but the cash-filled envelopes were generous. A $2000 gift was commonplace.

Professor Eiichi Kato, who served for twenty years in the Ministry of Home Affairs, which polices the nation, once explained to me that Japan is a land of patient people. "If a government official gives a favor to one citizen he doesn't expect a reward at once, but some day in some form or another he'll receive something. It will never be mentioned that this is a reward for his favor. The person will just say, 'This is a token of my thanks for everything.' You Westerners may be very uneasy about that, but the Bible says 'cast the bread upon the waters.' You believe in the God system, and we Japanese believe in our system, which works well and everyone can rely on it."

EPILOGUE

In the rapidly changing world of the approaching millenium, nations East and West are seeking cultural anchors. In Japan, even some critics of the institution concede that for many the emperor has that enduring, symbolic value. The continuation of the Imperial institution seems assured, in any case, and if its style and substance is to become modernized, it will be done by Akihito, the first emperor to have been educated outside the palace grounds, and the first to marry a commoner.

Change in Japan can be deceptive. What may be significant change to the Japanese is a mere variation on a theme to outsiders. But after assuming office and before his official enthronement, Akihito broke tradition and called a news conference, even inviting some foreign correspondents to it. During the session he was asked whether he thought the people should be free to discuss such things as his father's wartime culpability. His response was immediate: "Upholding freedom of expression is the foundation of democracy, and I believe it is very important to defend it."

The foreign ministry official who briefed Akihito when he

assumed the throne, said, "He, and especially the empress, want so much to be like ordinary persons, but if they are normal, nobody would be interested in them. Many people want them to be more regal. Their attitude may cause some antagonism in some quarters, but one must realize that nobody can please everyone."

An unknown number of Japanese such as Professor Shuichi Kato consider the Imperial institution a "fantasy" to be done away with. There are nearly one hundred civic groups in the movement for abolition of the imperial institution, though polls show there is still widespread support for it. The polls also indicate that among young people there is more indifference than enthusiasm. Extremists on both sides are vocal. Shusuke Nomura, a militant nationalist activist who spent eighteen of his fifty-five years in jail for arson and kidnapping in the name of ultranationalist causes, insists that the institution of the emperor satisfies a need within the Japanese people:

> The Emperor's significance to Japan is best understood with the heart, not the mind. The emperors of Japan have never been men of power or autocrats. To regard them as tyrants is a fundamental error. Leaders like Hitler, Mao Tse Tung, and Pol Pot had both prestige and absolute power; the people were completely at their mercy. The only solution was to remove them. Japan's monarchy is different. . . . Compulsory worship of the emperor is not necessary. We do not have to be told to love our wives, children, and friends, or to feel pride and affection for our fatherland. We should spontaneously love our emperor in the same way. . . . When Japan is in danger, the people turn to the emperor for solace and reassurance.

Emperor Akihito is not likely to allow a cult of worship to develop around him. He is certainly the most cosmopolitan and the least stiff of Japanese emperors. Hirohito's overseas experience as a young man induced him to expose Akihito to the wider world. Hirohito and Nagako took the unprecedented step of requesting that Crown Prince Akihito continue at the Peer's School through high school. How much influence the Occupation authorities may have had in this decision is not known, but the authorities of occupied Japan were not keen on seeing the next emperor trained by private tutors, who might inculcate him with nationalistic propaganda. Occupation officials attempted to purge such teachers from all the conquered nation's schools.

For the twelve-year-old Akihito, the world of 1946 was much different from the world of his father at the same age. It was decided that while he continued his education outside the palace, he would also get a special tutor. So one was sought, preferably an American, a Christian ("But not a fanatic" was the caveat), who would spend about one hour a week with Akihito privately, and also tutor other members of the royal family. Through the American Friends Service Committee, a tall, handsome, and charming writer of children's books, Elizabeth Gray Vining—a modern Anna of Siam—was chosen. After first turning down the surprising proposal, she relented under urging and signed a contract for $2,000 a year and all expenses. The Grand Steward of the Imperial Household counseled her to "open windows on a wider world for our Crown Prince." She insisted in her book, *Windows for the Crown Prince*, written in 1952, that the decision to hire a foreign tutor was wholly Hirohito's and Nagako's, and not imposed on them by the occupation authorities.

In class at the former Peers' School, which opened its doors to a general student population after the War, Akihito proved an apt pupil. The self-possessed Akihito also began to make decisions for himself, independent of the court chamberlains, who were accustomed to deciding everything. His most stunning decision was to become the first crown prince to marry a commoner. He had chosen Michiko Shoda, daughter of a flour milling magnate, after turning his back on some fifty prospective brides suggested by his parents and the household agency. Akihito was smitten by the classically beautiful Michiko on the tennis courts in the resort town of Karuizawa and at the Tokyo Lawn Tennis Club. The romance was widely discussed and wildly popular outside the palace. (The wedding in 1957 is remembered fondly by Japanese electronics companies because of the gigantic spurt in the sales of television sets, for it was the first televised Japanese royal wedding.)

One of Akihito's first acts on assuming power was to do away with the system of testing his food for poison before every meal, the minute weighing of his food intake and the leftovers, and the routine examination of the royal stool. He ordered the palace drivers and escorts to obey all traffic signals, stopping on red, just like every other citizen, and asked for less security than the stifling overkill of police, bodyguards, and functionaries that normally attend the emperor. When he called a press conference, it was the first Imperial press conference in fourteen years, the last one being in 1975 when Hirohito and the empress were about to embark on a trip to the United States.

Although Akihito required reporters to submit their questions in writing in advance, the smiling, shy emperor and the demure empress quickly put everyone at ease. They asked all to be seated and to remain seated during the questioning. They answered the questions freely and with good humor. Akihito said he wanted to strike a tone "appropriate to the present time." He would, he said, perform his duties as outlined in the Constitution, seeking no further role. He joked that his tennis game had deteriorated and that his children could beat him on the courts. "Quite a good show," commented one of the Japanese participants later, "but not much news."

Asahi Shimbun editorialized that the moves made by the new emperor boded well for a modernization of the imperial household, making it more accessible to the people: "The time has come when we can think about the relationship between the people and the Imperial family while keeping away from nostalgia, grudges and repulsion."

Members of the family have helped to show the change. Breaking tradition, the second son of the emperor, Prince Aya at age twenty-five announced his engagement to Kiko Kawashima, a fellow student at the Peers' School, now known as Gakushuin University. (His older brother Hiro, now the crown prince, vowed to marry by age thirty, but at thirty-two was still searching for a bride.) "Storybook Romance," headlined one newspaper. "Cinderella Charms Japan," said another. Kiko's father, an economics professor, and his family lived in a modest apartment on the school campus, which led one newspaper to nickname Kiko the "Apartment Princess."

For all his supposedly endearing ordinariness, Emperor Akihito is a strong-willed man, but palace watchers believe it will be difficult for him to successfully exert that will over all the strong minds of the palace bureaucracy. Too, no matter how "democratic" an emperor he wishes to be, his separation from ordinary Japanese is inescapable. Although Akihito has more freedom than his father or any of his predecessors, the institution of the royal family has never been similar to any modern Western model. Rigidities of style, tradition, and fashion are its very framework.

There has been no serious scandal in the royal family that has reached the mainstream press. Only the hard-drinking Tomohito, seventh in line to the throne, has kicked up his heels in a way that raised eyebrows. He began attracting attention in the early 1970s, when at thirty-six he said he wanted to be excused from his royal family duties because it took too much time from other, less ceremonial work, which he preferred. The rejoinder from the Imperial Household Agency was to persuade him to enter a hospital to recover from "fatigue."

Royal merrymaking is simply not the order of the day in Japan, perhaps because the access of the press to affairs of the palaces is more restricted than anywhere else. Furthermore, there is a kind of unwritten code of press morality in Japan that tends to keep unflattering news of speculation about the royal family out of the pages of the major publications. Even Japan's outrageous weekly magazines find little grist for the mill in the royal family. The Japanese press and its television outlets, including the publicly financed television network, NHK, are careful not to offend, for to do so would bring down the wrath of the palace power structure, which can dispense or withhold privileges of access and information.

Distressed over the attention being lavished on the royal family by the press, the agency demanded restraint after the papers ran a charming, informal photo of Princess Kiko smiling and brushing back a lock of her husband's hair. It was too informal, the agency said. A few months later, during the search for a bride for the Crown Prince Naruhito, the agency called in the press and demanded a three-month moratorium on coverage. The newspaper publishers association agreed to hold back stories for the period. They were later prevailed on to extend the blackout, and agreed.

How the public image of the new heads of the royal family will eventually change depends on how open they can manage to be. There was little sign of openness in the formal enthronement ceremony of Akihito, which took place immediately after the death of Hirohito on January 7, 1989. The first "democratic" enthronement ceremony held under the postwar constitution, the enthronement, with its panoply and pomp, its costumes and tradition, gave no hint of modernity.

According to tradition, the ceremony, in which Akihito took his seat on the *takamikura*, a thirty-one-foot tall, black-lacquer throne, should have taken place in Kyoto. But so severe were the threats from anti-Imperial groups and vows of defense from right-wing groups that police informed the palace they could not guarantee security if the ceremony were held outside the capital city. The ceremony was designed, then, to be held on the palace grounds in Tokyo, well secured and far from any possibility of interruption.

On November 12, Akihito began the ten-day period of ceremonies and banquets, called the *sokui-no-rei*, with the enthronement ceremony itself. Dressed in the style of the Heian Court of the eighth to twelfth centuries, the emperor and the empress appeared in multilayered robes of exquisitely embroidered silk. While colorful banners—purposely devoid of any religious symbology—hung in the courtyard and drums and gongs beat out accompaniments, the pair participated in the ceremony under a clear blue winter sky. They moved with a deliberate gait to their separate elevated and elaborate thrones, where they remained screened from view by curtains. After a long silence, the curtains were drawn aside at the sound of a bell.

From his throne topped with the mythical phoenix, the emperor intoned words not spoken by any of the 124 of his predecessors as they assumed the role of emperor: "I pledge anew that I shall observe the constitution of Japan and discharge my duties as symbol of the state and of the unity of the people, always wishing for the well-being of the people." Also in deference to the secular nature of the ceremony, the prime minister of the time, Toshiki Kaifu, wore western formal dress, rather than court dress, when he stood before the royal couple to deliver the traditional cry of "Banzai" (the equivalent of "Long live the emperor," but, literally, "10,000 years").

The final event in Akihito's ceremonial affairs connected with taking the throne, the *Daijosai*, or Great Food Offering, became the most controversial event because it is essentially a religious affair, in which the emperor is said to commune with the sun goddess in a night ritual. The experts disagree, but critics maintain that the ceremony signifies the transformation of the emperor into a god, and acknowledges the direct descent of the emperor from the sun goddess, known as Amaterasu Omikami. In the discussions leading up to the enthronement of Akihito it was argued that the *Daijosai* might be dispensed with. Seiji Okada, for one, a professor of Japanese history at Mie University, pointed out that it would not have been unusual to skip the controversial ceremony. The enthronement rites have varied through the years, and from the mid-fifteenth until the late seventeenth century, the *Daijosai* was dispensed with at various times because of civil war or financial difficulties.

Writing in Tokyo's *Asahi Shimbun*, Professor Okada also noted that the enthronement and the Great Food Offering ceremonies "do not follow the procedures of antiquity, despite government claims." They were radically changed in

1909 when the ritual-loving autocrat, Hirobumi Ito, modern
Japan's first prime minister, drafted detailed procedures for
imperial rites. Even the prime minister's *Banzai* cheers were
a new wrinkle added by Ito. "What the government calls
'tradition,' " wrote Okada in *Asahi*, "actually was done only
for the last two sovereigns." Okada asks: "Are rites that were
used for living gods invested with an absolute right of sovereignty appropriate for the symbol of national unity under
popular rule?" Obviously he and many others think not.

Of the $160 million spent for the ceremonies, fully $35
million was for security, with no fewer than 36,000 police
inspecting cars and guarding approaches to the palace and
Shinto shrines in the city. Nevertheless, nearly three dozen
incidents of protest took place. Left-wingers fired home-built
rockets at American military bases, and near Kobe, in western Japan, two small bombs damaged the American consu-
late. Right-wing supporters of the Imperial system
complained that police kept them under surveillance and
would not let them display their signs of encouragement, but
out of respect for the institution they vowed to refrain from
clashing with foes or creating any disturbance.

Among the 2500 official guests from 158 nations were a
dozen heads of state, including former president Corazon
Aquino of the Philippines and President Suharto of Indonesia, King Baudoin and Queen Fabiola of Belgium, and King
Carl Gustav of Sweden. The United States was represented
by Vice President Dan Quayle. Great Britain, whose royal
family Akihito and his family have said they admire, was
represented by Prince Charles and Princess Diana. The ceremony took only thirty minutes, after which the new emperor
and his consort changed into western dress and made a brief
tour of a carefully guarded route through the streets of Tokyo
to the Akasaka palace.

As the date for the Great Food Offering approached ten
days later, the experts from the government, the Imperial
Household Agency, historians, ethnologists, religious leaders, and politicians seemed to contradict each other trying
to explain what it was all about. If it is a religious ritual,

should the government pay the $20 million it cost to construct the separate buildings and all that go with them for the two day ceremony? Scholars differed. Missions overseas explained the ceremony differently. In Los Angeles the consulate invited guests to a celebration of the occasion where they could see a videotape of the ceremony. "This controversial ceremony is of a religious nature," explained the consulate staff in a statement on the ceremonies. "Critics feel that this ceremony signifies the transformation of the emperor into a god incarnate . . ." Despite the simple and straightforward language of the constitution, so carefully thought out by western experts in 1946, Japan was asserting its storied and defiant ambiguity.

The Imperial Household agency issued a statement explaining that the *Daijosai* is a ceremony in which the emperor merely expresses thanks to the sun goddess and is definitely not "an effort to gain divinity." In that case, editorialized *Mainichi*, one of Tokyo's largest dailies, "the *Daijosai* is inherently a private ceremony to be conducted by the Imperial Family and the government's intervention in this ceremony is problematical."

The ceremony, however, was held as scheduled. On November 22 at 6:30 P.M., Akihito entered the first of three wooden buildings constructed in the palace compound just for this use. No foreigners were invited to the Great Food Offering, and although all members of the diet and top provincial officials were invited to be present at a distance during the ceremony, many, including top socialist and communist figures, boycotted it.

After a ritual bath in a boat-shaped wooden tub, the emperor, dressed in pure white, moved under a white canopy from the first building, the *kairyu-den*, to an inner chamber of the structure called *yuki-den*. There the emperor offered rice and fish to the sun goddess. He then read a statement of gratitude to the gods for a rich harvest and for peace, after which the emperor ate the same rice and fish meal as a gesture of communion with the gods. The controversial bed in the center of the inner chamber was not for Akihito, it was explained, but for Amaterasu, although the new emperor was to wrap himself in bedclothes, symbolically inheriting the spirit of the gods. (Some versions have it that in this ceremony the emperor symbolically enters the womb of Amaterasu and is reborn a god.) Early in the morning the same rituals were performed in the second building, the *suki-den*.

A government official, Misoji Sakamoto, tried to explain: "This does not mean that politics is meddling in religion, or that religion is increasing its influence in politics." To the nation at large the argument seemed moot, a matter for scholars and critics to argue and not for public debate. Mainly it seemed to worry foreigners, fearful of a resurgence of a strong and militant Japan filled with religious fervor and emperor worship. Some critics do worry that a relaxed attitude toward the question could encourage right-wing elements, who wish to assert Japan's power and prestige in the world and would do it by reviving old traditions.

Questions persist. Is it possible that Japan as the most economically successful nation in Asia could tread the old path to Asian political, if not necessarily military, hegemony? If it was true that Hirohito was powerless to stop his generals and political schemers, could a less powerful and symbolic "emperor of the people" do any better? Or even as well? It is theoretically unlikely Akihito will ever get the chance. The reforms of the Occupation and the resulting constitution purposely drained power from the Imperial institution, giving the emperor no voice in what course Japan's political leaders choose in future.

Japan's growing military strength, partly encouraged by the United States, is being eyed warily by Asian neighbors. And its economic dominance as the world's major creditor nation is even more worrisome, a situation that nobody forsaw in 1945. There are those who believe that Japan continues to feel its destiny is to exercise hegemony over Asia; but they must reckon with the fact that Japan has already accomplished much as Asia's economic engine that military arms could not. Now that Japan has wealth, facing Japan's own internal problems and contradications is a prime task for the nation. Progress toward that end is slow. Japan's international role is far from clear to Japanese or foreigners. Cool and persistent heads in the international community must bring the economic superpower to a position of acknowledged equality and responsibility. A seat on the United Nations Security Council for the nation with the world's second largest economy should be a foregone conclusion. Forced to make decisions and participate fully in the affairs of the world in a context larger than its own self-interest, Japan could find its rightful place in world society. Such a prominent role could also serve as an instructive message—to Japan's insular people and to non-Japanese—that Japan's transformation is complete.

BIBLIOGRAPHY

Books:

Abegglen, James, and Stalk, George. *Kaisha, The Japanese Corporation*. New York: Basic Books, 1985.

Aida, Yuhi. *Prisoner of the British* (Louis Allen, Hide Ishiguro, trans.). London: Butler & Tanner, 1966.

Abbott, James Francis. *Japanese Expansion and American Policies*. London: Macmillan Co., 1916.

Adachi, Barbara. *The Living Treasures of Japan*. Tokyo: Kodansha International, 1973.

Agawa, Hiroyuki (John Bester, trans.) *Reluctant Admiral*. Tokyo: Kodansha International, 1979.

Akamatsu, Paul. (Miriam Kochan, trans.) *Meiji 1868: Revolution and Counter-Revolution in Japan*. New York: Harper & Row, 1972.

Akimoto, Shunkichi. *The Lure of Japan*. Tokyo: The Hokuseido Press, 1934.

Alperovitz, Gary. *Atomic Diplomacy: Hiroshima and Potsdam*. New York: Penguin, 1985.

Anesaki, Masaharu. *Art, Life, and Nature in Japan*. Boston: Marshall Jones, 1933.

Barr, Pat. *The Coming of the Barbarians: A Story of Western Settlement in Japan 1953–1970.* London: Macmillan and Co., 1967.

Barthes, Roland (Richard Howard, trans.) *Empire of Signs.* New York: Hill and Wang, 1982.

de Bary, Theodore William., ed. *Sources of Japanese Tradition.* New York: Columbia University Press, 1958.

Behr, Edward. *Hirohito: Behind the Myth.* New York: Villard Books, 1989.

Benedict, Ruth. *The Chrystanthemum and The Sword.* New York: New World Publishing Co., 1967.

Bergamini, David. *Japan's Imperial Conspiracy: How Emperor Hirohito Led Japan into War Against the West.* New York: William Morrow, 1971.

Berry, Mary Elizabeth. *Hideyoshi.* Cambridge: Harvard University Press, 1982.

Blond, Georges (Edward Hyams, trans.). *Admiral Togo.* New York: Macmillan, 1960.

Borg, Dorothy and Okamoto, Shipsei (eds.). *Pearl Harbor as History.* New York: Columbia University Press, 1973.

Borton, Hugh. *Japan's Modern Century.* New York: Roland Press, 1955.

Bowers, John Z. *Western Medical Pioneers in Feudal Japan.* Baltimore: Johns Hopkins Press, 1970.

Brackman, Arnold C. *The Other Nuremberg: The Untold Story of the Tokyo War Crimes Trials.* New York: William Morrow and Company, 1987.

Braisted, William Reynolds (Assisted by Yasushi Adachi and Yuji Kikuchi). *Meiroku Zasshi: Journal of the Japanese Enlightenment.* Cambridge: Harvard University Press, 1976.

Buruma, Ian. *Behind the Mask.* New York: Pantheon Books, 1984.

Butow, Robert J.C. *Tojo and the Coming of the War.* Stanford: Stanford University Press, 1961.

———. *Japan's Decision to Surrender.* Stanford: Stanford University Press, 1954.

Bywater, Hector C. *The Great Pacific War.* New York: St. Martin's Press, 1991.

Cabinet Commission on The Constitution. *Comments and Observations by Foreign Scholars on Problems Concerning The Constitution of Japan, 1946.* Tokyo: Secretariat of the Commission, 1964.

Carew, Tim. *The Fall of Hong Kong.* London: Anthony Blond, 1960.

Chamberlain, Basil Hall, trans. *The Kojiki. Records of Ancient Matters.* Rutland, Vermont, and Tokyo: Charles E. Tuttle, 1981.

Cohen, Theodore (Herbert Passin, ed.). *Remaking Japan.* New York: Free Press, 1984.

Choate, Pat. *Agents of Influence.* New York: Alfred A. Knopf, 1990.

Close, Upton (Josef W. Hall). *Behind the Face of Japan.* New York: Appleton-Century, 1934.

Coffey, Thomas M. *Imperial Tragedy.* New York: World Publishing Company, 1970.

Cole, Robert E. *Japanese Blue Collar.* Berkeley: University of California Press, 1971.

———. *Work, Mobility, & Participation.* Berkeley: University of California Press, 1979.

Cooper, Michael. *They Came to Japan: An Anthology of European Reports on Japan, 1543–1640.* Berkeley: University of California Press, 1965.

Cosenza, Mario Emilio, ed. *The Complete Journal of Townsend Harris.* New York: Japan Society, 1930.

Couperus, Louis. (John de La Valette, trans.) *Nippon.* New York: George H. Doran, 1926.

Craig, William. *The Fall of Japan.* New York: Dial Press, 1967.

Cram, Ralph Adams. *Impressions of Japanese Architecture.* London: George G. Harrap & Co., 1931.

Cummings, William K. *Education and Equality in Japan.* Princeton: Princeton University Press, 1980.

Curtis, Gerald L. *Election Campaigning Japanese Style.* New York: Columbia University Press, 1971.

Doi, Takeo. *The Anatomy of Dependence.* New York and Tokyo: Kodansha International, 1971.

Dore, Ronald. *Taking Japan Seriously.* Stanford: Stanford University Press, 1987.

———. *Land Reform in Japan.* New York: Shocken Books, 1985.

Dower, John W. *War Without Mercy.* New York: Pantheon Books, 1986.

Dull, Paul S. *The Imperial Japanese Navy.* Annapolis: Naval Institute Press.

Earl, David Magarey. *Emperor and Nation in Japan.* Seattle: University of Washington Press, 1964.

Entwistle, Basil. *Japan's Decisive Decade.* London: Grosvenor Books, 1985.

Esthus, Raymond A. *Theodore Roosevelt and Japan.* Seattle: University of Washington Press, 1966.

Francillon, Rene J. *Japanese Aircraft of the Pacific War*. Annapolis: Naval Institute Press, 1988.

Fuchida, Mitsuo and Okumiya, Masatake. (Clark K. Kawakami, Roger Pineau, eds.) *Midway*. Annapolis: Naval Institute Press, 1955.

Fujiwara Hirotatsu. (John Clark, trans.) *Tanaka Kakuei: Godfather of Japan*. Tokyo: Fujiwara, 1985.

Fukuzawa, Yukichi (Eiichi Kiyooka, trans.) *The Autobiography of Yukichi Fukuzawa*. New York and London: Columbia University Press, 1966.

———. *Fukuzawa Yukichi On Japanese Women*. Tokyo: University of Tokyo Press, 1988.

Gayn, Mark. *Japan Diary*. New York: William Sloan Associates, 1948.

Gibney, Frank. *Five Gentlemen of Japan*. New York: Farrar, Strauss & Young, 1953.

———. *Miracle By Design*. New York: Times Books, 1982.

Gluck, Carol. *Japan's Modern Myths*. Princeton: Princeton University Press, 1985.

Goedertier, Joseph. *A Dictionary of Japanese History*. Tokyo: Walker/ Weatherhill, 1968.

Guillain, Robert (William Byron, trans.). *I Saw Tokyo Burning*. Garden City: Doubleday & Company, 1981.

Hane, Mikiso. *Reflections on the Way to the Gallows: Rebel Women in Prewar Japan*. Berkeley: University of California Press, 1988.

———. *Peasants, Rebels, and Outcasts: The Underside of Modern Japan*. New York: Pantheon Books, 1982.

Hearn, Lafcadio. *Kokoro*. Boston: Houghton Mifflin, 1896.

———. *Japan: An Attempt At Interpretation*. New York: Grossett & Dunlap, 1904.

———. *Out of the East*. Boston: Houghton Mifflin, 1985.

———. *Letters From the Raven*. New York: Brentano's, 1907.

Hersey, John. *Hiroshima*. New York: Alfred A. Knopf, 1946.

Honan, William H. *Visions of Infamy: The Untold Story of How Journalist Hector C. Bywater Devised the Plans that Led to Pearl Harbor*. New York: St. Martin's Press, 1991.

Honjo, Shigeru (Mikiso Hane, trans.). *Emperor Hirohito and his Chief Aide-de-Camp. The Honjo Diary*. Tokyo: University of Tokyo Press, 1982.

Hozumi, Nobushige. *Ancestor Worship and Japanese Law*. Tokyo: Hokuseido Press, 1943.

Heusken, Henry (Jeannette C. van der Corput and Robert A. Wilson, trans. and eds.). *Japan Journal.* New Brunswick: Rutgers University Press, 1964.

Hunter, Janet C. *Concise Dictionary of Modern Japanese History.* Berkeley: University of California Press, 1984.

Ienaga, Saburo. *The Pacific War 1931–1945. (Taiheiyo Senso).* New York: Random House, 1978.

Imai, Masaaki. *Sixteen Ways to Avoid Saying No.* Tokyo: Nihon Keizei Shimbun, 1981.

Irokawa, Daikichi (Marius B. Jense, trans.). *The Culture of the Meiji Period.* Princeton: Princeton University Press, 1985.

Ishihara, Shintaro (Frank Baldwin, trans.). *The Japan That Can Say No.* New York: Simon & Schuster, 1989.

Johnson, Chalmers. *Conspiracy at Matsukawa.* Berkeley: University of California Press, 1972.

———. *MITI and the Japanese Miracle.* Stanford: Stanford University Press, 1982.

Kawasaki, Ichiro. *Japan Unmasked.* Rutland: Charles E. Tuttle, 1969.

Keene, Donald (trans.). *Modern Plays of Chikamatsu.* New York: Columbia University Press, 1961.

———. *Some Japanese Portraits.* Tokyo: Kodansha, 1978.

———. *Dawn to the West: Japanese Literature in the Modern Era.* Two volumes. New York: Holt, Rinehart and Winston, 1984.

Kido, Takayoshi (Sidney Devere Brown and Akiko Hirota, trans.). *The Diary of Kido Takayoshi.* Three volumes. Tokyo: University of Tokyo Press, 1983, 1985, 1989.

Kikuchi, Makoto. *Japanese Electronics.* Tokyo: Simul Press, 1983.

Kinoaki, Matsuo. (Kilsoo K. Haan, trans.) *How Japan Plans to Win.* Boston: Little, Brown, 1942.

Kitagawa, Joseph. *Religion in Japanese History.* New York: Columbia University Press, 1966.

Knapp, Arthur May. *Feudal and Modern Japan.* Two volumes. Boston: Joseph Knight, 1897.

Kosaka, Masataka. *One Hundred Million Japanese.* Tokyo: Kodansha International, 1972.

Kutakov, Leonid N. (George Alexander Lensen, ed.) *Japanese Foreign Policy on the Eve of the Pacific War: A Soviet View.* Tallahassee: Diplomatic Press, 1972.

Lea, Homer. *The Valor of Ignorance.* New York: Harper & Brothers, 1942.

Lebra, Takie Sugiyama. *Japanese Women: Constraint and Fulfillment.* Honolulu: University of Hawaii Press, 1984.

Lee, Sherman. *Reflections of Reality in Japanese Art.* Cleveland: Cleveland Museum of Art, 1983.

Manchester, William. *Goodbye, Darkness.* Boston: Little, Brown, 1979.

Maraini, Fosco. *Japan: Patterns of Continuity.* Tokyo and Palo Alto: Kodansha International, 1971.

———. (Eric Musbacher, trans.) *Meeting With Japan.* New York: Viking Press, 1960.

Michener, James A. *The Hokusai Sketchbooks: Selections from the Manga.* Rutland, Vermont, and Tokyo: Charles E. Tuttle Co., 1958.

Midorikawa, Yoichi, and Magoichi, Kushida. *These Splendored Isles.* New York, Tokyo & Kyoto: Weatherhill/Tankosha, 1970.

Miller, Roy Andrew. *Japan's Modern Myth: The Language and Beyond.* New York and Tokyo: Weatherhill, 1982.

Minear, Richard H. *Victors' Justice: The Tokyo War Crimes Trial.* Princeton: Princeton University Press, 1971.

Moloney, James Clark. *Understanding the Japanese Mind.* New York: Philosophical Library, 1954.

Moore, Charles A. (ed.) *The Japanese Mind.* Honolulu: East-West Center Press, 1967.

Morris, Ivan. *The Nobility of Failure: Tragic Heroes in the History of Japan.* London: Secker & Warburg Limited, 1975.

Morison, Samuel Eliot. *Victory in the Pacific.* Boston: Atlantic, Little, Brown, 1960.

———. *The Two Ocean War.* Boston: Atlantic, Little, Brown, 1963.

Morita, Akio (with Edwin M. Reingold and Mitsuko Shimomura). *Made in Japan.* New York: E.P. Dutton, 1986.

Mosley, Leonard. *Hirohito, Emperor of Japan.* Englewood Cliffs: Prentice-Hall, 1966.

Mydans, Carl. *More Than Meets the Eye.* New York: Harper & Brothers, 1959.

Naito, Hatsuho (Mayumi Ichikawa, trans.) *Thunder Gods: The Kamikaze Pilots Tell Their Story.* Tokyo: Kodansha International, 1989.

Nakae, Chomin (Nobuko Tsukui, trans.). *A Discourse by Three Drunkards on Government.* New York and Tokyo: Weatherhill, 1984.

Nakane, Chie. *Japanese Society.* Berkeley: University of California Press, 1970.

NHK (Nippon Hoso Kyokai). *Unforgettable Fire.* Tokyo: 1977.

Oka, Yoshitake (Shumpei Okamoto and Patricia Murray, trans.). *Konoe Fumimaro, A Political Biography.* Tokyo: University of Tokyo Press, 1983.

Olson, Lawrence. *Japan in Postwar Asia*. New York: Praeger Publishers, 1970.

Omura, Bunji. *The Last Genro: Prince Saionji, the Man Who Westernized Japan*. Philadelphia and New York: J.B. Lippincott Co., 1938.

Onoda, Hiroo (Charles S. Terry, trans.). *No Surrender: My Thirty-Year War*. Tokyo: Kodansha International, 1974.

Orwell, George (W.J. West, ed.). *The War Commentaries*. New York: Pantheon Books, 1985.

Otis, Cary et al. *War-Wasted Asia*. Tokyo: Kodansha International, 1975.

Oxford, Wayne H. (with Eiichi Kiyooka). *The Speeches of Fukuzawa: A Translation and Critical Study*. Tokyo: Hokuseido Press, 1973.

Pacific War Research Society. *Japan's Longest Day*. Tokyo: Kodansha International, 1968.

Packard, Jerrold M. *Sons of Heaven*. New York: Charles Scribner's Sons, 1987.

Passin, Herbert. *Encounter With Japan*. Tokyo: Kodansha International, 1982.

Perrin, Noel. *Giving Up The Gun: Japan's Reversion to the Sword*. Boston: David R. Godine, 1979.

Plath, David W. (ed.) *Work and Lifecourse in Japan*. Albany: State University of New York Press, 1983.

Prange, Gordon W. (With Donald M. Goldstein and Katherine V. Dillon). *Miracle at Midway*. New York: McGraw Hill, 1982.

Price, Willard. *Japan's Islands of Mystery*. New York: John Day Company, 1944.

———. *Children of the Rising Sun*. New York: National Travel Club, 1938.

Pyle, Kenneth B. *The New Generation in Meiji Japan: Problems of Cultural Identity, 1885–1895*. Stanford: Stanford University Press, 1969.

Reischauer, Edwin O. *The United States and Japan*. Cambridge: Harvard University Press, 1965.

———. *Japan Past and Present*. New York: Alfred A. Knopf, 1967.

———. *The Japanese*. Cambridge: Harvard University Press, 1977.

———. *My Life Between Japan and America*. New York: Harper & Row, 1986.

Reischauer, Haru Matsukata. *Samurai and Silk: A Japanese and American Heritage*. Cambridge and London: The Belknap Press of Harvard University Press, 1986.

Richie, Donald. *The Inland Sea*. New York: Weatherhill, 1971.

————. *A Lateral View*. Tokyo: The Japan Times, 1987.

————. *Different People*. Tokyo: Kodansha International, 1987.

————. *Where are the Victors?* Rutland, Vermont: Charles E. Tuttle, 1986.

Roberts, John G. *Mitsui*. Tokyo: Weatherhill, 1973.

Rudofsky, Bernard. *The Kimono Mind*. Garden City: Doubleday & Co., 1965.

Saga, Junichi (Garry O. Evans, trans.). *Memories of Silk and Straw*. Tokyo: Kodansha International Ltd., 1987.

Sansom, George. *A History of Japan*. Three Volumes. Stanford: Stanford University Press, 1958, 1961, 1963.

Scalapino, Robert A., and Masumi, Junnosuke. *Parties and Politics in Contemporary Japan*. Berkeley: University of California Press, 1962.

Seidensticker, Edward. *Low City, High City*. New York: Alfred A. Knopf, 1983.

————. *Tokyo Rising*. New York: Alfred A. Knopf, 1990.

Shioya, Sakae. *Chushingura: An Exposition*. Tokyo: Hokuseido Press, 1940.

Sievers, Charon L. *Flowers in Salt: The Beginnings of Feminist Consciousness in Modern Japan*. Stanford: Stanford University Press, 1983.

Statler, Oliver. *Japanese Inn*. New York: Random House, 1961.

————. *Shimoda Story*. New York: Random House, 1969.

Storry, Richard. *Japan and the Decline of the West in Asia*. London: Macmillan Press, 1979.

Takakura, Shinichiro (John A. Harrison, trans.). *The Ainu of Northern Japan*. Philadelphia: American Philosophical Society, 1960.

Terasaki, Gwen. *Bridge to the Sun*. Chapel Hill: University of North Carolina Press, 1957.

Thayer, Nathaniel B. *How the Conservatives Rule Japan*. Princeton: Princeton University Press, 1969.

Togo, Shigenori (Fumihiko Togo and Bruce Blakeney, trans.). *The Cause of Japan*. New York: Simon and Schuster, 1956.

Toland, John. *The Rising Sun*. New York: Random House, 1970.

Tolman, Mary S. and Norman H. *People Who Make Japanese Prints*. Tokyo: Sobunsha, 1982.

Totman, Conrad. *The Collapse of the Tokugawa Bakufu, 1862–1868*. Honolulu: University of Hawaii Press, 1980.

Varley, H. Paul. *Imperial Restoration in Medieval Japan*. New York and London: Columbia University Press, 1971.

Vining, Elizabeth Gray. *Windows for the Crown Prince.* Philadephia: J.B. Lippincott Co., 1952.

———. *Return to Japan.* Philadelphia: J.B. Lippincott Co., 1960.

Weglyn, Michi. *Years of Infamy.* New York: Quill, 1976.

Wigmore, John Henry, (ed.). *Law and Justice in Tokugawa Japan.* Vol. VII. Tokyo: University of Tokyo Press, 1972.

Williams, Harold S. *Shades of the Past.* Tokyo: Charles E. Tuttle, 1959.

Williams, Sr., Justin. *Japan's Political Revolution Under MacArthur.* Athens: University of Georgia Press, 1979.

van Wolferen, Karel. *The Enigma of Japanese Power. People and Politics in a Stateless Nation.* New York: Alfred A. Knopf, 1989.

Womack, James P., et al. *The Machine That Changed the World.* New York: Rawson Associates, 1990.

Wyden, Peter. *Day One.* New York: Simon and Schuster, 1984.

Periodicals:

Asahi Shimbun and Asahi Evening News
Business Tokyo
Chuo Koron
The Daily Yomiuri
The Japan Times and *Japan Times Weekly International International Edition*
Los Angeles Times
The Mainichi Daily News
The New York Times
Nihon Keizei Shimbun
Sankei Shimbun
Time Magazine (international edition)
Tokyo Business Today

INDEX

283

ABOUT THE AUTHOR

Edwin M. Reingold has been a practicing journalist for more than four decades. As a correspondent and bureau chief for *Time* magazine, he has covered political, economic, and diplomatic affairs in the United States, the Caribbean, Central America, East and Central Africa, the Philippines, Korea, the People's Republic of China, and Japan. He has reported on subjects as diverse as the failed Bay of Pigs invasion of Cuba, the beginnings of America's manned space program, Project Mercury, the independence and nation-building struggles of new countries in the Caribbean and Africa, the Detroit automobile industry, and the Hermit Kingdom of North Korea. Mr. Reingold has reported on Japan continuously since his first of two assignments there as bureau chief in 1969, with interim assignments in Detroit and Beijing. He was president of the Foreign Correspondents Club of Japan. Since 1986 he has been based in Los Angeles, where he continues to report on Japan and other subjects, including the world aerospace industry. He is a collector of Japanese prints and is a trustee of the Pacific Asia Museum of Pasadena.